Table of Contents

Contents

Table of Contents 1

What Can Brown Do for You? 7

So, Why Be an Actor in Atlanta? 7

What kind of roles can I expect to book out of Atlanta? 11

The Roadmap 11

1.   Move Here and Get Settled 12

2.   Have/buy a Reliable Car 14

MARTA 15

Living Costs 17

3.   Get a Survival Job 17

My experiences in survival jobs 18

Passive Income Streams 20

Passive Income Resources 20

Flexible Jobs 21

Sample List of Flexible Jobs and Freelance Gigs to Consider 22

Corporate Job Opportunities 23

Temp Staffing Agencies in Atlanta 24

4.   Get Training 25

Acting Studios and Teachers 25

Theatrical Acting 30

Improv-focused Training 31

Sketch Acting 32

Visiting LA Teachers / Seasonal Classes......................33

Classes for the Business Side of Acting........................34

5.   Get Headshots 35

Headshot Photographers List 35

Headshot Printing and Reproductions.........................37

6.   Find Work and Build Resume.................................38

Background Work 40

7.   Create More Marketing Tools 41

Get Listed on IMDB..41

Put Up Your Own Website...42

Create a Demo Reel 43

8.   Audition 44

Audition Taping Services 45

9.   Get Representation (aka Talent Agents) 47

10.   Know the Casting Directors 48

11.   Practice, Practice, Practice 49

12.   More Marketing..50

Atlanta Actor Interviews..52

Alex Collins 53

Al-Jaleel Knox...72

Anna Enger 78

Bill Murphey 88

Dane Davenport 97

David Kronawitter..109

Edward Bryan 115

Elizabeth "Beth" Keener-Dent..123

Eric Esquer..131

Eric Goins...138

Eric Kan..151

Gabriela Rowland 164

Jamie Moore...168

Jessica Leigh Smith 178

Jyn Hall..192

Kara Michele Wilder 210

Karen Ceesay 221

Kristen Shaw 226

Lee Armstrong 238

Mark Ashworth...250

Matt Cornwell...266

Michael Cole 272

Mike Pniewski...287

Omer Mughal..299

Parisa Johnston...306

Ravi Naidu..313

Ray Benitez 333

Scott Poythress...337

Tasia Grant...342

Tony Guerrero 348

Towanna Stone..355

Vince Canlas...367

Vince Pisani...379

Wilbur Fitzgerald 400

Yolanda Asher...421

Additional Resources on Acting in Atlanta 430

About Rafiq..430

Hello, Hola and Namaste!

If you'd told me 10 years ago when I was a freshly minted MBA that I'd be pursuing acting in Atlanta, much less writing a book about it, I would have laughed at you (politely, because that's how I am). Firstly, I was an analytical, hardheaded business school graduate destined for a great corporate career. Secondly, I never imagined Atlanta becoming the powerhouse of production it is today. Thirdly, I was a first generation *Indian* man with a hybrid Indian-American accent in the American South. My opportunities would be limited, to say the least.

But today, all that's changed. Acting in film and TV is a viable career in Atlanta. I've certainly had opportunities to audition way more than I imagined. And if I can be an Atlanta actor, so can you! More about Atlanta's awesomeness later. Let me tell you what this book is about.

This book is a guide to getting an acting career started in film and TV in Atlanta, with a suggested list of resources you can use at every step. I've also included interviews with established actors here who share tips and insights on everything – how they got started, how they go about their craft and managing their career, and what they see as the future of acting in Atlanta.

This book is only a starting point though. I recommend you do more reading, researching, and talking with other Atlanta film and TV professionals to build on what you read here.

Throughout this book, there are links embedded to classes, photographers, audition websites etc. These are not affiliate links; I make no money from including these links. Every link included is because I've personally used that particular resource or service, have had others in the industry recommend them, or pulled them from other reputable sites (like well-known talent agencies' websites).

That said, Atlanta is a dynamic, fast growing market. If you notice that I've missed listing a resource here (acting studio, photographer, audition taping service, talent agency, etc.), please email me at actinginatlantabook@gmail.com.

Thanks for reading. I'd love to hear your feedback. Break a leg (not literally, please).

~Rafiq
Some coffee shop in Atlanta, sometime early 2015
Update March 29, 2016 from an office complex in LA:

1. Ironically, since publishing this book, I've moved to Los Angeles because of my day job. Luckily the move brought me to LA and not to some middle-of-nowhere town!
2. I still think ATL is absolutely the best place to start your acting career. So keep reading!

What Can Brown Do for You?

...As the famous tagline from UPS (an Atlanta based company) goes. Perhaps you are wondering, "Hang on a sec, why am I listening to you, a "no-name" Indian actor in...of all places, Atlanta?" Precisely because I am a "no-name" (I prefer "rising") Indian actor in Atlanta. Pretty niche category. If I am able to find opportunities here, I think most other folks would be able to as well.

I began acting in 2010 just as Atlanta started becoming a hot market and have, since then, been working the craft and career regularly while working a day job to pay the bills. I've taken workshops and classes here, got headshots done with local photographers, haunted networking events and all the other stuff we actors do.

Over the years, I've made many mistakes and learned a lot. And I've met other actors who have accomplished so much, have such awesome insights and most importantly, are wonderful human beings and willing to share their knowledge. In this book, I've shared what I've learnt and what others, more successful than I, have learnt. Hope you find it useful.

So, Why Be an Actor in Atlanta?

The Walking Dead, Vampire Dairies, Hunger Games, Ant-man...perhaps you've heard of these TV shows and movies? These were/are all filmed in and around Atlanta. Atlanta is happening.

To be honest, when I first moved to Atlanta, I thought it was going to be temporary. Atlanta had never figured in my plans but, back when I was a hot shot engineer, I got a job with a tech startup in Norcross that kinda fizzled out. Facing an existential crisis, I decided to go to b-school at Emory. I always figured I'd get my MBA and leave. But I've stayed here for more than 10 years now ☺. In many ways, Atlanta is an ideal city – moderate climate, reasonable cost of living, great job market. And whaddaya know, now one of the hottest acting markets in the nation!

Being an actor in Atlanta could be one of the smartest decisions for the beginning actor because the competition is less intense (but growing, beware!) and the acting support structure of agencies, CDs, classes and such is growing deeper and wider every year. Established Hollywood talent agencies are setting up shop here. There are also actors moving from LA to Atlanta or at least getting representation with Atlanta agencies and willing to work as a local Atlanta hire. It's a juggernaut.

The reason so many productions are shooting here is because of the "Georgia Entertainment Industry Investment Act" (aka The Georgia Film and TV tax credit) which allows production companies to get back up to 30% of their production budget, quickly and with minimal red tape. This attracts plenty of big budget Hollywood film and TV productions to shoot in Atlanta. Basically, with this tax break, it becomes cheaper to film a movie or show in Atlanta than in Los Angeles. These productions then hire actors from the local Atlanta talent pool to play recurring and supporting roles, and as extras.

But you might say, "How is this any different from Louisiana? Or North Carolina? Or any of the other states offering similar incentives?" Atlanta and the whole state of Georgia really have many other advantages that position them especially well to be the "Hollywood of the South" for the long term:

1. **Favorable business climate:** Remember, film and TV are show **business**. And Georgia consistently ranks as one of the top states in the country for its business climate. Source: http://www.areadevelopment.com/Top-States-for-Doing-Business/Q3-2014/survey-results-top-states-analysis-2624441.shtml

For example, Site Selection magazine rated Georgia number 1 in the country. Atlanta has the 3rd highest number of Fortune 500 company headquarters in the US. And most recently in June 2014, CNBC named Georgia the number 1 place for business in the nation. So long as Georgia remains a great state to do show business in, there's no reason for the studios and the film community to leave.

2. **Studio presence:** Home to Turner Studios, Tyler Perry Studios, EUE/Screen Gem Studios, and Pinewood Studios and more. Coming soon is the "largest film and television media complex outside of California" by Jacoby Development which will be a 107 acre mixed use campus with 464,800 sq. feet of studio space, a 310-room hotel and 1,000 multi-family units. (Source: http://thejacobygroup.com/movie-studios). Also coming up is the massive Third Rail Studios at the site of a former GM plant (Source: http://thirdrailfilm.com).

3. **Amount of work available:** Did we mention all the work that's available here? 29 TV shows and feature films in 2014 as of May 2014 (Source: http://www.projectcasting.com/casting-calls-acting-auditions/29-movies-and-tv-shows-now-filming-in-georgia/)

4. **LA-level training:** Well-known LA teachers like Ted Brunetti, Crystal Carson, Margie Haber and Sam Christensen all include Atlanta in the list of cities they travel to teach to.

5. **No SAG required:** Georgia is a right-to-work state. This means you don't have to be a union member to book SAG work. Which means it's a great place to kickstart your career.

6. **Moderate climate:** It snows here maybe 2-3 days a year tops. Atlanta almost never suffers from hurricanes or tornadoes, and is one of the greenest large cities in the US. In fact, when you fly into Atlanta, you will be amazed at the lush canopy of green you see stretching to the horizon in every direction. This also makes Georgia more attractive than the Midwest or Northeastern states which face severe snowstorms during the winter months.

7. **ATL:** The busiest airport in the whole wide world with direct flights to over 200 cities everyday. It's a monster airport that still operates very efficiently (rated the most efficient in the world in 2011, for example) and almost never shuts down due to weather (I'm looking at you, Chicago) or strikes (Paris CDG, looking at you). Great connections to the rest of the world, metro train station right inside the airport terminal, and recently renovated world-class facilities and dining. And 10 non-stop flights to LAX and 40 non-stop to NY airports, every day.

8. **Great lifestyle for the price**: Of all the big cities in the US, Atlanta has one of the most affordable real estate markets and overall cost of living. Combined with the variety of landscape within driving distance (Savannah Beach and Smoky Mountains in 4 hours, awesome trails and Stone Mountain within city limits), amazing food choices (you name the cuisine, we probably have it) and neighborhoods to suit your style, it's probably the best bang-for-buck large city in the US today. Here's a pretty cool Huffington Post article about how Atlanta is the "Big American city you've been missing out on".

9. **Close enough to the other Southeast states** such as North Carolina, Florida and Louisiana so you can expect to book work in those states as well as a local hire (416 miles to Wilmington, NC and 469 miles to New Orleans – both within 500 miles).

What kind of roles can I expect to book out of Atlanta?

So far, lead roles are still not being booked out of here. But over time I've been invited to audition for recurring roles in TV shows. Most of the actors interviewed here have been asked to read for recurring and guest star roles as well and quite a few have even booked them. As the Atlanta talent community continues to grow strong here and even attract established talent from LA and NY, the caliber of opportunities offered to local actors is expected to go up. Of course, in terms of the range of characters you get to read for, that really depends on your training and your "type".

The Roadmap

Now that you are convinced that you should choose to pursue acting in Atlanta (right? RIGHT?), let's look at what you need to get you plugged into the scene and get started. Here's the basic list of steps:
1. Move here and get settled
2. Have/buy a reliable car
3. Get a survival job
4. Get training
5. Get headshots
6. Get listed on casting sites
7. Find work
8. Create a demo reel

9. Audition
10. Get representation (aka Talent Agents)
11. Know the Casting Directors
12. Practice, practice, practice
13. More marketing
14. Audition, audition, audition
15. Audition more
16. Audition some more
17. One more audition
18. Maybe book a job
19. Repeat steps 4 through 18 (repeat Step 9 only if not happy with current agent)

1. Move Here and Get Settled

Atlanta, like LA, is a sprawling metropolis though not quite on the same scale.

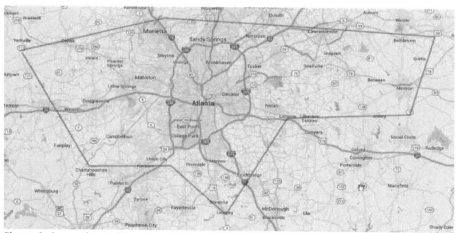

Figure 1: Approximate LA metro area over Atlanta metro area

The image above shows a rough outline of Los Angeles (LA) in blue line overlaid over the map of Atlanta. The area of LA in blue above includes Santa Monica to the west, North Hollywood to the north, San Bernardino to the east and Newport Beach to the South. Of course, the Greater LA area is much bigger.

So yes, Atlanta is huge but not as massive as LA. And definitely not as dense. So good news, Atlanta is more manageable and the layout is easier to grasp, though the traffic is quite bad here too.

Like LA, Atlanta is really a collection of cities and towns. There's the City of Atlanta, which is really quite small, around 500,000 people. Then there's a whole bunch of inner and outer suburbs. The Interstate 285 is like a perimeter that encompasses downtown, midtown, Buckhead and Decatur areas. Atlantans typically refer to the area within 285 as **Inside-The-Perimeter (ITP)**, and the areas outside as **Outside-The-Perimeter (OTP)**. See map below:

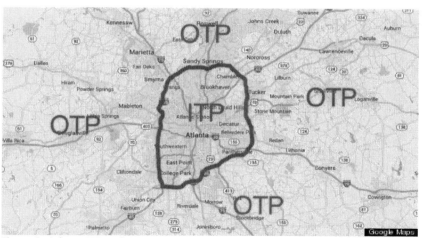

Figure 2: Atlanta ITP and OTP

Source:
http://www.huffingtonpost.com/2014/04/05/atlanta_n_5008299.html

2. Have/buy a Reliable Car

Again, like LA, you really can't get around much with Atlanta's woefully inadequate public transportation system, MARTA (Metro Atlanta Rapid Transit Authority), which includes subway and buses. So it's important that you have a good reliable car with:

- Decent gas mileage.
- A good sound system to chill out with music or to listen to podcasts, to enjoy the stop-and-go traffic in.
- Working heating and air conditioning – Georgia summers, 'nuff said. The winters, though mild in comparison to the Northeast or Midwest and with little to no snow, can be cold.
- Working turn signals because I HATE people who don't use their turn signals!

Most of the big car dealerships are along Peachtree Industrial Boulevard or in Marietta. Carmax.com has locations in Marietta, Roswell and Norcross. Of course, you can always check out Carvana.com. Or just check out Atlanta.craigslist.org.

MARTA

Though it has limited reach, the <u>MARTA subway system</u> is quite useful to beat the rush hour traffic and it goes right into Atlanta airport (domestic terminal). So when the time comes for you to fly to LA or NYC for that big job, consider using MARTA. MARTA has two major paths – North-South and East-West. See the map below.

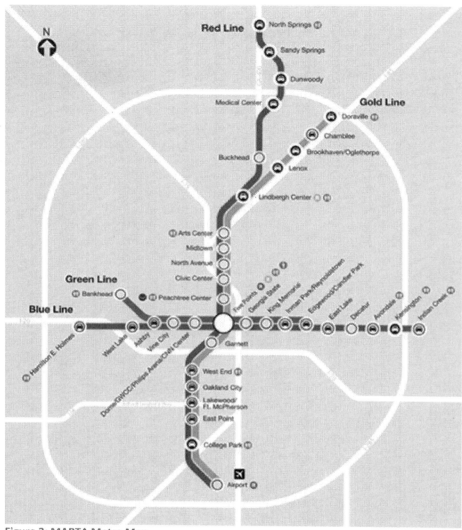

Figure 3: MARTA Metro Map

Source: http://www.itsmarta.com/IMAGES/system-map-2014.png

Living Costs

Atlanta is cheaper than LA and NY. No question. It's part of its awesomeness.

The biggest difference in cost of living will be due to lower rent or mortgage and cheaper gas. For example, you could rent a newish 1-BR apartment for around $900 inside the Perimeter near Chamblee or Doraville area. It's even cheaper outside the Perimeter. However, like across the country, prices are going up steadily as folks realize what a bargain Atlanta is and move here in larger numbers.

Similarly, gas is 15-20% cheaper. You will notice the difference adds up when you dash from home to work to audition to audition to class.

3. Get a Survival Job

Having the means to sustain yourself while you build up your acting career is probably THE key to having a successful acting career. If you, like me, weren't smart enough to have chosen to be born into a wealthy Sheikh's family, you gotta work a day job while pursuing acting.

As an actor you need a survival job that:
1. Pays you well enough that you are able to pay your bills and live comfortably enough that you don't need the money from booking an acting job.
2. Gives you the flexibility to be able to take time off for an audition as and when needed, and when you do book, to take time off to go work on the project.

With the right combination of skills and focused search, you should be able to find a job that meets these criteria. Some of the stuff in the rest of this section is not necessarily Atlanta specific but I felt I needed to share because I've struggled with and thought so much about survival jobs.

My experiences in survival jobs

By the time I figured out that I really wanted to act for a living, I was already married and had just graduated from business school. I had a wife to support and student loans. Also, I needed visa sponsorship to stay in this country. So I definitely needed to work a corporate job that would sponsor my visa. I ended up in a management consulting job that needed me to travel pretty much every week for client projects around the country. It was demanding work.

During this time, I submitted myself via Craigslist for some extra work and remember being called in to be a featured extra on a Tyler Perry show. It was to shoot in the middle of the week, when I was out at a client site in Indiana. I got a call and was so excited at the opportunity that without thinking I immediately said, "Yes, I'll be there!" And then, try as I might, I couldn't get my manager to let me leave mid-week back to Atlanta. I had to call back and leave a message with the casting agency that I couldn't make it. It was terribly unprofessional of me and I felt really bad. I was so torn – on the one hand a chance to be on a real TV show, albeit as a featured extra, and on the other hand, scared of losing my job. I decided then that I really needed to become the master of my destiny. I would create my own feature film, shooting on weekends and during vacation. That was the film *Mumbhai Connection*, and the pressures and pleasures it put me through will fill up a whole separate book. But the reason I mention all this is to drive home the point that often times (but not always!), a corporate job doesn't lend itself to an acting career.

In 2009, I left my consulting job and tried to be an entrepreneur. I partnered with a b-school buddy of mine importing baked goods from France and trying to sell within the US market. I also tried my hand at freelance graphic design, video production services and a few others. Suffice to say, they didn't pan out. Some, like options trading, actually lost me money. The importing or video businesses might have succeeded given enough time but for me personally, the worry of making rent and paying my bills every month was just too much pressure.

So finally, slightly over a year after I quit consulting, in fall 2010, I started working again in Corporate America at a large global technology company doing "Product Marketing". The job pays the bills and though I do have to go into the office, it gives me the flexibility to go for auditions and take days off when I do book acting jobs. I'm very thankful for it.

However, this job can be demanding too, though less so than management consulting. I've had to miss auditions due to work-related travel and the days I have to take off, I do need to ask for permission. Also it is still a career, not just a job. I have to strike a fine balance between providing enough value to be kept at my job but not seeming too eager to rise up the corporate ladder (and getting more responsibilities).

So here's my preference of job types/income streams, in decreasing order:
1. Win the MegaMillion or PowerBall lottery (please share 15% of your winnings with me)
2. Passive income streams – where you make money even when you are not working

3. Location independent businesses / Freelance – where you work for yourself to make money but not bound by location or time
4. Flexible and/or telecommute jobs – where you work for Corporate America to make money but not bound by location or time
5. Other jobs

Passive Income Streams

Passive income is generated by a business you own and operate that, with some upfront investment in time and work, provides you with regular income, with little effort required to maintain it. There are many different ways to do this. For example:
1. Create a high traffic website with affiliate links
2. Sell physical or information products on Amazon or other websites or on your own website
3. Rent out real estate properties
And many more.

This is, of course, not specific to Atlanta. And the topic of passive incomes is vast. There are tons of websites, courses and "gurus" teaching you how to do it. I can't do any justice to it in one paragraph here. That said, here are a few resources to check out:

Passive Income Resources
1. The 4 Hour Work Week book by Tim Ferriss, or just read his blog. In the blog post I've linked to, Tim talks about creating a "muse", a low-maintenance business that generates significant income. Tim gives many real life examples of such muses that others have created. I also love his podcasts.
2. The $100 Startup book by Chris Guillebeau. His whole philosophy is that starting a passive income stream doesn't even have to cost much money at all.

3. Warrior Forum: This is an Internet forum where people share ideas about various Internet businesses and marketing, and their experiences. Just subscribing to their newsletter gives you many, many ideas to consider. For example, this is a fantastic post about how one user spent $1,440 on a very simple cold calling process and landed $69,400 in new business for website design.
4. Shopify.com is an ecommerce platform that lets you create an online store to sell physical products. Here is a fantastic free course on their site about how to find ideas for what to sell online, where to find products to sell and much more. All free!
5. Sourcing and selling products on Amazon, eBay, etc. For this, I trust Jordan Mallik. He has a free eBook where he compares four of the courses available and includes an incredible 365-day "no questions asked" money back guarantee. That's an amazing deal. Link to free eBook.

Flexible Jobs

If the passive income option is too daunting or you need to earn cash ASAP while still having flexibility, consider being a freelancer or getting a flexible job.

To find freelance gigs:
1. https://www.elance.com
2. http://www.guru.com
3. http://atlanta.craigslist.org (look under "Jobs" and "Gigs" sections)

To find flexible jobs:
1. http://www.flexjobs.com
2. http://remoteok.io

Sample List of Flexible Jobs and Freelance Gigs to Consider

Waiting tables and bartending – these are the classic actor survival jobs. With the huge number of restaurants and bars in Atlanta, opportunities are plentiful. But there are many other options! Check these out:

1. Teach acting, especially if you have solid training and credits under your belt. This is one way to keep your instrument sharp while helping others also develop their craft.
2. Offer audition-taping services. Again, make sure you know what you are doing in terms of the technical skills required regarding light, audio and taping. This is a great option because it helps you also hone your own craft each time you get to be a reader for another actor. Just be careful about providing input and feedback that is misplaced or wrong.
3. Work at a film/TV production company, casting director's office or talent agency. This can be a great way to stay connected with the industry.
4. Design websites and apps – if you have a knack for technical stuff, this can be very lucrative.
5. Become a certified real estate agent.
6. Become an independent financial advisor.
7. Do sales for a large company. Typically, sales is a remote work, flexible hours job. Plus, sales is a useful life skill that is also very relevant in an acting career.
8. Get trained as a massage therapist.
9. Be a pharmacist – especially if you can work the night shift at a 24-hour CVS pharmacy.
10. Become a tutor – Help children and adults prepare for specific tests such as SAT, GMAT, GRE, whatever. You could even join Kaplan or other such prep courses' companies and get an evening job. Or do this freelance.
11. Be a recruiter – help IT and other firms recruit talent and place them in jobs.
12. Be an Uber or Lyft driver.

13. Become a technical and business writer – if you have a way with words, this can be great because here you focus on businesses which typically have a budget for this kind of stuff
14. Be a DJ – I know two South Asian friends of mine who actually make a full time living doing this at weddings, community events, corporate events and such. It's great because you typically work on weekend nights only.
15. Be a wedding photographer – again, great money and you typically work weekends only. Plus, you might be flown to some cool wedding location, all expenses paid. What's not to like? ☺

Corporate Job Opportunities
Atlanta is home to the third largest number of Fortune 500 companies such as Delta Airlines, UPS, Coca Cola, Home Depot, Turner Broadcasting, and Porsche. And consistently ranks as one of the top places in the US for young professionals. Here's a list of Fortune 500 companies in Atlanta, to give you an idea of the companies based here.

If you can find a corporate job that provides a decent paycheck and the flexibility, take a moment now and pat yourself on your back, and thank The Flying Spaghetti Monster because, my friend, that is awesome. Just one tip, don't slack off at this job – create value in whatever you do while pursuing what you want to do. And over time, after proving yourself to be reliable and making your manager look good, you can ask for flex hours and remote work options.

The standard job sites are:
1. AJC Jobs (Atlanta Journal Constitution, the biggest newspaper in Atlanta): http://www.ajc.com/s/ajcjobs/
2. Monster: http://jobs.monster.com/l-atlanta,-ga.aspx

3. LinkedIn: https://www.linkedin.com/job/jobs-in-atlanta-ga
4. Dice: http://www.dice.com
5. Indeed: http://www.indeed.com
6. Glassdoor: http://www.glassdoor.com/index.htm

With universities like Georgia Tech and Emory, Atlanta also has a vibrant technology and startup culture. For startup and entrepreneurship-like jobs, check out:
1. https://angel.co/atlanta/jobs
2. http://atdc.org/atdc-companies/

For government jobs:
1. https://www.governmentjobs.com/jobs?location=Atlanta%2C%20Georgia
2. http://www.atlantaga.gov/index.aspx?page=1137

Or simply use Google to search "Atlanta jobs" ☺

Temp Staffing Agencies in Atlanta

There are plenty of staffing agencies as well that give you flexible job or not-too-demanding job opportunities. Some of these are:
1. Randstad USA
2. Kelly Staffing
3. TRC Staffing
4. Horizon Staffing

And many, many more. Look up "Atlanta temp staffing agencies" online.

4. Get Training

Once you've settled in Atlanta and figured out a way to pay your bills, you need to work on your acting career. **The number 1 way to get started is to enroll in classes.** This has two HUGE benefits – 1) you hone your skills and 2) you network with other actors, your teacher and learn what's happening in the industry.

Whether you are a new actor looking for On-Camera Acting 101 or an experienced actor looking to hone your craft, there's always a class that is bound to be useful to you. Almost all these acting studios offer a variety of classes and additional services as well such as audition taping, special casting director workshops, showcases and so on. Check out their websites for the latest information.

Acting Studios and Teachers

Here are some of the acting studios and teachers in Atlanta, in alphabetical order:

Actors Complete Training
This studio is run by Bob Harter, one of Atlanta's most respected actors, working frequently on-camera. He is also in demand as a voice-over artist, known for his many celebrity impressions and character voices. Classes include On-Camera Audition and On-Camera Acting Basics.
Website: http://www.actorscompletetraining.com
Address: 695 Pylant Street, Atlanta, GA 30306
Phone: 770-335-0690

Actors Breakthrough Film Actors Training Studio
Actor's Breakthrough provides rigorous and practical instruction for children, teens, and adults as they develop the advanced skills required to win roles in episodic television, feature film,

and commercials. In this studio, there is only one standard to evaluate acting skills: "Does the audience believe in you?" The studio's mission is to help actors meet this single, simple, standard; the standard by which every professional actor is judged—both in the audition and on the screen. The studio is run by accomplished actor Greg Alan Williams.
Website: http://actorsbreakthrough.com
Address: 674 Mt. Zion Road, Suite F, Jonesboro, GA 30236
Phone: 678-422-2990

Actors Express
Actor's Express was founded in 1988 and has long been considered one of the most daring, provocative and consistently excellent theatres in Atlanta. Most recently, Creative Loafing named Actor's Express the Best Local Theatre Company of 2011. Classes include acting, improv and playwriting.
Website: http://www.actors-express.com
Address: 887 W. Marietta St. Suite J-107, Atlanta, GA 30318
Phone: 404-875-1606

The Actors Scene
Located in Buford, GA, this is a great studio for actors living to the northeast of Atlanta. The studio offers programs for all skill levels, ages 4 onward, in acting. The programs have two sessions: February–May, and August–November. Throughout the yearlong program, students will cover all aspects of the acting industry from TV to Film to Theater. They also offer audition-taping services.
Website: http://www.theactorsscene.com
Address: 4484 Commerce Dr., Suite A, Buford, GA 30518
Phone: 770-904-6646

Chez Studios

Chez Studios is the training wing of The Chez Group, which started out as a premier casting agency in Atlanta, under the direction of three-time Emmy nominated casting director, Shay Bentley-Griffin. This studio was created with the primary focus to strengthen the talent pool available to the filmmakers working in the Southeast. It offers a variety of workshops throughout the year focused on various aspects of acting and writing.
Website: http://www.chezgroup.com/training.html
Email: prepare@chezstudios.com
Address: 2221 Peachtree Road NE, Suite D, Box #335, Atlanta, GA 30309
Phone: 404-603-8755

The Company Acting Studio
The Company Acting Studio was founded in 1996 by Lisina Stoneburner in Atlanta. This studio offers a structured training curriculum for all kinds of acting: film, TV, stage and commercials. The methods and techniques, while based in the teachings of Stanislavski and Stella Adler, are a combination of practical work experience and years of training with various instructors and in various styles over the years. The staff members have their own required training program to qualify as instructors. The owners share a combined 30 years in the business. The founder, Lisina, was trained in Conservatory programs including The Stella Adler Conservatory, The New York School of Performing Arts and Boston University School of Theatre Arts.
Website: http://www.thecompanyactingstudio.com
Address: 500 Amsterdam Avenue Northeast D-1, Atlanta, GA 30306
Phone: 404-607-1626

Drama Inc.
This studio was founded in June 2013 by four working Atlanta actors: Jason MacDonald, Scott Poythress, Catherine Dyer and Claire Bronson.
Website: http://www.dramainc.net
Address: 650 Hamilton Ave. SE, Atlanta, GA 30312
Phone: 404-600-6070

Get Scene Studios
Address: 500 Bishop St NW, Suite: E4, Atlanta, GA 30318
Website: http://www.getscenestudios.com
Email: info@GetSceneStudios.com

Kristen Shaw Acting Studio
Founded in October 2011 by Kristen Shaw who honed her skills during her 15 years in the Los Angeles professional film industry. Probably the only acting studio in Atlanta using the Strasberg Method, it also offers On-camera Audition technique classes as well as Marketing/Living the Actor's Life to strategize the business side. Also offers audition taping and coaching services with convenient ability to book appointments online.
Website: http://new.kristenshawactingstudio.com
Address: 3040 Holcomb Bridge Road, Suite E-1, Norcross, GA 30071
Email: kristenshawactingstudio@gmail.com
Phone:??

Michael H. Cole Studio
Michael Cole is a prolific actor and a great coach, focusing specifically on on-camera audition technique. He also features guest speakers regularly and hosts stage plays every year, which is another way for his students to audition, perform and be seen.
Address: 4650 Flat Shoals Parkway, Decatur, GA 30034

Email: colemichaelh@gmail.com
Phone: 404-561-5132

Nick Conti's Professional Actors Studio
Also locally called Nick Conti Studio because it is owned and operated by Nick Conti, this studio is located in Buckhead. Easy access from GA 400. Nice facilities. Great improv classes. I've personally taken the improv classes here with Matt Cornwell and loved them.
Website: http://www.proactorsstudio.com
Address: 2849 Piedmont Road NE, Atlanta, GA 30305-2767
Phone: 404-943-1873

The Rob Mello Studio
The Robert Mello Studio is the only acting studio in Atlanta offering complete Meisner-based training by an instructor with over 15 years of teaching experience. Students from The Robert Mello Studio have worked on dozens of hit TV shows, in feature films, Broadway and off-Broadway.
Website: http://therobertmellostudio.com
Email: rob@therobertmellostudio.com
Address: 3041 N. Decatur Rd., Scottdale, GA 30079
Phone:??

yourAct Acting Studios
yourACT has been one of the leading acting schools in Atlanta for over 10 years. They are an affiliate of the prestigious Margie Haber Studio, voted the Backstage Reader's Choice Award two years in a row for Favorite Cold Reading and Audition Class in Los Angeles. They offer a complete program of on-camera and Voice-over classes for Adults, Kids and Teens including Film, Television, Voice-over, Teleprompter, theatre and improv training.
Website: http://www.youract.tv

Address: 6251 Smithpointe Drive NW Building B, Peachtree Corners, GA 30092
Phone: 404-499-9996

The Alliance Theater Acting Program
Celebrating over 30 years of excellence, the Alliance Theatre Acting Program has developed a comprehensive curriculum in stage, film, and television acting. One of the most successful and respected programs in the country, the Acting Program offers students of all ages, experience, and abilities a chance to work with professional theatre and film educators in one of America's most renowned regional theatres. They have a wide range of classes including: adult acting classes, youth acting classes, drama camps, specialty workshops for adults including playwriting, screenwriting and voice-over as well as Master Series: Artist to Artist.
Website: http://alliancetheatre.org/content/acting-classes
Other details:??

Atlanta Workshop Players (AWP)
AWP's "Actor's-Track" is designed to exercise creativity and develop a love and appreciation for the arts in an exciting, joyful atmosphere. Their "Pro-Track" trains and inspires the serious student who wishes to pursue a career as a performer. Classes are held at AWP's Studio of the Arts.
Website: http://atlantaworkshopplayers.com
Email: info@atlantaworkshopplayers.com
Phone: 770-998-8111
Address: 8560 Holcomb Bridge Rd. Suite 111, Alpharetta, GA 30022

Basement Theater
Focused on improv classes. They also have improv and stand-up shows. Other classes include corporate training and team building workshops.
Website: http://www.thebasementtheatre.com
Email: info@thebasementtheatre.com
Phone: 404-277-3071
Address: 175 West Wieuca Rd NE, Suite B3, Atlanta, GA 30342

The Brink Improv
Improv training for adults and children. Also has corporate training classes.
Website: http://www.thebrinkimprov.com
Email: kristy@thebrinkimprov.com
Phone: 404-989-3672

Dad's Garage
Founded in 1995, Dad's Garage Theatre has grown from a small volunteer led organization to a thriving mid-size theatre led by professional artistic and administrative staff. They put up original scripted products and improve shows year-round. Classes include structured, progressive improv classes (Level 1 – Fundamentals of Improv to Level 4 – Performance Skills and Theatresports).
Website: http://www.dadsgarage.com/classes
Phone: 404-523-3141
Address: 1105 Euclid Ave. NE, Atlanta, GA 30307

Improv Atlanta
Focused on stand-up comedy shows and classes. Classes cover both the craft and business side of stand-up.
Website: http://www.theimprovatlanta.com/comedy-class

Email: info@TheImprovAtlanta.com
Phone: 678-244-3612
Address: 56 E Andrews Dr NW, Atlanta, GA 30305

Village Theatre

The Village Theatre offers an extensive 5-level improvisational comedy-training program in addition to occasional workshops. Over the course of the 5-level program, you will learn and continue to improve your understanding of the rules of improv acting and the fun behind improv games. As you progress through the levels, you'll receive instruction from experienced Village Theatre improvisers.
Website: http://villagecomedy.com/classes
Email: classes@villagecomedy.com
Phone: 404-688-8858
Address: 349 Decatur St., Suite L, Atlanta, GA 30312

Whole World Theatre

Classes include various levels of improve for adults and kids.
Website: http://wholeworldtheatre.com/classes
Phone: 404-817-7529
Address: 1216 Spring St NW, Atlanta, GA 30309

Sketch Acting

Founded in 2001, Sketchworks is Atlanta's premier live sketch comedy company and troupe featuring some of Atlanta's top working pros. The group also conducts classes in both writing and acting, always developing and launching the next generation of Atlanta's funniest artists and talent. Classes include sketch acting and writing for adults, and kids' summer camps.
Website: http://www.sketchworkscomedy.com
Address: 349 Decatur St SE, Atlanta, GA 30312

Email: sketchworkstheatre@gmail.com
Phone:??

Visiting LA Teachers / Seasonal Classes
Some of the top instructors from LA regularly come down to Atlanta to teach as well.

Crystal Carson
Crystal is an LA-based acting coach and teacher. She teaches "auditioning by heart", utilizing students' emotional, intellectual and spiritual sensibilities to generate a character's life. She holds weekend workshops in Atlanta.
Website: http://www.crystalcarson.com/weekend-workshops

Margie Haber
Margie is an LA-based audition technique and acting coach. She travels to teach in Atlanta twice per year to teach at YourAct Studio.
Website: http://www.margiehaber.com/home/classes/haber-in-atlanta

Sam Christensen Studios
The Sam Christensen Program of classes and workshops provides a tested, research-based system that adapts as careers grow and change by defining an image, an individual 'Personal Brand' for actors. Sam's classes in Atlanta are held at Drama Inc. acting studio.
Website: http://samchristensen.com/cities/across-the-us/#atlanta

Ted Brunetti Studio South
Ted is one of the last protégés of the famous acting teacher, Uta Hagen. A passionate teacher with great insights into the

industry and a solid framework for script analysis, he visits Atlanta every year for focused classes and workshops at the Lovett School near Cumberland Mall area. I completed a 4-day class with him recently and loved it.
Website: http://www.tedbrunettistudiosouth.com

Classes for the Business Side of Acting
Most acting teachers usually spend some time at the beginning of class going over what's happening in the industry in Atlanta and offer career management tips. But sometimes it's hard to know how to move forward. Sometimes you need some personalized coaching. The resources below help you with that.

Acting Career Management Coaching with Mike Pniewski
Mike Pniewski is a very well established actor with a long string of credits under his belt. He offers one-on-one coaching to actors on the business side of acting – from planning to strategizing to actionable goals to accountability. Mike's guidance helps a lot. Check out his website: http://www.acttowin.com. I personally continue to work with him and can tell you that I've found his guidance and insights very valuable.
Phone: 404-863-6768

Kristen Shaw Acting Studio
This is another studio that, in addition to offering classes on acting skills, also has a class called "Living the Actors' Life" (http://kristenshawactingstudio.com/class-descriptions). If you prefer to work on your career in a group setting, this is worth considering. I've had friends take this class who've absolutely loved it.

5. Get Headshots

Headshots are probably your #1 marketing tool. Atlanta has great photographers that help you get comfortable in front of the camera and get the photos you need to bring out your essence. There is no one best headshot photographer – you must evaluate which works best for you by checking out their work on their website, their location, their rates, and asking around during class or asking your agent. Some agencies even have a list of photographers on their website. For example: Houghton: http://www.houghtontalent.com/links.htm
PeopleStore: http://peoplestore.net/resources/
AMT: http://amtagency.com/client-resources/headshot-photographers-guidelines/

Tips –
1. Make sure you know what Acting headshots are. They are not glamor shots. They are not supposed to make you look good. They are supposed to capture you, as close to how you would look when you walk into a casting session or put yourself on tape.
2. Know yourself and the market you are in to know what looks you want to capture. Perhaps an archetyping / personal brand class would help?

Headshot Photographers List
Sample list of headshot photographers in Atlanta:

- Actor Boutique, Natalia Livingston, 404-596-8556, http://actorboutique.com/services/head-shots-for-actors
- Angela Morris, 404-314-4789, http://www.angelaphotography.com
- Anna Ritch, 678-522-2322, http://www.annaritchphoto.com

- Barbara Benvil, 323-969-4944, http://benvilphotography.com (I've used her, love the pics)
- Brenda Lajoan, brendalajoanphotography@gmail.com, 678-576-1655, http://www.brendalajoan.us
- C. Dyer Photography, catherine@dramainc.net, http://www.catdyer.com
- Christian Morris Photography, 678-315-3083, photographybycm@gmail.com, https://cmpd.carbonmade.com
- CMK Photography, http://www.cmkphotos.com
- Daniel Parvis, daniel@danielparvis.com, 678-699-0484
- Derek Blanks, 678-457-5332, http://dblanks.com
- Dwayne Boyd Photography, 770-873-8974, http://dwayneboydphotography.com
- Jackie Goldston, 678-662-7425, info@jackiegoldstonphotography.com, http://www.jackiegoldstonphotography.com
- John Scott Randall, 404-218-9516, jsrandall@mac.com, http://www.johnscottrandall.com
- J. Renee Photography, 678-481-4609
- Kelsey Edwards, LA-based photographer who also does work in Atlanta. Can book appointments online. 323-936-6106, kelsey@kelseyedwardsphoto.com, http://www.kelseyedwardsphoto.com/atlantacontact.php
- Leigh Germy Photography, http://www.leighgermy.com, leigh@leighgermy.com, 434-426-2614
- Lou Freeman, 404-697-1113, http://www.loufreeman.com
- Megan Dougherty, 770-309-8711, megan919@gmail.com, http://megansimage.com
- Michael Stothard, http://www.michaelstothard.com, Michael@michaelstothard.com, 404-202-0963
- Offhand Photography, 404-312-5392
- Paul Amodio, 770-423-1654, http://paulamodio.com

- Photography by Raquel, 404-454-1878
- Richard Mellinger, 404-622-5998
- Stacey Bode, 404-622-5998, http://staceybode.com/category/headshots
- Ted Westby, http://www.niceshotted.com, NiceShotTed@yahoo.com, 678-548-3655 (I've used him, love the pics)
- Teryl Jackson, 770-218-6138, http://www.terylphoto.com
- Tracey Page, Babycake Studios 404-910-3259, http://www.babycakestudios.com
- Travis Sawyer – Mellow Photography, 770-355-1362
- Vii Tanner, 678-366-5946, http://www.viitanner.com

You will typically get your headshot pictures on a CD or as a zip file using an online file transfer service like HighTail.com or WeTransfer.com. Once you get your headshots, do a couple of things:
- Copy them to your computer or to another external hard drive – so you have multiple backups.
- Also upload them to cloud storage like DropBox or Google Drive - so they are accessible even away from home.
- The files will all have some weird names based on the camera used. So choose 2 or 3 from each look and rename them into some easily recognizable form. For example, "Rafiq_Batcha_Headshot1.jpg" or "RafiqBatcha_Headshot1.jpg" or some such uniform manner. Casting Directors and Agents can easily see what the file is (a headshot) and whose it is (yours).

Headshot Printing and Reproductions

Once your headshots have been shot, you also need to get them printed. These days, with the use of online submissions and self-taping, you really don't need a lot of printed headshots. But in the few instances you are asked to audition in-person, you do need one or two printed headshots with your resume printed or attached on the back. You could, of course, print as and when needed on your home/office printer but too often, I've found myself in situations where the printer was out of ink or having paper issues *just* when I needed to print color headshots. Then I end up making a mad dash to a FedEx Kinkos or worse, taking whatever terrible colors end up on my home printer and hope the casting directors don't notice (yeah right).

Bottom line, I highly recommend getting at least 50 headshots printed from a professional lab such as below:

- ABC Pictures / Headshots, http://abcpictures.com, 888-526-5336
- Bunker LA, https://bunkerla.com, 323-463-1070
- Genesis Printing, http://www.genesis-printing.com, 323-965-7935, upload@genesis-printing.com
- PhotoScan, https://www.photoscanonline.com/atlanta-comp-cards.php, 800-352-6367
- Prima Atlanta, http://www.primaatlanta.com, 404-355-7200
- The Pixel Pusher, http://www.thepixelpusher.biz, 404-781-1111

Remember to always keep a couple of up-to-date headshots in your car and/or backpack (briefcase, whatever) too.

6. Find Work and Build Resume

When you are starting your career, you will most likely not have any credits or agent representation. You will have to find projects and self-submit to build your resume. This is absolutely key, even if you have representation. You have to constantly look for opportunities to perform at auditions because that is one of the few aspects of this career that is in your control. As you do more of it, you get better at it. You also hone your craft and comfort level, and get better known by the buyers (casting directors, producers, directors).

A note on your initial resume – it's okay to start with no credits. Everybody has to start somewhere. If you've done some student films or shorts before, list them. Also list classes you've taken. Just don't lie about work you didn't do.

Create your profile on these websites and self-submit to projects. All these sites have email notification systems to alert you when projects have roles that fit your profile. Make sure you are signed up for these and submit yourself as promptly as you can.

- Actors Access (http://www.actorsaccess.com) – Most commonly used by casting directors working on the big SAG projects. Creating a profile is free but additional services such as uploading a demo reel or modifying pictures cost money. You can sign up for email notifications to receive breakdowns based on your geographic preference (in this case, "Southeast") and your gender, age range, etc. Submission is $2 per role you submit for or free if you buy the $68 annual membership.
- 800Casting (http://800casting.com) – This is a paid website, i.e., you need to pay to even create a profile. Basic membership starts at $49.95/year and goes up from there. You can sign up for email notifications here too. But submitting to projects is free.

- NowCasting (https://www.nowcasting.com) – Another "free to register" website with extra services costing money.

Other such websites are:
1. http://home.castingnetworks.com
2. Backstage (Atlanta Auditions) – http://www.backstage.com/casting/open-casting-calls/atlanta-auditions
3. Love2Act.com – mostly non-union independent projects
4. http://atlanta.craigslist.org/search/tlg – a lot of hip hop related opportunities. Though I have booked some work through this when I was starting out, there is the element of scammers and unreliability involved. Overall, be careful about Craigslist and use your judgment.
5. IndieFilm Casting – as the name suggests, focused on indie, non-union projects. You can sign up for email alerts. The email subject will mention the project name and location. If it is Atlanta-based, you will know right away and can then choose to self-submit.

Background Work

Background, or extra, work is **not** the same as being a principal actor on a project. The pay rates and treatment on set are vastly lower for extras. Typically $64/8 hours or $72/10 hours but it really depends on the project. That said, if you do not have a day job to support you, or if you wish to get a glimpse of the enormous work and complexities of a professional SAG production, this is one way to do it and get paid. There are plenty of opportunities to do background work. Just sign up for alerts from these:

- Bill Marinella Casting: http://www.facebook.com/billmarinellacasting
- Catrett Locke Casting: http://www.facebook.com/CLCastingCo
- Cherrix Casting: http://www.facebook.com/CherrixCastingATL
- Christopher Gray Casting: https://www.facebook.com/groups/250424711642058
- Cordon Extras Casting: https://www.facebook.com/bacatlanta
- Extras Casting Atlanta: http://www.facebook.com/ExtrasCastingAtlanta
- Hylton Casting: http://hyltoncasting.com
- Last Looks Casting: https://www.facebook.com/groups/lastlookscasting

7. Create More Marketing Tools

Get Listed on IMDB

It is totally worth it to get an IMDBPro account. This gives you access to casting directors' and agents' info, and a ton more information that helps you prepare for agency interviews, find and book jobs, etc. Cost is $149.99/year or $19.99/month.

Getting listed on IMDB is not as simple as just creating a profile and adding yourself.

If you worked on a film, TV show or other project that is already listed on IMDB and you are credited as an actor, or any other role (producer, writer, director etc.), you should automatically have a page on IMDB under the same name as you were credited.

If you worked on a project that is listed but you don't have credit or if the project you worked on is not listed on IMDB, you can submit to have it added.

Once you do have an IMDB page, you must get a vanity URL that looks like http://imdb.me/<ACTORNAME>. For example, http://imdb.me/rafiqbatcha. This will make your IMDB Page easy to read and remember. And it's free! To learn more about setting up a vanity URL, see this IMDB help page for Vanity URLs.

Put Up Your Own Website

These days, it's a given that people will google your name at some point. So it's useful to create an online presence that, at the bare minimum, consists of your website with your name or some variation of it (say "JohnDoeActor.com").

Step 1: Register your domain name.
Preferably your website domain name should be "yourname.com" or "yournameactor.com". Registering a website domain name is cheap, usually around $10/year. There are many places to do this: https://www.godaddy.com, https://www.namecheap.com or just look up "cheap domain names" online. For steps on how to register a domain name, check out http://www.wikihow.com/Register-a-Domain-Name.

Step 2: Build a website, either on your own or through some low cost providers.
1. You can create your own site using http://www.weebly.com, or https://wordpress.org or some such free website building service. My own website http://www.rafiqbatcha.com is built on Weebly.

2. Or hire a website design and hosting service like http://www.easyactorwebsites.com or http://atomicbell.com , you can alo look up "actor websites" online and see what pops up.

If you don't want to spend money on registering a domain name, here are some other options to consider:

3. Create a blog at https://wordpress.com, https://www.blogger.com, or https://www.tumblr.com. This typically will be not a dedicated website name but rather something like ActorName.blogspot.com or ActorName.wordpress.com. For example, http://markruffalo.tumblr.com.

4. Or just create a Facebook fan page. This can be done even to complement your website that you create above. Here's a good guide to create a Facebook fan page: http://www.wikihow.com/Create-a-Facebook-Fan-Page

Of course, in addition, you have a whole range of online presence options such as Twitter, Instagram, and LinkedIn. Ideally, when people search for your name on Google, you want the first result to be your website or your profile on IMDB.com.

Create a Demo Reel

Most probably a lot of the work you book initially, without a professional agent's representation, is going to be unpaid work in student films and webisodes. But hopefully, the final result will at least look and sound great so you can start to build a demo reel. The key is that it really does have to feel professional – the lighting, the sound quality, the editing. Otherwise, it is better to not have a demo reel.

Here are some resources that help you cut together a demo reel after you have managed to get a copy of your work in an indie feature or short, a web series, a commercial, etc.

- Video Impact, http://videoimpactatlanta.com, 404-325-1444
- Chris Paul, 404-663-6920
- Paul Ryden, 678-777-7825
- Viviana Chavez, 404-725-5500
- Alexander Williams, 404-735-4043

8. Audition

When you do get invited to audition, chances are you will be asked to self-tape the audition and send it in. More and more casting happens directly off your audition tape and in some cases the tape is used as a first level screening. There are some very clear guidelines about how the audition should be taped – the background should be clean and plain, the lighting should be good, the audio should be clear, you should have a reader and much more.

IMPORTANT - here are some websites that explain how to self-tape correctly:

- Do's and don'ts of self-taping by Matt Cornwell, local actor and teacher: https://www.youtube.com/watch?v=GZoG3mFGlrc. And on a related note, a really funny sketch about an actor self-taping, doing almost everything wrong possible: https://www.youtube.com/watch?v=9mPNzyom0bM
- 3 videos by Kristen Shaw Acting Studio that give examples of a bad self-tape, a good self-tape but with bad audition, and finally a good self-tape and audition performance: http://actortapingservices.com/services/audition-taping/ (scroll down to the "Example Auditions" section)

Audition Taping Services

If you are unable to create good quality audition tapes as mentioned above, here's a list of audition taping services that you can use. Typically, the cost is $15-$20/15 minutes with no coaching. Check out the respective websites or call for current info and rates.

Actor Taping Services

This is the audition taping service at Kristen Shaw Acting Studio. I love the fact that they have a convenient online booking system where you can select the day and time slot.
Address: 3040 Holcomb Bridge Rd, Norcross, GA 30071
Website: http://actortapingservices.com
Email: contact@actortapingservices.com
Phone: 682-233-4863

Actors Taping Actors

This is run by my fellow actor at Houghton, Omer Mughal. Also love that there's a convenient online booking system here.
Address: The Company Acting Studio, 500 Amsterdam Ave NE, Atlanta, GA 30306
Website: http://www.actorstapingactors.com
Phone: 404-388-4882

Audition Recording Services, Brian Childers

Address: Near Chamblee Tucker Rd & I- 85 Access Rd, Atlanta, GA
Website: http://www.auditionrecordingservices.com
Phone: 678-644-6908

Drama Inc.
Address: 650 Hamilton Ave SE, Atlanta, GA 30312
Email: info@dramainc.net
Phone: 404-600-6070
Website: http://www.dramainc.net/audition-taping.html

Get Taped!
Address: 2849 Piedmont Rd NE, Atlanta, GA 30305 (same as Professional Actors Studio)
Website: http://www.get-taped.com/Get_Taped/Welcome.html
Email: get_taped@comcast.net (best way to schedule appointments)
Phone: 404-913-9ACT (228)

Michael H. Cole Studio
In addition to teaching, Michael Cole also helps put actors on tape at a very reasonable price. And being a phenomenal teacher, he will also offer some coaching if you so desire.
Address: 4650 Flat Shoals Parkway, Decatur, GA 30034
Email: colemichaelh@gmail.com
Phone: 404-561-5132

Randall Taylor
Located near North Druid Hills Rd and Briarcliff Rd, Atlanta, GA
Email: randyready21@gmail.com
Phone: 404-786-4168

Suzanne Salhaney
Address: Alpharetta-Johns Creek Area
Phone: 770-598-6057
Website: http://suzannesalhaney.com/audition-taping-services-atlanta/

9. Get Representation (aka Talent Agents)

So now that you've got <u>great training,</u> great marketing tools (<u>headshots</u>, <u>website</u>, <u>online profiles</u>) and some credits under your belt, it's time to get professional representation. There is, of course, nothing stopping you from submitting to agencies before you have any credits but typically the top agencies in Atlanta want to see that you are willing to do the work and are self-motivated. Remember that you are a product and the talent agency is a sales agency. If you can prove that your product is polished, has great sales tools to go along with it and has some market traction, that's when the agencies will be more than happy to represent you. But you have to show that you believe in yourself first.

The benefit of having a talent agency is that they are working to get you auditions. They have the established relationships with the top producers and casting directors to get you the right opportunities, with access to breakdowns and knowledge of projects that don't even show up on the casting sites.

With the vast increase in the amount of filming happening here, the number of agencies has also increased. Each agency has its own requirements in terms of how they accept new submissions (via email or online form or mailing in, etc.), when they accept, what information they need from you, etc. Please review the websites of each of these agencies for the latest information.

Here are some of the better-known agencies, in alphabetical order.
- Alexander White Agency: http://www.alexanderwhiteagency.com
- Atlanta Models and Talent: http://amtagency.com
- Atlanta's Young Faces: http://atlantasyoungfaces.com
- Bloc South: http://atl.blocagency.com

- The Burns Agency: http://www.theburnsagencyonline.com
- Convention Models and Talent (CMT) Agency:
  http://www.cmtagency.com
- East Coast Talent: http://www.ectagency.com
- Elite Model Management Corp – website??
- Houghton Talent: http://www.houghtontalent.com (my
  agency, GREAT PEOPLE!)
- J. Pervis: http://www.jpervistalent.com
- Jana VanDyke Agency: http://www.jvagency.com
- People Store: http://www.peoplestore.net
- Salt Model and Talent: http://www.saltmat.com
- Stewart Talent: http://stewarttalent.com/atlanta/index.php

10.   Know the Casting Directors

This is not necessarily a step in the roadmap to becoming an
actor but rather a "know the Atlanta market" section. Typically,
there's not much for you to do with casting directors except
interacting with them if and when you get invited to audition in
person. However, this is not very common because of the
prevalence of self-taped auditions.

But still, it's good to know that the casting directors are in town
and what shows they are casting for. Sometimes they do
workshops, which might be worth checking out. Other times
you might want to do some targeted marketing to them. The
following Casting Directors have offices in Atlanta:
- Alpha Tyler: http://www.imdb.com/name/nm1858087
- Big Picture Casting: http://bigpicturecasting.com
- Carolyn Jenkins Casting:
  http://www.carolynjenkinsagency.com
- Cherrix Casting: http://cherrixcasting.com

- Corrigan & Johnston Casting : http://cjcasting.com (located in Charlotte, NC, but audition Atlanta actors as well)
- Chez Casting: http://www.chezgroup.com
- Feldstein | Paris Casting: http://feldsteinpariscasting.com
- Fincannon Casting: http://www.fincannoncasting.com
- Jackie Burch: http://jackie-burch.squarespace.com
- Kris Redding Casting: http://www.castingbykrisredding.com
- OAS Casting (Olubajo Sonubi): http://www.oascasting.com
- Pierre Casting: http://www.pierrecasting.com
- Rhavynn Drummer: http://www.rhavynndrummer.com
- Stilwell Casting: http://www.stilwellcasting.com
- Tag Team Casting: http://www.tagteamlocationsandcasting.com/Casting.html

11.   Practice, Practice, Practice

There are plenty of ways to keep acting and performing in between jobs:

1. Do theater – there are many theaters in Atlanta such as Alliance Theater, 7 Stages, 14th Street Playhouse, Atlanta Workshop Players and Theatrical Outfit. One way to get seen by all regional theaters is to audition at the Atlanta Unified Auditions that are held every year where actors get a chance to audition before approximately 50 Atlanta area and regional theater companies.
2. Student films – sign up to be notified for student film auditions at Art Institute of Atlanta: aiaauditions@gmail.com. You can also check out the film departments at Georgia State University and SCAD.
3. Do improv – typically, upon completing advanced level classes at any one of the improv studios in town, you will get a chance to perform improv in front of a paying audience.

4. Do sketch comedy at SketchWorks, upon completion of the Advanced Workshop Group.
5. Every year, the 48-Hour Film Festival happens in Atlanta, where teams have one weekend (48 hours) from writing to having a finished movie ready for screening. Check out the website http://www.48hourfilm.com/en/atlanta and sign up to be notified when they hold auditions.

12.   More Marketing

As an actor, you must constantly make your presence known to the decision makers (casting directors, producers, etc.) in a non-annoying way. As the interviews with actors in the second half of this book will make obvious, the #1 way to market yourself and network is to take classes. Additionally, here are some more ways to do just that:

1. **Casting Director (CD) workshops** – This is typically a one or two-day event where a casting director teaches and shares their insights about the industry. This can be a great way to be seen by a CD that you've not auditioned for before. Each acting studio typically has some workshop like this. Check out the acting studios' websites and sign up as and when a workshop is available. Some, like Chez Studios, let you sign up for a newsletter that then notifies you when a workshop is coming up.
2. **Attend monthly Georgia Production Partnership (GPP) meetings at Manuel's Tavern** – Firstly, I love the food at Manuel's Tavern – great burgers, thick cut fries and beer at affordable prices. The GPP is a coalition of companies and individuals who are active in the state's film, video, music, and interactive game industries. GPP meetings typically feature a few speakers talking about current issues and trends that affect the entertainment industry in Atlanta/Georgia.

3. **Volunteer at film festivals** – In addition to the Atlanta Film Festival, there are many other festivals as well, such as: Atlanta Underground Film Festival, BronzeLens Film Festival, Atlanta Shortsfest, and many more. Volunteering gets you free screening passes in many cases, and a chance to help out filmmakers and be known.
4. **Join the "Georgia Film TV" Facebook page** – Run by Atlanta actor Lawrence Van. It's not an open group, so you will need to request approval to be added. With 4000+ members, it's a great way to stay in touch with what's happening in the Atlanta film and TV scene.

This concludes the roadmap section of this book. It's a lot of info so take your time to go back and review sections, check out links, and take notes. Know that as you continue to pursue acting in Atlanta, you will absorb this info just by being in class and interacting with fellow actors. Don't rush or fret. Enjoy the ride and take frequent bathroom breaks.

Atlanta Actor Interviews

In this second half of the book, I've included interviews with Atlanta actors. Many thanks to all the actors who have graciously spared their time to share their experiences and insights. I've tried my best to include a variety of actor types (gender, ethnicity, age range), and experiences (ATL to LA, LA to ATL, long list of credits, relatively new, formally trained, etc.).

I asked the same set of questions to all the actors here, though not necessarily in the same order, and we took some interesting detours as they popped up in the conversation.

The idea is to show you the diversity of the journeys of actors pursuing acting in Atlanta. There is no one-size-fits-all. The interviews are listed in alphabetical order of first names.

Alex Collins

Born and raised in both England and Atlanta, Alex Collins is a 12+ year member of SAG-AFTRA, and a co-founder and former Managing Director of Straitjacket Society, LA's wildly popular sketch company whose alumnae include Jillian Bell (Saturday Night Live, 22 Jump Street, Workaholics), Lenny Jacobson (Nurse Jackie, Big Time In Hollywood, Fl), Kelly Levy (Producer, writer, sketch performer on E's Soup!), and Sarah Tiana (national and international touring standup comic), to name a few. Collins has worked in independent and award winning films, episodic television, national and regional commercials, industrials, voice-overs, and new media and recent credits include his role in The Accountant with Ben Affleck and Anna Kendrick, Sleepless Nights with Jamie Foxx and Mena with Tom Cruise as well as roles on Sleepy Hollow (Fox), Satisfaction (USA), The Game (BET) and a recurring guest-star role on The Haves And The Have Nots (OWN).
IMDB Page: http://www.imdb.com/name/nm1180204

When did you know you wanted to be an actor and how did you go about starting that?

I grew up in England, and I was always an energetic and expressive kid. I really enjoyed watching American television. As a kid in England, we only had four channels. One of the TV shows that I remember watching was *The Fall Guy*. And he was a stunt man. That seemed like a glamorous way of making a living. I thought that's what I wanted to do but there weren't any avenues for that. I moved into athletics, and then playing soccer. My family moved to the US right before I started high school, which is where I took a few drama classes and got my first opportunity to actually work on stage.

Where was high school?

I went to a few different high schools. But my opportunity came here in Atlanta at the Lovett School. Through Jay Freer, who is still the Fine Arts director there today - he gave my first true acting opportunity on stage. I'm sure I was quite awful. I went on to college and I wanted to act but it never worked with my schedule. I got a degree in finance and a degree in marketing and ended up working for a couple of different Fortune 500 companies in a couple of different cities. Then I ended up back in Atlanta.

One of my lifelong friends would email me or call or leave a voicemail everyday saying, "Quit your job you know you want to act, quit your job you know you want to act". After about six months of that, I did it. I didn't really have a plan in place at that point. I promptly returned the favor to him and told him to quit his job. And he did! We ended up bartending and working at restaurants, got in a few different classes together, studied, took an introductory acting class at the Alliance Theatre, took a very early improv class and then found our way to the Professional Actor's Studio. At that point, it was one of the only schools that had an LA mentality. There were places that were teaching theatre technique like at the Alliance Theatre. The Professional Actor's Studio was really the only place teaching on-camera work. After a few years, I had learned a few skills and felt like I was doing a reasonably good job. I was represented as an actor in Atlanta. I got some different projects. The landscape back then was very different, back in the early 2000s. Very different from what it is today. And then I was fortunate enough to get my union eligibility here. My friend and I then decided to make a move to California.

You were working at Fortune 500 companies in corporate jobs. Was it a challenge for you going from that into the starving actor mode?
It was tough. I think back then I didn't know what I didn't know. Ignorance is bliss for lack of a better term. Personally, I'm a planner, very methodical, a list-maker. Had I actually taken the time to plan out what I was going to do, I probably wouldn't have ever done it because the odds are overwhelmingly against success as a career as an actor, depending on how you define success. If financial measure is the only measure of success, it's going to be very difficult to make a living as an actor. But if you can define success in other ways, then you can find success. For me, in the corporate world, making that decision to leave was a reactionary decision - like jumping in the deep end of the swimming pool and then figuring out how to swim.

You were born and brought up in England, so you are originally British?

Yes, I carry both citizenships. I carry a British passport and an American passport. My family and I moved here from England. It took about 10 years going through the natural channels to become a citizen. So fortunately for me, as an actor, I was able to obtain a British accent and about half of my work comes as an English actor, a British actor. Most people can't tell. My day-to-day life, I live as an American. But when I need to, I go back to being English. It's a little hidden thing.

Well, there's something going on in England that they're all booking these roles in the US. So it's good that you can leverage that in some way...

There's always been a different sort of respect for British actors. It's that they tend to have a theatre background, a lot of training in the theatre from a younger age. There's definitely an influx of Australian actors as well working in the past 10 or 15 years. And I think folks in England and Australia tend to really understand the work, the years that it takes. We're still sort of in this paparazzi, tabloid economy in the US, where we think that the shortest distance between two points is the easiest one, the path of least resistance, and that's not necessarily correct.

You don't have a formal degree in drama?

No, not at all.

Do you sometimes wish you had something like that?

No, I'm glad that I don't have a degree in theatre. It's a wonderful thing to have - it provides you with an immense amount of training, in theory, in different acting techniques, in the history of the theatre whether it's Greek, Roman, what have you, classical English theatre, knowing how to break down a script especially Shakespeare, a bit of that. But in the on-camera world, it's two totally different disciplines. Being a great theatre actor is no way to indicate that you're going to be a great on-camera actor. It goes to support the notion that you must have discipline to work hard, to rehearse, to take direction but it doesn't mean you're going to be a good actor, a good on-camera actor, by any stretch. A lot of people who just have an undergraduate degree, a Bachelor in Fine Arts, there's no guarantee that where they're coming from is teaching them anything relevant to today's industry on-camera. It changes so quickly.

After nine years in LA, what prompted your return to Atlanta?
I was in Los Angeles from 2003 to 2012. Right in the middle of that, in 2008, there was a writer strike that had a big impact on how television was made. That also coincided with some shifting paradigms in the way technology was being used to make television. And still, there was a conversion from film to digital, conversion from SD to HD. There was much more presence on the web, at new media around that time frame. Everybody freaked out. Nobody knew where their next job was coming from. As a result, film actors started taking on roles on television. That's why you see people like Steve Buscemi doing Boardwalk Empire. Now that these megastars were doing series leads, those roles were never available to television actors so

57

they had to take recurring roles. Those actors who did recurring roles had to ripple down to take smaller recurring roles, who had to ripple down to take guest star roles, who had to ripple down to take co-star roles. It was a massive saturation. It became a lot more competitive. And you combine that with the fact that there was a lot of runaway production happening, film and television was going to Toronto, it was going to Vancouver, it was going to Michigan, to New Orleans, and ultimately to Atlanta. A lot of the work in Los Angeles had dried up, so opportunities dried up. Actors, who the year before may have been getting 3 or 4 or 5 auditions a week, were getting 1 or 2 auditions a month. It changed the landscape for the entry level actor, and even folks who had credits. There's also a gatekeeper mentality in Los Angeles where certain casting directors are only going to see certain actors who are represented by a certain agency. If you're not with that agent, a right agent, you're never going to get it to the office, which means you're never going to audition. There's a lot of political maneuvering in Los Angeles. It's a really difficult uphill marathon. If you're there long enough, you can navigate it. You can get through a lot of the gatekeepers and access points. But it's not, by any means, an easy road.

You happened to have a base in Atlanta and then you saw Atlanta is booming. It worked out well that way that you were able to say I want to go back to Atlanta?
Yes. I had always maintained communication with my Atlanta agent when I was in LA and I've always maintained communication with my friends who are actors. I saw that they were able to keep a pretty good pulse on what was happening.

Between 2008 and 2012, technology really changed, primarily with Facebook. It allowed people to stay in contact with each other in a much easier way and MySpace was a precursor to that. It was easy to passively observe what was going on in Atlanta. There was a theatre company that had a Facebook page. Someone was making a short film and fundraising, they had a Facebook page. So I could always see what was going on. And when the tax subsidies were enacted in 2008, around 2009, 2010, things started to turn into a positive note in Georgia while the economy nationally was going down outside the industry. The economy was especially hit hard in California. Combine that with the writers' strike, California was not looking as wonderful as it had. I thought about moving. I thought to come back in 2010. I just stayed longer in LA because LA is gorgeous, the weather is great and my friends are there, the other sketch comedy people. Ultimately, it was the right decision to move back when I needed to.

Since you already maintained relationships with your agent in Atlanta, you were able to continue that and get back in the Atlanta scene quite quickly?
Correct. I moved back in October 2012 when the industry was closed down for Christmas. Which was fine because I had to move back, get settled, and get organized so I was ready to hit the ground running when production hit back up in 2013.

Can you talk a little bit more of how you supplemented your income once you moved back here?
I'm very fortunate. I think actors need to be adaptable. They need to be good at a wide variety of skills. Los Angeles is such a

massive city. It's built around Hollywood so the great majority of people who are actors are bartenders, waiters, valet guys. That's just a commonly accepted practice in Los Angeles that you're going to work in the service industry. It doesn't hurt if you're young and good-looking. You could make a lot of money. But Atlanta is not so directly correlated or entrenched in Hollywood. It's starting to get that way but there's still a novelty here. If you have a good relationship in a corporate environment with your job and they find out that you're an actor, a lot of times they're supportive so long as you get your work done. If you don't let your acting interfere with your work, I find a lot of employers to be relatively or reasonably supportive. If that's not the case, I think it's important for actors to evaluate their skillsets. Sometimes actors are great writers and they can work as copywriters or copy editors or freelance ghostwriters on projects. They can live a freelance lifestyle. I know other actors who are web designers or graphic designers or trying to be in a realm where they can set their own schedules like personal trainers, yoga instructors and Pilate's instructors. It's about understanding that making money as an actor is certainly no guarantee so you have to be able to think on your feet, and look at both the long game and the short game, and how you can make money.

Technology-based opportunities and home-based businesses are changing the landscape for actors. Uber is a great thing. I'm fortunate enough that I have a corporate job that I've had for 10 years. I had it in Los Angeles and I still work for that company from my home office. I'm able to set up a schedule that works for me. I can go to auditions or work on projects. I also teach and coach actors at Drama Inc. in Atlanta. In a corporate environment, actors need to show their value as an employee first. Do your job, show up. Be valuable to your employer. When you've been there for a while without asking for too many favors and too much flexibility, you can approach, you can understand who your boss is and how your boss is a communicator. Present that you're an actor and could maybe work a couple of days a week from home? The business landscape is now changing and teleworking is becoming more of an option because employers understand that the work-life balance is important. That eases into an actor's schedule.

What do you do in terms of marketing and networking in Atlanta?

There's active and passive marketing and networking. For me, passive networking and marketing are unchangeable all the time, which can be good or bad. It depends on your ambitions. But it also allows me to see who in my peer network is booking. Agents are posting congratulations. I can see who my competition is or who among my friends is doing well. I can read about what productions are coming to town - I learned instantly that Sleepy Hollow relocated from North Carolina to Georgia through a Facebook article. There's definitely value there. The active type of thing – definitely in the acting classroom environment, being open and listening to what's happening. You hear about "Oh my friend's producing a short film. My friend is producing a web series." And just through those organic circles with people that you study with or people who you respect, teachers that you work with, they all hear about casting, they'll hear about opportunities. I've been fortunate enough to be referred for a few jobs and that's been great. That's the best opportunity there, when somebody believes in you enough to refer you and you're able to work for someone else.

What about casting director mailings or workshops?
There are a lot of different schools of thought on that. LA has a very different market than Atlanta in that respect. There has been a big uprising in Los Angeles currently against the "Pay to Play" workshop scenario. In essence, what's happening in Los Angeles is a lot of workshops, the great majority of workshops, are taught by casting assistants or casting associates who have no ability to be a decision-maker in the casting process. They're just supplementing their income. But actors are filling these classes up to capacity because they feel like they don't have an access to the casting office otherwise. You can see where these connect here. Casting associates make $2,000-3,000 a month supplementing their income. Also, the fact that hardworking actors are paying $40, 50, 60 a workshop. I'm against that segment of the industry. Atlanta's not there yet but I'm firmly against 1 day, 1 night workshops. Why? Because if you are here in Atlanta and you're studying, and you have a good headshot, an agent will sign you. Sooner or later an agent is going to get an opportunity for you and you're going to get an audition. There's not enough casting, there's really a dozen casting directors in the region. You will get an opportunity to see that casting director, to read for that casting director, to go on tape for that casting director. An actor shouldn't have to pay for access to that sort of casting director.

I don't believe that can happen in a 1 or 2-hour workshop format. All you're learning is what particular casting directors need you to do, or what kind of headshots they like, or how do they get into the business, that kind of thing. That's all well and good but I'll rather spend $50 to pool that with all my friends and make a web series. Or you take that money, instead of doing a 1-page, 2-hour casting director workshop, take a scene-study class. Take a Meisner class. Take a film weapon class, any of those things. You can use your money to invest in yourself and your training and that's ultimately going to make you a more desirable actor to casting in the long run.

A lot of actors produce their own content that shows their type in the best light. Would you say that's one of the best marketing tools?
No question. Self-production, proactive production is one of the best things you can do. You can write something, or have someone write something that is in your wheelhouse, your branding, your type. You can package it in such a way now with iMovie and Final Cut. You can make something look quite high budget for very little investment. Have somebody who's a really talented editor? Great, they're on your team. Know somebody who's great with music? Great, he's going to compose your score. It's about people doing favors for each other and ultimately everybody can raise their level.

Looking forward, where do you see acting opportunities in Atlanta? Do you think we're going to see bigger and bigger roles being offered to Atlanta actors?

There's a short answer and a long answer to that. The first part of the answer is yes. Within that, we have to be careful. There has been a yellow brick road idea with Atlanta. And everybody's seen all the work. There's all the production and they see the celebrities coming to town. People are blinded by the glitter and glamour of that. What's happening, as a result, is that there are hundreds, if not thousands, of people who are hobbyists and getting into the industry. They don't have headshots, they're not taking classes, and they're calling themselves an actor. I wouldn't act in an episode of E.R. and call myself a doctor! The analogy is very similar. Or somebody worked background for 1 day for Captain America, now they're an actor. That's not true, and it demeans the value of what it means to be an actor. It demeans the value of people who've been working for 10, 15, 20 years seeking out a career through lean. We have to be careful that we give those people on the periphery of the industry too much visibility or too much credit. We need to be careful because too many of those people get audition opportunities. When they tank those audition opportunities, it continues to enforce the glass ceiling here in Atlanta for actors. That, in turn, continues to limit access to the larger roles here.

That said, I believe that producers are starting to see the talent here, not just for the under-five, not just for the costar roles but in larger roles. We have a number of people who've been through thick and thin who are doing great things. Michael Cole on Being Mary Jane. Lori Beth Sikes who was practically a series regular on Resurrection. There's a number of the Walking Dead cast, obviously. Studios continue to invest in Atlanta heavily. There's Screen Gems here, Pinewood here. There are multiple other construction projects going on here. Those people don't make multi-million dollar decisions quickly or lightly. Productions are going to be here for many, many years to come. The bottleneck now is in crew. They still have to bring out a lot of the top line crew, department heads, from Los Angeles and that's very expensive to do. So the next step for the industry behind the camera is to train qualified crew people to ultimately pick up the reins and manage large projects.

Bringing it back to the actor front, yes, I think what we're starting to see now is actors reading for larger roles. It's a matter of economics. Series regular roles on television will almost never be cast out of Atlanta. The simple reason is creative people are not making the final casting decision. Network people are making the casting decisions. They're called suits, or network suits. They are making the decisions. Often they're accounting people, numbers people. They say, well this person hasn't done anything before. This person hasn't been a series regular before. This person doesn't have the Q factor or the Q rating that another actor has. He's not a name, that sort of thing. I do believe that series regulars for television and series leads for film will continue to be cast out of LA. There's no reason for me to be given a lead role for Captain America. That's just not art. That's not going to sell tickets. But what's happening is that feeling is breaking down and you're finding Atlanta actors now doing multiple episodes, 3-5 episodes in a season in a TV show. And that didn't happen in the past. So that's really, really changing.

What do you think needs to happen, if anything, to Atlanta, for actors to be ready for the bigger opportunities?

Training. If an actor is not in class every week, they're doing themselves a disservice. One of my friends, a series regular in a TV show that shoots here, spoke to my class end of last year. She talked about before she became a series regular. For her first several years in LA, she had multiple roommates so her rent was low. She worked as much as she could to make as much money as she could. And she was in 2 or 3 classes all week. She was coaching. She was paying for private coaching for every audition she could afford. So the difference between LA and Atlanta is actors who are finding success in Los Angeles are making it their priority, their main reason for existence. The going out, partying in the club, going out surfing, going out to rub elbows with celebrities...that's not the priority. Studying seven pages for class tomorrow, two lines for my audition and coaching for this guest star audition, that's the priority. In Atlanta, we still don't have that mentality, and I can't blame a lot of people for not having that mentality. But in Atlanta people have work, family, life, and then acting is somewhere like 3rd or 4th in the list of priorities.

It's basically about making acting your #1 priority and pursuing it every day?

Yes, but then the follow up to that is - what is each individual's definition of success as an actor? If you want to be a series regular, if you want to be a known commodity, you're probably not going to achieve that in Atlanta, you're probably not going to achieve that if it's not your #1 priority. If you want to make a reasonable living, enjoy a quality of life when you can still see your kids in the morning, your kids when they come home from school, then maybe have a supplementary income or something freelance. Or you have a nice accommodating boss in your corporate job, and you act here and there when it comes along, Atlanta's a great place to be. But you have to have realistic expectations of what's going to happen.

It's funny though how British actors and Australian actors didn't necessarily live in LA but they still are able to book these big roles.
It's because a lot of those folks have been working for 10, 15 years in their home country before making it in the American public sphere. You can take Cate Blanchett, Sam Worthington, Guy Pearce, Tom Hardy. All of them were all working for double-digit years before anybody in America ever knew who they were.

You are SAG?
I'm SAG-AFTRA. That's correct. I have been in the union for 12 years now.

Do you continue to have representation outside Atlanta?
Not at this time. When I came back to Atlanta, I left LA behind for the time being. But I certainly consider all opportunities. I look at other markets like Los Angeles, New Orleans, as opportunities to secure representation whether through an agent or a manager.

Do you use tools like Actors Access or 800Casting to look for opportunities outside Atlanta?

Not so much. Being union changes things a little bit. I advocate non-union actors using all of those tools. Whether it's Actors Access, Casting Networks, 800casting because there's a large number of student films, independent shorts, independent features that are all non-union. That's a big slice of pie that I can't look at because I'm union. There are still projects here in Georgia that are independent and are union. There's SCAD or GSU, or through the 48-hour film project, those have a range of agreements with the union so I can work on those. But the lion's share of my opportunities come directly through my agent.

You have no plans right now to move back to LA at any point?
No. I'm there every few months just connecting with my friends, going out for a long weekend. I would love if I were so busy that I had to move back out there, that'd be great. I don't envision that happening. I would love to be in a financial place where I could live in both cities but the economics of Los Angeles are very, very expensive.

How do you stay positive? This is a very, very tough profession. Do you ever feel like giving up?
I think we all do, we're all human. And it's something that you have to get used to quickly as an actor. It doesn't make it easy, you just have to know. You are statistically going to hear overwhelmingly more no than yes in this business. The majority doesn't give feedback as to why you got a no. In other professions, if you are interviewing for a job, generally you'll get feedback as to why someone is not hiring you. At least you could move forward and learn from that. In acting, you don't know. Was my audition terrible? Or was my audition great but

they just went with somebody they thought was a better fit? What If they scrapped the role altogether? You have to trust your instincts as an actor and that comes from just constantly being in class, and trusting that the work that you're doing in auditions is good work. It's not that they don't like you. There are a million reasons why you don't get tapped and usually only one reason why you do. You just have to have a short, short memory. The way I assume, everything is I'm not getting the job. And that's a very defeatist attitude.

It's not that I don't think I'm good and I don't deserve the job. I deserve every job I audition for. Every audition I put forward is a good audition. I just understand the statistics. It's easier to function if I compartmentalize things. I'll do the audition and then the three most words I believe an actor can understand is "Let it go". I'll use a different analogy and this may make sense. When you've taken your math midterm, turn it in left the classroom, you can't suddenly walk in and go, can you give me my test back? I need to change number seven. You don't get to do that, and it's the same thing in auditions. You go on, do the work, take the test, and when you leave the room, let it go. Because you can't change your grade, you can't change the outcome. So do your work upfront, notice you did the good work and then let the chips fall where they may. It is very difficult and hard to understand that because you think somebody doesn't like you as an actor or doesn't like your choices but majority of the time that's not the case. It's just that someone else was more right for the role than you were.

What do you wish someone had told you at the beginning of your career and what mistakes do you think you've made, if any?

I've made dozens, if not hundreds, of mistakes and I continue to make mistakes everyday in this industry. Understand that you will make mistakes and you have to pick yourself up, dust yourself off and stay at it. You have to develop a thick skin as an actor because this is a thankless industry. Many people don't understand the sacrifice that it takes to do this, especially if you ultimately want to move to a place like Los Angeles. Let it go. If an actor can really remember that, that will help them. Having a thick skin, not taking things personally, will really help. There are a million things that you can learn as an actor. Technically, how to act on-camera, how to deal with improv. Those things come with time and experience. Those things come with the variety of classes that you take over time, and experience that you have on set.

Fundamentally, as a person, if somebody told me stop chasing your tail, stop trying to fit a square peg into a round hole or stop trying to mold yourself into what you think they want you to be. A lot of actors do that. They try to guess what casting wants at any given time. They try and guess what agents want and so they'll dye their hair blonde because blondes are in right now or they'll get a tan because ethnic actors seem to be more in right now. But trends will change. And they're cyclical. What's hot today won't be hot for a year and then they'll be hot every year. It's really weird. Having confidence in who you are, as a person, as a being. When you step into the room, having the confidence to say, here's what I am giving you. This is my representation of the character, this is why I believe this is the right interpretation of the character. I'm open to take direction from you if I like your direction.

You may not get the job. More often than not, you won't get the job. But if you could do that, its a lot easier to absorb that rejection, and absorb the no, knowing that you did all the things that you needed to do, and understanding that it's not you. They don't dislike you as a person. So many actors, especially younger actors chronologically, especially younger actors in terms of tenure to the business, they constantly seek out this magic formula, or this magic potion. But there isn't one. They invest all the time and the money trying to change who they are, based on what they think someone else is going to like. That's definitely one of the things that I struggled with earlier too in my career. But now I do what I do and leave with my head held high.

Al-Jaleel Knox

Al-Jaleel Knox started rapping at the age of 9, performing in many talent shows around Atlanta. As he grew up, he continued to write poetry and raps. His original goal was to use acting as a foot in the door technique for his music career but once he began to pursue acting in film and TV, he was bit by the acting bug. In 2010, Jaleel began to appear in local theatre and independent films. Then he discovered The Company Acting Studio where he began to truly understand and love the craft. He is represented by Houghton Talent.
IMDB page:
http://www.imdb.com/name/nm5287030/?ref_=fn_al_nm_1

Where are you from and how did you get started in acting?
I'm from Atlanta, Georgia, born and raised. Lived in Houston for a little bit. I got into acting because I wanted to be in music at first. I wanted to make beats and I wanted to rap ...I didn't know how to really go about making it in the music industry. So I

figured, "hey, how about I get myself into movies and that way I have a fan base, then I can switch my career over to music". I thought that acting was gonna be super easy, I'm gonna get in a movie in a few days. But I did not know how hard it was gonna be. This was fresh out of high school.

When I graduated from high school, I had no excuses, I had to go after my dreams now. At the time, it wasn't necessarily acting, it was mainly music and acting was a way to get there. I started looking up and finding some agencies. I started auditioning and the more I started going out for it, I just started to like it more and more. But when I really started to fall in love with it was the first time I did extra work. I felt I liked this more than music and then eventually I was pursuing acting and I wasn't even pursuing music anymore.

Have you done any acting at all in high school or college?

I did a play. I did some plays in high school. I never saw myself as being a huge actor at the time. I always thought I was gonna do it, but just for fun. I never actually thought I was gonna be fully pursuing it like I am now.

Your family has been supportive?

Definitely they are, everybody is.

Do you do anything else to supplement your income or is this it?

I just stopped working a 9-5 job about two months ago.

It gives you the flexibility to go out for auditions?

I wouldn't say the job is too flexible but I find ways to maneuver because I don't want to let it get in the way of my career.

Did you go about getting any training as well when you decided you wanted to act?

Yes, definitely. I'm still training. When I first started getting into acting, I started auditioning for independent stuff. But nine months into acting, I felt the need to start taking classes so I can really learn my craft and know what I'm doing. I enrolled at the Company Acting studio and I'm still there. I've been there for about four years now.

How did you end up signing with Houghton Talent?

At a workshop. Because it was like years and years that I did not ever hear back from an agent and it got to a point where I just had to do something. Because I was submitting like crazy. I was not hearing anything back. And it got to a point where I felt like I knew I had to be creative. I knew I had good enough material to get signed. But no one was calling me back, that means they are not seeing me. I had to find a way to get in front of them in person. I started seeking out workshops and showcases. I found Get Scene ATL workshops. I saw People Store was there, Houghton was there. People Store called me in, I auditioned for them but they eventually declined. I went back the week after to Houghton and Mystie loved me, she offered to sign me on.

What do you do in terms of marketing and networking?

That's probably one thing for me that I probably don't do enough. But then I do get that naturally, just from class, I'm always meeting people, just being on set and being friendly, naturally, you just meet people that you, I guess, have a connection with. But I'm not particularly the person who goes out to meet people at networking events. I just never was that guy. I always was just kind of focused on...like I know who you know does matter sometimes in the business, but for me I never really focused on that. I always just tried to focus on being a good actor and doing good stuff. So I meet people just being in the business myself.

What else do you do in terms of finding work? Do you follow people on social media? Do you check out certain websites?

Yes, I'm listed with all those websites. And Houghton's doing a lot of it for me for me. I'm so grateful for and definitely happy with the work and auditioning they're finding me. At the same time, I still look on my own through Actors Access, because they have all these opportunities to submit ourselves.

Do you feel that you might be able to book bigger and bigger roles out of Atlanta or do you think you might have to move to LA or to New York?

I feel like eventually we will have it as long as we keep all the business out here. It's gonna happen, no matter what. But at the same time, I feel like right now it wouldn't hurt for me to go to L. just so I could be up for those bigger roles. Over time, no matter what, it's definitely gonna happen here. We will be up for lead roles, we are already getting series recurring roles. I've seen a lot of people book good stuff.

What do you think we need to do here in Atlanta to be able to book bigger roles, to stay competitive with actors coming in from LA?

Push ourselves a little harder, just fight a little harder. One thing about Atlanta is a lot of actors here have a really hard time keeping up. A lot of people are getting into it and they don't know what they're doing and they're not making Atlanta look that bad but they're just making it seem like we're all like that. Being educated and trained is important, so you look professional, like you know what you're doing and you don't embarrass yourself. Taking classes is the best thing anybody could do. It sets you on the right path.

How do you stay positive and motivated?

One thing I do is, whenever I have a slightly negative thought, I repeat positive things over and over. Every time I go to some audition, I rehearse the same belief - I got it. I come home, I meditate. I don't do that enough, but whenever I really do it...I don't know if it's a coincidence, but I feel like I book a lot more whenever I'm persistently meditating. I always get a call back or I get on set for something.

What kind of meditation do you do? Do you just sit in a quiet room?

I've been trying to learn more about it. Because I don't do a lot, I don't know about it, but my mom does it a lot and I listen to her and try to do what she tells me. One thing is when I go to my room, make sure it's quiet and I just clear my mind and focus on my breathing. I clear my mind, rest my mind and when I come out of there, I feel pretty energetic. Ready to go.

How long have you been acting now?
Altogether almost five years now.

Do you wish you had done something differently when you started your career?
Yes. I would have taken classes earlier than I actually did.

Anna Enger

Anna Enger is a film and television actress appearing next in the anticipated Nicholas Sparks film, The Choice. Anna has recurring roles on television shows including The Vampire Diaries and Complications, and has appeared in several major motion pictures including Anchorman 2, Endless Love, and opposite Vince Vaughn and Owen Wilson in The Internship. She is represented by People Store in Atlanta.

Where are you from originally and when did you decide you wanted to be an actor?

I was born in the Philippines and raised in Guam. I've always enjoyed all things creative – especially theater and dance. As a child, I can vividly remember begging my mom to enroll me in classes, but we just didn't have the resources growing up. When I was 13-years-old, we moved to Savannah, Georgia. A couple of years later, The Savannah Arts Academy opened and accepted me as a new student. Such a blessing – it was then when I was able to dive into training for performing arts. I developed even more of an appreciation for theater and seriously thought about becoming an actor.

Did you pursue acting in college too?
The whole Hollywood acting world was such a foreign concept to me so after high school, I pursued a degree in communications. I felt that the communications field certainly had creative elements and again, the whole concept of Hollywood didn't really seem tangible or obtainable at the time. Ultimately, I wasn't as taken with the communications field as I thought I'd be. I ended up going a safe route and took classes toward a degree in nursing. I never gave up on acting though—I just pursued it outside of my education.

Did you move to Atlanta for college or did you move after you decided you wanted to act?
I moved to Atlanta with the intent to finish the college education I started in Savannah. I wasn't in Atlanta very long when I had an opportunity to move to LA.

So you were in LA?
Yes, I pursued acting in LA for several years.

Did you have any plan for LA or did you say "I'm just gonna go" and went with it?
I didn't have any concrete plans but I did have some friends out there who I could stay with until I was settled and they introduced me to a lot of great people. It all just kind of fell into place and I was able to enroll in acting classes, go on auditions and live the lifestyle I thought was only a dream. Don't get me

wrong, it wasn't at all easy; a lot of hard work—even to get the auditions, never mind landing the role!

Has your ambiguous ethnicity helped you?
My mother is Filipina and my father is of Norwegian descent so it does give me an ambiguous look, which I thought would be beneficial. I can distinctly remember going to my first commercial audition, where the casting agent had requested a 5'6, half Asian, half American young woman and being shocked to see about 30 other girls that look so similar to me! It was an immediate awareness.

LA really has an abundance of talent no matter how unique you think you are?
We forget that Los Angeles is the *international* hub for people trying to get into the industry. I have friends from Australia, England and Japan who traveled to LA with goals of breaking in. It's a hugely saturated town—some people get lucky and come into success right off the bat, but that just wasn't the case for me.

What made you decide to move back to Atlanta?
My (now) husband and I started a family and I moved back to Georgia. My thought was, I'm leaving LA and the acting world and I'll go back to school, maybe pursue photography and take part in local theater productions. Little did I know, the move was actually amazing for my acting career; I had no idea the opportunity that lives here. I was fortunate to sign with The People Store pretty early on and shortly after I had my son, I was working. It's just been a nonstop blessing in such an

unexpected market. I would have never thought to move here specifically for acting. It's really fantastic how life just works itself out. Humble beginnings made me a super hard worker so I can say for a fact that LA didn't work out at the time, not for lack of effort. It wasn't until I was three months pregnant with my son, leaving Hollywood, that I booked my first professional job in Los Angeles. I had no idea the market in Atlanta was on the verge of this great explosion. We (actors) are very fortunate to be in this market with so many opportunities.

When you came back, how did you get your agent?
While I was eight months pregnant on a maternity photo shoot in Atlanta, the other models recommended reaching out to several agencies, including The People Store. I met first with The People Store and thought they were wonderful. I've been here with them since.

Did you have a survival job?
Not at the time; I was fortunate enough to have been able to save money where I could take leave. My son was born in December and I started auditioning actively in March, and was working by May or June. During those first few months of my son's life, I took up photography and that has been my side job since. I started in family and children's portraits and transitioned to headshots solely — being in the acting industry, it was a natural fit.

Did you get back into classes here when you returned to Atlanta from LA?

I did. I took a few workshops here and there and eventually started taking classes more actively. Most recently, I have studied with Rob Mello at the Rob Mello Studio in Decatur. Rob is a gifted teacher and the Meisner technique is one that has always resonated with me.

Having a kid even when you're working a regular job is such a challenge because kids require a lot of attention. So how do you manage that? Do you have family here that supported you too?
I do. I'm in a fortunate situation to where I'm able to have ample family help. Family assistance has enabled me to continue to pursue my artistic endeavors. My husband's parents have been some of our biggest supporters--I really couldn't do it without them. It really does take a village. I don't think anyone who is successful in any capacity has ever claimed, "I did this all by myself".

What do you do as far as marketing and networking?
Photography has been a great networking tool for me because of all the headshots I'm hired to shoot. Also, I think just being in an acting class, taking workshops and being involved in the local community is a great networking tool in itself.

Do you recommend those other activities such as workshops?
Sure. I think there's value in everything. Early on in my career, I had a hard time with the whole idea of "paying to be seen", but my first professional job was from a casting director workshop so I can't say it doesn't happen. The biggest value is the

community you become a part of when attending workshops; that's priceless in itself.

What do you think about social media or sending postcards to casting directors?

It absolutely can't hurt. Social media has never really been my thing – it's always felt a bit unnatural to me. In order for it to be effective, you have to fully embrace it.

What do you do in terms of staying aware of what's happening in the industry?

Elizabeth "Beth" Keener and Greer Howard have this super cool show called "The Local Lense" where they do a terrific job of keeping everyone updated on industry news. They are so lovely and so fun to watch!

What about industry events like Get Connected or GPP or any other mixers or actors help groups?

Why not? Why not be as involved as possible? For new actors, the more you can get out there and meet new people, the better.

What do you think has been the biggest difference pursuing acting in Atlanta versus LA?

Everyone's journey is different. The big difference for me is that it has afforded me an opportunity to have a family and still pursue acting. I think overall, we (actors) are very fortunate with the amount of opportunities we have here. Being able to be a working actor in a secondary market is such a blessing.

Do you think we're going to get bigger roles and maybe even series regulars and leads out of Atlanta?

Absolutely! It's already happening. I know several people within my core circle that have landed series regular roles. Is it going to become as common as it is in LA? Not immediately. It will take time for the talent pool in this market to really establish, but it will happen.

You got a recurring role in Vampire Diaries, right?

Yes! It definitely happens.

Maybe in the past there was this perception that the depth and level of talent in Atlanta was not up to the mark but do you think that as the Atlanta actors are stepping up their game, the perception is changing too?

I hope so; time will tell. More than anything, it's a numbers thing. The Atlanta talent pool here is a fraction of what it is in Los Angeles, but there is great talent to be found here in the south.

What can Atlanta actors do to step up their game?

Treat it like a job and not a hobby. Give acting the attention it deserves. Pay attention to every part of it. If you want to be a professional actor, you have to treat it as a professional job.

And so that means continuously training?

Training is a very important part of it – you can never stop learning.

Being in Atlanta, has your ethnicity helped you set yourself apart?

I think it's been helpful, especially starting out. When I first started out in 2007 here, I worked a good bit of industrial jobs that called for ethnically ambiguous actors.

Do you have representation outside Atlanta?

I do. I have theatrical representation and a manager in Los Angeles.

For LA opportunities, you do get a chance to self-tape and get yourself submitted there?

I work closely with management in Los Angeles. I do most of my tapings here and fly out for callbacks whenever I have the opportunity for a larger role. This is a team I started working with post moving here. After working here in Georgia, I found myself back and forth to California with bigger audition opportunities out there. Life is funny like that.

How do you stay motivated? How do you stay positive?

When I made the decision to pull the time limit off, it took the pressure away and ultimately positivity comes rather easy. I am so grateful to have the opportunity to pursue a career that I love, so it's effortless to stay positive. It's been remarkable and I am so very grateful. I feel like I live in a perpetual state of excitement! The more I let go of results and really just enjoy each opportunity to audition, the more I work. I love the process and I never take a job for granted.

Recognizing that rejection is always going to be a part of this journey at any level. What do you do? You move on to the next audition. It's only over when you decide to quit. If you give yourself a time limit, you probably shouldn't have started. This is a lifelong journey. To be a successful actor, you really truly have to love the process. You have to love auditioning. You have to love meeting people. You have to love performing. You have to love the grind.

What do you wish someone had told you at the beginning of your career or if you had to re-do your career all over again, what would you do differently?

To be more fearless would be my number one answer. Robb (my husband) used to always tell me this early on. Not necessarily just acting related, but in all aspects of life. When I first started out acting, I had such a fearful mentality of everything. I wouldn't even want to go on vacation because I was afraid I was going to miss a big audition. I didn't start consistently working as an actor until after I became a mother – ironically, I used to think it would have been the opposite for females pursuing an acting career. Live life outside of the industry. There are no rules.   Every experience you have outside of acting only enriches your work even more.

One of my biggest mistakes early on as an actor is that I was so "act or die." Everything for me revolved around acting and I couldn't do anything that wasn't going to further my career. Consequently, I never worked. Which was the ironic thing - it wasn't until I moved away from Los Angeles, started a family, pursued other interests like photography and nursing.

A bit of advice I would give any new actor is how important it is to live life outside of this industry. Don't underestimate the amount of work it takes to be a working actor, but don't overvalue it either. Work hard. Work really, really hard. Have fun and be kind.

Bill Murphey

Bill Murphey has been a constant presence on the Atlanta stage since the late '80s. He has performed at nearly every professional theatre, in over 60 productions, and has been awarded two Suzi Bass Awards for his work. His film and TV credits include The Revised Fundamentals of Caregiving, The Fat Boy Chronicles, Devil's Knot, The Game, Army Wives, and Constantine. He is represented by Houghton Talent in Atlanta. More info at his IMDB page:
http://www.imdb.com/name/nm1705421/?ref_=fn_al_nm_1

Where are you from originally and when did you know you wanted to be an actor?
I'm from here; I was born in Decatur. And so I've always lived here, except when I was away at college. I was interested in movies and theatre from a very young age. There wasn't a lot of theatre being done in my school but I tried to participate in everything I could, and also did church plays and anything around that I could find to be in. Once I got into high school and it got close to graduation, I decided I wanted to study theatre.

But I thought if I'm going to do this, I need to make sure that this is something that I'm not going to regret having spent four years on once I'm done. I wanted to make certain it wasn't some passing phase I was going through. So I waited a year after high school to start college. I worked retail for a year, and at the end of that time, I realized I was serious about it. The passion had grown, if anything. I went to a small school in Alabama, the University of Montevallo, that had a pretty well respected department. I studied there for four years and went on to graduate school at the University of Mississippi. I studied there for three more years, got my Masters, and came back to Atlanta to get to work. I went all the way!

Then you came back to Atlanta and it was not quite the boomtown it is today, right?
It was not. There was a lot less theatre. There were the bigger houses - the Alliance, and the Academy Theatre, which had a much larger presence than it does now. Theatrical Outfit, the Performance Gallery and some dinner theatres. Some of the smaller theatres were just getting started - the Horizon theatre, and Theatre in the Square. No, it was a much smaller theatre town. There wasn't much going on in the summer except the Shakespeare Festival at Oglethorpe, and Theatre of the Stars, to my recollection. I spent every summer working out at an outdoor drama in North Carolina called UNTO THESE HILLS. I did that for 21 summers. It gave me a lot of experience - acting, directing, designing, and interacting with people, just a whole bunch of experiences in just about every aspect of theatre.

What made you come back to Atlanta though?
My family was all here. That's important to me. And I know this place. I thought there are 50 times as many people in New York or LA who are looking for the same number of jobs as there are here. I felt I needed to make sure that I could make it here before trying to make it there. That was my feeling at the time. I don't know if that's valid or makes sense. But I could try making

a reputation here with the safety and the comfort of my family in familiar settings. Or I could go on my own to someplace where I didn't know anybody and be terrified. I chose not to be terrified.

Your family has been supportive throughout?
Yeah, they have been. I think they were, of course, a little worried at first. They wanted to make sure that I was doing something that I was going to be happy in, and that I'd be able to support myself and a family, if I got a family, and wasn't setting myself up for disappointment. But they've always been very, very supportive.

Was it possible to make a living as an actor doing theatre, or did you have to do other things as well to supplement your income?
Till about eight years ago, I always had a day job. I worked full-time at the box office at the Woodruff Arts Center for a while. Then I worked full time for about nine years at a Starbucks. And then since 2006, I have not had a day job. I do other little things along the way. I house sit and do other odd jobs. I can bring in a little extra money doing that. And sometimes that's the only way I've gotten by. Once I didn't have a day job anymore, auditioning for film and TV became a lot easier. If you have a day job, you can't just take off in the middle of the day and say 'I have an audition' or 'I'm going to be gone for two days to shoot something.' They want you there at your desk or your register or whatever it is that you're doing.

It's a big challenge, not having that safety net. I'm pretty good with money; I know how to save. I don't spend a lot of money. But even so, there are times when you don't book something, nothing is happening. You have no idea what's going to happen.

Then you'll book something. I've been very fortunate that it's never gotten to a critical point.

How do you keep your acting skills sharp?
I need to take more classes. I haven't because when I can afford to take the classes, I'm probably working and don't have the time. And then when you're *not* working and have the time to take the classes, you need to be very careful guarding your money because you don't know when your next job is coming.

When you have a day job, is it easier to pursue theatre as opposed to on-camera work because on-camera work is typically during the day, as opposed to theatre where shows are typically on the weekends?
Exactly, it's so much easier to just do one or the other. If you're doing theatre, it's hard to be considered for on-camera work when you're doing a show five nights a week. You tell your agents, 'yeah I'm available to shoot this but I have to be done by 5pm,' or 'I'm available all day Monday, and Tuesday, and Wednesday until 5', and then they'll say, 'well, why don't we just not submit you for this because we can't guarantee it'll be done in time.' It gets a little frustrating. You want to be at a point where people will work around your schedule rather than you working around theirs, but I'm not at that point yet. Most of us in Atlanta aren't.

Has doing theater been helpful in terms of marketing you?
I think it has been, yes. I've been around here for so long and worked at most of the theaters, so I'm guessing that most people in the theatre community who are in a position to hire me, know who I am. Whether we've actually met or not, they've probably heard of me or seen me in something. Some agents are very good about coming to theatrical productions, seeing

the actors they represent do their stuff, and scope out potential new talent.

Do you do any other marketing and networking?
I'm not really good at marketing myself or networking, other than just posting something on Facebook. I'm not even sure how I would go about it. My mom is much better at marketing me than I am.

What about staying aware of what shows are shooting in town and trying to stay on top of industry news?
That's a hard one. You want to trust that your agent is on the lookout and knows what's going on, and wants to submit you for anything that you're available for. There are times you'll compare auditions with other actors you're usually up against for the same parts and say 'Did you get called in for this project?' And they won't have, but they'll have been called in for something you weren't. And you wonder 'Why didn't *I* get called in for that Robert Duvall movie?' But I am determined to feel that if I'm right for something, my agent will submit me. Whether the casting director chooses to see me is beyond my control. But all sorts of conspiracy theories can race through your head.

What about casting websites?
I'm on Actors Access and 800casting and sometimes I look at those. A lot of those things are for little or no pay, and I'm not looking to do things now just because 'they'd look good on my reel.' When this run of employment I'm on right now winds down, I'll reconsider!

How many shows are you having for this current show you are doing?

I just finished the first half of a coproduction between two theatres, a play called VANYA AND SONIA AND MASHA AND SPIKE. It ran at the Horizon theatre for six weeks, and then it will run again in October, at the Aurora Theatre for a month. In between that time, there's another show, a musical called MEMPHIS, which is a coproduction between the Aurora Theatre and Theatrical Outfit. Both the shows that I am now working on, or am about to be working on, will show in two different theatres for a full run. That's an unusual and really nice position to be in. It's great for me theatre-wise. I think it might limit me for on-camera work, though, in that I'm not going to have my nights available for a while.

How do you get your theatre work? Do you have a different agent for that?
In Atlanta, at least, your agents don't send you out for theatre work. It's all on your own, it's networking. Casting directors will call you in, or if you're a member of Actor's Equity as I am, you can request to be seen for an audition. I'm in a pretty good position where most of the theatres at least know who I am, have at least heard of me, and I've worked with most of them. And I think I have a pretty good reputation.

You think all that formal training has made a difference?
I think the main benefit of the seven years I spent at school was the people I met and learned from. I've remained friends with many of them, and have worked for them and with them since then. It's networking. A friend of mine from my undergraduate school is a director and producer in California now. We've kept in contact, and some years back he wrote a movie and offered me a small part in it. I have friends in the business all over the country - New York, Chicago, LA, and here. None of my schooling taught any of the methods of different acting teachers like Stanislavsky or Meisner, though I wish they had, but I did

get introduced to a lot of people who've opened a lot of doors for me. That was the major benefit.

What do you see the future of acting being in Atlanta? Do you see us booking bigger roles out of Atlanta?
A couple of years ago, the most that you could hope for might be landing a bit role as somebody's secretary saying "Your 3 o'clock appointment is here". And that's it. But that's changing; people are booking really nice parts. The more work that's done here, and the better showing we make, the more the directors and producers are going to trust Atlanta talent with larger roles. *If we step up our game!* Anytime I see a familiar face on a locally shot project, an actor friend who's up on the screen and holding their own with the New York or the LA talent, it's inspiring. It allows one to say 'okay, good for them. Next time, that could be me.' Hard work and ability - you've got to trust it will pay off. Now we've got so many things that are shooting here, and around the Southeast, the opportunities are really taking off.

What do you think actors in Atlanta need to do to step up their game?
We need to bring it in every audition and every time we book something. We need to come in prepared; we need to come in with confidence. We need to give them no reason not to use us, no reason to say 'well, we can't find anybody here; we're going to have to bring someone from LA to do this part.' We're here, we're ready, and we're cheaper. They don't have to put us up in a hotel. They don't have to get an airline ticket. But proximity can't be the only reason to use us. We have to be just great. In fact, we have to be *better*. I get irritated with theatres or production companies that think having a 212 area code or a zip code beginning with 902 makes you a better actor. I want just the 303-- zip code and the 404 area code to be a gold standard.

The whole mindset of "We can't cast this out of Atlanta," that's baloney.

Do you have representation outside Atlanta?
No, I don't. As long as the work is here, I would love to work locally. Now, I'd be happy to take a job out of town if offered. I'd love to tour with a show. I'm not glued here, but I haven't really tried to get work outside Atlanta.

No plans to move to LA or New York?
No, I've got my house here, my family...I've got my whole life here. Having to move would be...not *traumatic* – that's probably too harsh a word, but I don't see the need to yet.

Being an actor, you're being rejected day in, day out. It can take its toll on you emotionally and financially. How do you find the motivation to keep going on?
Yeah, it does. Absolutely. This happens to every actor - you get rejected all the time. It's part of the job. You can't be thin-skinned and remain in this business long. You go through a barrage of auditions for plays or for on-camera work, and think 'I would be *great* for these roles,' but those casting the projects think someone *else* would be great for them. It's frustrating. It's often completely out of your control. Maybe they had somebody blond in mind for the role, or maybe you look like the producer's ex-husband, and they'll say 'Nope, not him."

But you start questioning yourself and your career choice, and the bank account starts running low...It's heartbreaking and you think maybe it's time to get a day job now, just to tide you over. The bills don't stop coming just because the paychecks do. Last year, I'd been in one of those slumps, and then I booked three straight things in one week. Things turned around. Often it's hard to have that confidence that things will turn around, that you will work again. But that confidence in yourself and your ability is what has to keep you going.

I have friends that I went to school with who are running businesses and they have expensive houses and multiple cars and families and kids and go on vacations all the time and are preparing for retirement down the road. I can't even imagine what that life is like. They can't imagine how I can be happy knowing I have work lined up through October. They think, "October?!...and then?!" I don't know; we'll see! And that's the life of an actor! There really has to be nothing else that makes you happy to make this work. If you can't imagine yourself doing anything else, that's really the only time you should do this for a living.

What do you wish someone had told you at the beginning of your career, or if you had to redo your career all over again, what would you do differently?
I'd probably try harder from the beginning and take more chances. I probably played it safer than I needed to do. Maybe I should've given up the day job earlier, just taken that big leap, taken that jump and see where it landed me. But it can be hard to do that when you're a kid. Some do. I wish I had. You've just got to commit 100%. Sometimes it's hard to, because you want that safety net. I think if you're not worried about the safety net and take that leap of faith, you might succeed spectacularly or you might fail spectacularly, but whatever you do, it will be *spectacular*. Everything in between is less dangerous. But the rewards might be not as great either.

Dane Davenport

Dane's credits include Flight (2012), Let's Be Cops (2014) and Anchorman 2: The Legend Continues (2013). He is represented by People Store in Atlanta. More information can be found at his IMDB page:

http://www.imdb.com/name/nm2474245/bio?ref_=nm_ov_bio_sm

Your IMDB page says that you're from Plano, Texas. How did you end up Acting in Atlanta?

I grew up in Plano but went to high school here in Atlanta and spent my teenage years here. When I got out of college, I was a sports broadcaster. I started working with my sister, who's also into sports broadcasting. There's nothing more demeaning than talking about sports and having your sister be better at it. I wasn't terrible but I wasn't going to go anywhere with it. I knew that right off the bat, I wanted to be in front of the camera but this is not the right avenue. That's when I got into acting. I was in Wilmington, North Carolina, at the time and they were filming One Tree Hill and other things there. So I said, let's try that out.

You didn't study acting in college?

I didn't. I minored in theatre but I didn't concentrate on acting in any way. It was more theatre production. When I quit broadcasting to pursue acting, the first thing I did was background extra work, just to see how things were done and see if it was something that I was interested in. The good thing about that is you talk to a lot of people on set. Some have either done it for a while and know what they're talking about, and some don't know what they're talking about. But, you get a lot of good insights doing that. People told me, you need to get headshots, resumes, agents, classes, credits. So that's what I did. I also started taking a class and read some books on how to become an actor. I was still in North Carolina at that time. I stayed about six months out and then moved back to Atlanta. I started off with the usual real low budget stuff, just to get some filming credits wherever it may be. I also did some more classes and courses to put on my resume.

How did you get your Atlanta agent?

I got my first headshots in North Carolina. And quickly after that I moved to Atlanta. So I had headshots. I built some kind of a resume. I did my research and just found out who the Atlanta agents were and if they were respectable. I started sending out my headshots and resume to them.

Back in the day, nothing was digital. It was all on a piece of paper - headshot and a resume. And you sent it out with a cover letter saying who you are. I probably sent it out to around 40 - 50 agents, not only in Atlanta but in Florida, New Orleans, and

North Carolina. It took me a while to get an agent. I sent out one batch of resumes and I got no call. I sent another batch, got no call. It was the third or fourth time I did it, that I finally got a couple calls. And immediately, I went up and met them and got interviewed, which is basically auditioning for them. I got lucky enough to sign with one of them - People Store here in Atlanta. Been with them for close to 10 years now.

You started in Atlanta and did some acting here for a couple of years before you moved to LA?
I did. I got my first guest star role on a TV show and that made me union eligible. It also gave me the feeling of wanting to do this my whole life. It was great. But I made the mistake of thinking that because I got one job, I'm going to get plenty of jobs out in LA too. I opted to move and basically started over. A lot of people do that and it's a whole different ball game out there. It's another different story in itself. I came back to Atlanta and made my home here after that.

It's been pretty good here since then?
It has been, yes. I've been here 4-5 years now. I came back when all the business started coming back. And got lucky enough that my agent took me back.

When you moved to LA, did you have to become SAG?
I didn't have to. I chose to. The union thing is very, very different in LA. Because by being union, they think that gives you some sort of reputation of being someone that they could sign. But I was so young and so naïve to the business that I wasn't anywhere near where I needed to be to book any of those jobs.

I was going up against guys who have been doing this for years, and knew the business, and knew that they wanted better actors than me. At the same time, if I wasn't union, I wouldn't have gotten those opportunities. Out here you can be non-union, you can still have opportunities and book those jobs.

Why did you move back from LA to Atlanta?
For me, personally, it was a lot of different factors. One of them was LA was not working out. And the other main reason was because of family. I'd just gotten married. My wife is from here. She wanted to start a family and our life in the southeast. Of course, it didn't hurt that there were more opportunities coming in Atlanta too.

When you started out, did you do anything else to support yourself? Do you still do stuff outside of acting?
Absolutely, yeah. I was a bartender and waited tables in North Carolina. I did it when I came back home to Atlanta. I did it when I was out in LA and even when I came back to Atlanta the next time. I was still bartending. I got lucky on a personal level, that the bar that I was working at was up for sale. I used whatever collateral I had and bought the bar and restaurant that I currently own now. That's where I make a living when I'm not acting. When I was bartending, I was responsible for finding some of the work and getting my shift covered. Now that I own it, it's really nice. I can be here and not be here whenever I want. I have the ability to do anything I need to do for my career.

It's tough to find such opportunities but it's out there. You don't have to buy a business or anything like that. You can find those types of jobs that give you that flexibility - that's one of the most important things for an actor. You can't just not have a job and hope to make some money on acting because you never know when you're going to work, or even if you are going to work. But on the other hand, it's also not fine if you have a 9 to 5 job that doesn't give you time for your acting career.

I have a good management team that basically runs the restaurant and bar. I'm more of just an overseer but occasionally, when I don't have anything to do and I'm not busy on my career, I'll spend some time, hang out, make sure everything's going exactly like how I want it to be, but most of the time they run it. They're really good at it and that's a blessing in itself.

From your experience, what kind of jobs have you seen other actors typically have in Atlanta?
I've seen a lot of variety, I'm sure that there are a lot of actors that do the restaurant type industry job. But something I do see a lot of is people doing work with computers. Or it's some sort of technology where they can work from home. Some people provide IT services, some sell stuff online. Whatever it is, it seems that a lot of people do that. And now with all the self-taping stuff, people are basically building their studios in their garage where they charge other actors for taping services. That's a great idea because your "other job" is still in the business. You're still learning and making connections. That's hugely beneficial.

Do you typically have your own setup for self-tapes or do you use a taping service?

I have my own setup and I also use a friend who has a taping service, depending on what my kind of schedule is like. Because I live in Peachtree City which is 30 minutes away from Atlanta. If I get an audition on Wednesday night and I need to turn it in by Thursday morning then I'm going to just use my own setup. But if it's something that I have a couple days for, I'll drive up and then have my friend do it.

What kind of training do you have?

I've had a lot of different teachers and all of them have given me something different to concentrate on. That's from when I was in Wilmington to Atlanta, to LA, to back here. My opinion is to find someone who you really connect with and who you really are learning a lot from, and just stay with that person. Always keep studying.

What do you think are maybe two of the most important skills for actors starting out to learn?

If they're just starting out, it's important to have business type training to it, because a lot of people will come into the acting business and want to be an actor, a star, but not understand how the whole process works. I've been told by some different people in the business that that's one of their pet peeves. A guy might be the greatest actor in the world but he doesn't know how to instruct himself or even steps over boundaries you're not supposed to go over, whatever it may be. It's hugely important. Because no matter how good you are, that's something that can ruin your career. For example, if you piss off the wrong person they're going to make sure that not only them but everyone else who they know is not going to use you for anything. Then you're in trouble. The next important thing is to find someone to teach you a style of acting that you feel comfortable with, that you can always keep training with. Once you're at that point, there are showcases you can do for agents and casting directors.

What do you do in do in terms of marketing and networking?
Back before I had an agent, sending out different letters was a great way to market. I know nowadays a lot of casting directors aren't very appreciative of getting things in the mail, from what I've heard. But, at the same time, if you don't have a way to talk to people, one of the things that everyone here struggles with, you have to find a way. I talk to my agents regularly, making sure that they still know that I'm willing and ready to work. I talk to them about other opportunities. I take the initiative instead of sitting around waiting for them to call me. Get known by the decision makers. If you have a choice between someone that you worked with, or someone that you know, and someone that you absolutely haven't seen around, you'll probably go with the guy that you know.

It's always ongoing too. You can't just get in front of somebody thinking they know who I am. You've got to make sure it's ongoing, whether it is sending them a thank you card or sending them your headshot, or getting in front of them in another workshop. You've got to make sure that you're fresh in their mind too because you're one of thousands and thousands of people who are acting in the southeast. They might remember you but in a week, they've also seen 1,500 different actors so they've forgotten about you. Keep them engaged. That goes for working on low budget stuff for free. You know you're getting in front of people. You're getting to know them. If you do a good job, they're going to remember. Personally, I want to make sure I'm going to do everything I can possibly to make it happen. I'm not going to wait around for something to happen to me.

Do you self-submit to projects? You are out there looking for projects?
Absolutely. I'm looking for projects on a daily basis, finding out what projects are coming to town even if I don't know what the breakdowns are or if I'm right for them or not. I still try to find a way to know. Do I know anybody that's working on it? Do I know any way that I could find a way to get in front of the casting director? Do I know a way of being on set that I can see if this goes somewhere?

I use Breakdown Express, Actors Access, NowCasting, Casting Network. There's a lot of websites and you can search to find out what projects are coming to town. Variety and Hollywood Reporter will tell you basically every project that's happening and where it's happening. For example, you look at the front page and realize Ant Man was filming here in Atlanta. Look on the Internet for low budget films and student films to work on. Get to know more people and as you talk to some of them, they might know a friend who's putting a film together.

For me, if it's a non-paying or student film, I would do it if it's something I truly believe in and feel I could connect to. When I first started out. I would do anything and everything. It didn't matter to me whether I really liked it or not. I had no credits. I had nothing. I wasn't at a place where I could be even a little choosy. I still don't believe I'm at a place where I could pick and choose my projects but I am a family man and I have other stuff going on in my life that maybe the time just to do everything isn't available.

Do you think it's worthwhile for actors to subscribe to the print versions of Hollywood Reporter and Variety?
No, they're pretty expensive. And that's one of the big problems. It's that we don't have any money being actors. There are ways to find out either just by being on IMDB and maybe doing Google searches for Atlanta films. That will get you started. If you find that is not enough, then maybe you start thinking of doing digital subscriptions to these publications.

Do you attend the GPP meetings, Get Connected and such events around town?
I have in the past and they are very beneficial for someone to go to. I would try anything once, and see if it's good for you, if it's something that you could attend regularly. The GPP meetings and other events are not the same thing over and over again. It's different news, different questions being answered and different speakers and topics. I don't think I've ever sat in any type of meeting or seminar or workshop where I haven't learned something. If you're debating whether to watch TV or

go to the meeting, you're going to be a lot better going to the meeting.

Do you think Atlanta is going to get to the point where they might be casting bigger roles from here?
I haven't quite made a decision on that. I know that any type of project that comes here is going to be more work for Atlanta actors. That being said, the bigger supporting and obviously the lead roles are coming out of LA and other bigger markets. That's not a knock on Atlanta actors. There's not a TV show film that films in Atlanta that doesn't have at least one Atlanta actor in it. The ones that are getting those roles are doing a great job. The more and more we do that, the more and more people will start trusting us, and the more and more roles we'll get. It's just that for all these producers and studios that are putting all this money into a film or a TV show, their main goal is to make money and it's easier to make money on someone that they know they can trust to do the job and also that they could sell to the public.

Do you have representation outside of Atlanta?
No. As of right now, for my career, I feel that Atlanta is where I'm going to get my best work. If at some point it gets to where I have to become more bicoastal, I will get representation out there. A lot of the agencies here in Atlanta do bicoastal. You might be reading for a project that's filming in LA that your Atlanta agent has submitted you for. That happens a lot ,so long as you can pay for a flight to LA to read for a casting director out there even if you don't book the role. If you're willing to do that

and you have the income to support that, by all means there's no reason not to.

What about New Orleans though?
I consider New Orleans and Wilmington, and Orlando, Miami, everywhere at the Southeast in general, to be local. I feel like the casting directors in the southeast, whether they're based in Atlanta or New Orleans, are casting from the same pool of people. I don't think there's any reason to have an agent in every single town that you possibly might work in the Southeast.

Atlanta is becoming the biggest market in the Southeast. If you're part of the southeast market in Atlanta then you should be part of the rest of the southeast as well. I know actors that are working and living in Atlanta who are getting jobs in New Orleans.

Do you ever struggle with rejection or ever wonder am I doing the right thing?
Earlier on, I did. We're actors so we always are very self-conscious of ourselves. We always wonder why didn't I get that job? I could have done something differently. Oh, this, that, the other. It's always going to be there but one of the huge things that I realized is that you can't think like that because if you doubt yourself then why is someone else going to give you money to do something that you're not even sure you could do.

I made that choice a few years ago to be comfortable with myself and confident that I could do it. Because if they know I'm confident, they trust me. And that comes with time. I didn't just snap a finger and say I'm thinking that. I had to work at it, and I had to keep taking classes and learning and getting jobs. Over time you get to a point where you say wow I can do it, this is what I want to do. It just comes to you and it makes you that much better of an actor. That's something you learn early on in the business - as long as you do your job and make sure that you've done the best work, put the best foot forward, you're not the reason you're not getting the job.

What advice would you give somebody starting out in Atlanta?
The simplest advice I could give and the most important is to never quit. It's a very tough business but if it's something that you want to do, you've got to go 110% into it and don't look back. That means when you're first starting out, do all the necessary steps, from the bottom, to get to the top. If you don't have any credits, find the non-paying credits that you can do. If you don't have an agent, do whatever you have to do to get in front of agents so that they want you as a client. If you haven't talked to casting directors, find a way to get to know those casting directors. You've got to do all those steps. You can't just say I want to be an actor and then you book the job. Have faith in yourself. Know what you're doing, and never stop learning and getting better, whatever it is.

David Kronawitter

David has been an actor in Atlanta since 2000. Some of his work has included such shows as Sleepy Hollow, Drop Dead Diva, Prison Break and Satisfaction, to name a few.
IMDB Page:
http://www.imdb.com/name/nm2909891/?ref_=fn_al_nm_1

When did you know you wanted to be an actor and how did you go about getting started?

The first inkling I knew I wanted to be involved was when I was in middle school. They had a Magnet Performing Arts troop come around to our middle school. Each county has a magnet school and in Cobb County it's Pebble Brook. For some reason it just called to me, I don't know. Then I went through the process of auditioning, got accepted - that was the beginning of my education. I went to that high school for four years. I was blessed with the best teacher imaginable. It was competitive. I liked that. It helped. That was the beginning of it right there.

You are originally from Georgia?
Yes.

And it's worked out well because Atlanta has picked up so much in terms of acting?
I never expected it to. Around the time I started acting, there were just one or two TV shows here - *I'll Fly Away* and *In the Heat of the Night*. After I graduated from Florida State, I went out to LA and some of my friends came here. I'd get in touch with them and compare stories. They all had agents here and had auditions. I didn't have an agent out there. I didn't have auditions except for theatre stuff and living in LA is expensive too. After a couple of years, I came back. I had great opportunities in LA outside of acting, with production stuff. I fell into a job logging video for Mark Burnett's show *Eco Challenge*. It's what he was doing before *Survivor*. That was my day job. All the doors were opening there. They asked if I would come back and be an assistant producer the next year but acting was still pulling at me.

I knew I had to really give it a good shot so I came back here in 2000. That was the best thing I ever did. I never thought I'd come back here. Didn't want to, but I'm glad I did.

You studied theater at Florida State University?
Yes, I got a performance degree. I started off going to college in Colorado for a couple of years as a ccommunications major. I chose that as a safe route thinking I could always pursue theatre

later. However, I found myself doing plays with the theatre department at the college I went to get a broadcasting degree from. Soon I realized I couldn't do journalism, took a couple years off to figure things out, and save some money for the last couple years of school in whatever capacity that was. I spent a couple years working and was passionate about nothing else as much as theatre so I decided to go for it. That's how I ended up at Florida State as an acting major. The setting truly felt like home. It was an incredible experience. It was the next phase of solid education after high school that I really needed. The program and the teachers were excellent.

After you completed that, went to LA and returned here, did it really pick up in Atlanta right away or did it take some time here too?

It took some time but there were signs that it was a good place to be because I was able to audition for good things and there was the ability to make money at it. From 2000 until 2006, it was mostly part-time and from then on things picked up enough to be full-time.

When you started out initially, did you have a survival job? Did you do other stuff to supplement your income?

I was a substitute teacher and I still do that when time permits. There were a number of theatre gigs that helped bring in some money too.

What else do you do to keep your acting skills sharp?

I'd say doing theatre is one of the best ways to stay sharp. To each his own though.

What do you do in terms of trying to stay positive and being grounded?

My faith is a big thing for me. It's what keeps me grounded. It keeps things in perspective and from not getting too wrapped up in it. There are so many things beyond my control.

When you moved to Atlanta, how did you go about finding work? How did you get an agent?

I'd kept in touch with a friend of mine, Jamie Renell, that I went to college with at Florida State, who came here when I went to LA. He was with People Store and offered to take my headshot and resume to Jen Kelly. She offered to represent me so I moved back and got started that way.

Were you SAG by the time you came back from LA?

While I was in LA, I was working towards becoming SAG. Everything out there is union-based but here it's not necessary. I became eligible but had not joined.

What do you do in terms of marketing and networking?

I don't do as much as I should or could, that's for sure. Houghton gets me out there quite a bit. After time, you build relationships with casting directors and people that you have worked for. Every chance I get, I try bringing the best I can for what is called for. Networking is definitely not my strength. I wish it were because I think I could benefit a lot more from it. It's a great skill, especially in this business.

You've booked a recurring role on *Drop the Diva*. Do you think the opportunities are going to keep increasing so that eventually they book series leads out of here?

As time goes on, it seems that larger roles are being booked in Atlanta. There is so much work here now that the opportunities have increased greatly. It's looking like it to me. Before the tax incentives, the roles seemed smaller...just a few lines. Now you have more scenes. So yes.

No move to LA planned in the future?

I think I'm cut out for Atlanta. I don't think I've got enough to be out there in LA or New York to stand out the way I need to. I make a comfortable enough living that I don't feel like I need to change anything. I really just want to make a living out of it. I can't see myself changing anything as far as moving unless something was already there waiting that was worth it.

Do you do any writing or try to put projects together that give you more opportunities for yourself?

No. If I had more time on my hands, I might. It's just enough right now, it's the perfect balance. And I get enough creative fulfillment through the stuff that I work on.

Do you ever go through any periods of self-doubt or handling a negative mindset?

To some degree, of course. But I've also tried to train myself over the years to do the best I can and then just forget about it. Of course, there are some things that I remember but overall I just get ready for the next thing.

Looking back, what decisions could you have made differently?

That's tough to say but being a better networker would help. I was trying to learn from my mistakes. I think that as long as I can do that, I'll be okay.

You believe that the formal degree has helped you?

For me, it has helped tremendously. There are many people who don't have formal degrees at all but still have great success in the industry.

If you can't afford to get into a proper film or drama school, the other option is also to immerse yourself in theatre?

If you really want to learn your performance craft, yes. You could do theatre anywhere, anytime, very close to you. Some are better than others but there's always the opportunity, especially for somebody who's starting now. The experience will teach you. You will start meeting people with the same interests and things will develop. Atlanta is a great place to get started.

Edward Bryan

Edward Bryan is a multi-faceted performer with various film and TV credits including Teen Wolf, Drop Dead Diva, Mean Girls 2, Lottery Ticket, and Stomp the Yard 2, to name a few. He is represented by Houghton talent. More info can be found at his website: http://www.ebryan.com.

When did you know you wanted to be an actor and how did you go about getting started?

I was an actor back in high school in 2002. I was always doing small productions for high school. I knew I wanted to be an actor but I joined the military instead. I did a couple productions for churches while in the military, and exited the military in 2006. I started to pursue acting professionally then. I moved back to Atlanta, my mother state. I moved here in 2007 when I started doing the acting thing, and started doing small stuff. I got an opportunity to work for Tyler Perry in Atlanta. I stayed in for about three months, and I learned so much in that time. That was very vital to me, the way I am as an actor.

It was a blessing for me to just get out of the military and get that opportunity. I've heard from so many people. I was so close to success, and still far away. Although I was right there were the man was changing lives, I still didn't get to be successful as I wanted to. I was still learning the ropes. I had the blessing, I had the opportunity but I didn't have the direction.

I did a lot extra work. I started taking classes at the Professional Acting Studio with Nick Conti and Matthew Cornwell. I started learning more of the craft of it than just the learning lines. The different techniques of how to prepare myself as an actor, how to cold read, how to sing study, and that was something that I took very hard because not knowing too much about acting but learning more about it, the technical side, is what prepared me to actually be better onstage as well as trying to get the audition, trying to get the part.

Was your family supportive?

At the time, I had no kids. I lived with my mother. All she wanted me to do was whatever made me happy.

Did you have any survival jobs, day jobs to support yourself meanwhile?

I have to say thanks to the military because although I didn't have a full-time job per se, I was still able to satisfy most of my basic needs due to the military giving stipends to go to school. I was still getting a Bachelor's Degree. The military was paying for my college and giving money in my pocket. I did a lot of the extra background work, it used to pay a lot of money when I was doing it. I started driving for limousines. I always had opportunities to be self-sufficient financially. So as of right now, I have three different titles. I'm still a national guard. I have a bounce house, inflatable party room for kids. Now marriage, I have kids I have to provide for. So I'm still grateful that I still do the business here and I still work and provide for my family.

If I can be the actor Edward Bryan as well as the family man, I would love it. Well I can't, I have to be actor Edward Bryan, military Edward Bryan, and driver Edward Bryan. I have to be that, I have to 'cause in acting you're not going to get paid continuously unless you're an A-list, B-list actor. So I'm just doing my best to maintain this, and do what I have to. People want to come here and get rich. It's not going to happen overnight. You can be rich in other avenues. But if you trample around, it's not going to happen. You have to get the love for it, and you've got to have that face to continue on with it. Continue on and be persistent with it.

How did you end up at Houghton Talent?

Houghton was a process. I got denied the first time. I resubmitted after six months, after I did more projects and I looked for more work and pursued it more, so I can show myself and prove myself that this is what I want, this is what I'm willing to do to get it. I'm willing to work hard for the opportunity, and then Houghton asked me to come in and do some of the interviews. A week later I got an email saying congratulations! I've been with Houghton since then, it's been a blessing to be able to be with them, and support me in my career, mold me with opportunities.

What do you do for marketing yourself and networking?

I've been to a lot of film events where you get connected. That's the big bit that you have to stay in Atlanta, get connected with a lot of different websites done locally. You can submit for four roles as well as connect with other actors and directors that are looking for roles. The indie films as well as the 48-hour film projects. I just go into the loop of the whole film industry, not just as an outsider submitting.

Do you read any particular websites or do any social media?
Yes, I stuck with Facebook as well as websites and just look on different social media websites.

Do you do postcard mailings to casting directors or emails to let them know what you're doing, keep them in the loop?
I've done that in the past. Maybe a lot of people did that as well because I didn't get as much of a response as I would've wanted.

What else do you do to stay aware of what projects are coming to town?

I set my ear to the street as well. Mostly my agents that tell me here that there's a movie coming to town or there's going to be an audition here. Or local actors will tell you as well yes we have a film coming here. And you can see a lot of the movement on social media. But most of the big casting, you won't see it due to confidentiality. The only time you'll hear about that is if you get invited to audition for a movie that was out.

Do you think you're going to get a chance to read for bigger roles, leads, guest stars in Atlanta?

Oh it's already happening. This year alone, I've auditioned for major films that I would never think that we Atlanta actors would be able to get. Because years ago the statement was that all the actors they were getting was always from LA because they didn't want any Atlanta actors because there were no actors here. Or there were actors but no professional actors in SAG.

But now I've auditioned for so many roles, Atlanta's the New York now. Their actors are coming here. And why are they moving to Atlanta? Because they see the work. I've been able to build a rapport with George Pierre and Pierre Casting. To be able to continue on to do that, that's a blessing to me because now I put my foot in there before everybody jumped into the water. So it's been good to see the roles diversify now. But the thing is everybody's coming here so you've got to get more focused and more competitive.

Are productions and casting directors seeing that the talent in Atlanta is improving?

Yes, that talent in Atlanta is improving because of the success of our education on acting now. Not just hanging out with important actors. No, there are a lot of different agencies out here that are teaching kids, teaching them how to act and how be a professional actor and just be an onstage actor, an onscreen actor, showing people the ropes of how to act. And so I give credit to all those who are giving those seminars, those 2-day seminars, weekend seminars, classes on a daily basis, to improve the talent base here in Atlanta. Some of the casting directors have auditions. They go through their self-tapes, audition tapes and in person casting. They see that there's talent here in Atlanta. So we don't have to go elsewhere to get talent.

The other part is that you've got to be able to compete with the rush of talent that's coming in from Hollywood or New York. What do you do to step up your game?

I continue to train as an actor, always staying busy, doing roles that will further more give me my success. When I say that, not just the normal roles like being a robber, being a doctor. Auditioning for roles that require more talent and more layers of acting. So being able to deliver anytime. Being able to be on time, being professional, having good set etiquette. And it's being able to be wanted. All in all, it's how you work and sometimes not your acting but how much you want to work, how much direction you can take. Being able to have a good heart and take constructive criticism.

Do you have any plans to move to a bigger market like LA or New York?

Right now I'd say no. I plan on staying here and continue to work on my craft and continue to work on my opportunity to get the roles that are coming that are bigger. Because I've seen a lot of my good friends. They get here, they get hot. And they move to LA, and they don't get nothing. They don't get any roles. They don't get any opportunities. They still stay stagnant to the point where they feel like they have to come back to Atlanta and start over, which you never have to. You just go back into the system and try to reinvent yourself. But it seems like I've seen them go to the bigger markets. They're small fish in a big sea, and they never get anything.

How do you handle rejection?

I tell people if you can't take a no in the next job, if you can't take someone telling you no or hey I didn't book you, then you can't be in this stuff. Because I will say I'll probably get 50 nays before I get that one yes, and that one yes makes it all worthwhile because they wanted me.

What do you wish someone had told you at the beginning of your career? What mistakes have you made, if any?

As far as I can tell young Edward, that before he started acting in Atlanta, about being patient. Being patient and know success won't happen in 30 days or a year. I was more sustainable to learning the craft harder everyday, and pushing myself to understand that I have to find my craft, find my niche, and work on that, and not try to put myself in everything I can to try to be successful because I found out that you could be in everything, try to put yourself in everything to be successful, it's not going to happen.

You've got to find what works for you and work as hard as you can so you can see the progress that you've made, and become what that is. Learning that would be awesome. I need to continue on to be a better actor by doing studies, getting to school, learning the craft, learning how to get an agent and work it from there. So now every casting and audition I get from my agency gives them a tip and that I'm getting paid for and that they're getting paid for. And last thing I want to add to it is never quit on yourself. Never quit on your dreams. Never quit on what can happen for yourself.

Elizabeth "Beth" Keener-Dent

Beth Keener is a Georgia native calling Atlanta her home for 10 years. She graduated from Kennesaw State University earning a bachelor's degree in Communications with a concentration in Journalism and Citizen Media. Atlanta's local market has enabled Beth to have a flourishing career in hosting, television and film. She has represented numerous household names as a spokesperson, also appearing in 25 local, regional and national commercials. Beth's TV/Film performances include: Death Sentence, My Fake Fiance, Battle: Los Angeles, Vampire Diaries, Reckless, One Tree Hill, Drop Dead Diva, and Necessary Roughness to name a few.

Beth is now the founder and co-host of The Local Lense, an entertainment news show that brings you the 411 on entertainment in the southeast. Check out the latest from The Local Lense on their website: www.TheLocalLense.com.

Where you are from and when did you know you wanted to be an actor?

Probably when I was in elementary school. I just had a knack for performing and I loved it. I asked my mom if I could get into theater and she let me. The first thing I ever did was *Oliver Twist* when I was 10-years-old and it kept on going from there. I moved to a performing arts high school in Cartersville from tenth grade to twelfth grade. At the same time, I also worked at a dinner theater as a professional singer/dancer. So I had to do both – my homework and a "real job". It taught me about managing finances and how to live on my own. Being a paid professional performer seemed like a dream come true. But I decided to come back home to Georgia and finish up my degree. I'm a Georgia girl, I grew up on a chicken farm. My dad was in the carpet business. My mom got remarried and my stepdad was a chicken farmer. We had about 50,000 chickens. It was insane, to say the least.

You were making money performing and then you decided to come back to Georgia to finish college. What did you do after that?

I wasn't performing on a scale that I really wanted, it was a lot of hard work and I knew that I was ready for a life change. When I came back to Georgia, I actually wasn't pursuing TV and film, I was just pursuing a communications degree at Kennesaw and I was helping my mom sell real estate. I realized I was unhappy and wasn't pursing my calling so I bought books online like "Breaking into Acting For Dummies" and the "Actor's Guide of the Southeast". I read everything I could and started taking on-camera classes, learned a lot and through that I got headshots. They helped you write a cover letter and I started sending my stuff out. So I did verbatim what the book told me to do because I didn't know how to do anything else.

Fortunately, I'm ethnically ambiguous. Because of that, there's a huge market for me now that the world is becoming more and more blended. Atlanta is a great market and it was even changing ten years ago, I just feel like I got really fortunate because I'm in a specific niche and because of that agents were looking for someone like me. I'm not your regular, run of the mill white girl.

What do you do to supplement your income?

Initially I was a server. I served for many, many years at Tin Lizzy's Cantina in Buckhead and I would help my mom sell real estate as well. My first supplemental income was working at Lacoste at Lenox Mall. I did that for about a year. And then I learned photography. A very important thing for actors to remember is the more skills you acquire, the better informed you are as a person and then the more opportunity you have to make alternate income to control your schedule. It's a win-win because it's not always easy to be self-employed as an actor, you have to come up with a side hustle for your main hustle. Because the most important thing that you can do is keep your lights on and eat food, as an actor you really have to be smart about the jobs you choose so that your schedule can maintain flexibility, so that you can go out and pursue your dreams.

Is your husband supportive? Does he have a day job that helps you in a way?

He does. He has a great job and he's very supportive of what I do. He's only come into the picture in the last two and a half years so I've really had to figure everything out on my own for the first eight years.

Do you do anything else in terms of marketing and networking?

I've always had a personal website. Initially I had postcards made and business cards made so that if I'm out, I always have a presence and I can always hand somebody a card and talk about what I do. Keeping your website up and running, if somebody's interested in how multifaceted you can be or the different things you can do, or the variety of work that you have already done, is a great way to send everyone to one place, it's a great marketing tool. Thank you cards are a great way to market, but it's a very difficult thing because your access to your work is through your agent. But some of my mentors have said to keep that running rolodex every time you have access to a production company, keeping their information in your back pocket, and if you hear something, an award they've achieved, or you've worked for them, always dropping a "Hey congratulations on that" or "Thank you for hiring me in this" or "Hey I heard you had a baby" or whatever it is, and being present that way, making it more about them then about you. Once I got an agent, I did less of that, and now it's frowned upon, I heard a couple of casting directors mentioned in different workshops that it's a very impersonal thing to do, that if you take an interest in who they are in their lives that means more than sending a post card with your face on it.

What about any events that you go to that have been helpful?

GPP is amazing. I'm an adjunct professor at Kennesaw State University now and I talk to my students about being a member of GPP, a member of the Atlanta Film Festival, supporting the Atlanta community. Networking, especially if you're starting out, is key. You have to be in class with other working actors, you have to have your name out there, you have to go to events where people can get to know you and start building your network.

What do you see the future of acting being in Atlanta, do you think we are going to get the bigger roles here now?

No doubt. When I lived in LA, there was a huge emphasis on training. You didn't meet an actor, working or not working, that wasn't well trained. Atlanta takes for granted the need to train, and that's why they still go to LA for these larger parts. But we have to really focus on being the best in our craft so that when we are offered opportunities for better roles, we are prepared, and that's the biggest thing lacking in this industry. If we can get to that same level of training and we have the same quality actors in mass quantities like LA, we'll be unstoppable.

Do you think the training available in Atlanta is good?

Yes and no. There are some great places to train, absolutely, but I don't think that there are enough great ones here. The problem is that anybody, especially here in Atlanta, can call themselves a teacher. And then you just don't know the value of the education, especially if you're new. It's important to really research and ask around, talk to people about where they've studied and figure out what the best programs are, get into those programs, even if you have to be put on a waitlist. It's remarkable how many actors I talk to that are not in class. They are not in any sort of acting troupe.

Are you SAG?

No, I've maintained just my SAG eligibility, I haven't joined the Union. A lot of hosting work is non-union, almost all of it actually. So it would really defeat the purpose for me specifically joining just because my goals are to host my own TV show.

Can you share more information about your show?

The Atlanta market is changing. I love people, I love being myself, I love being silly, and I love connecting and building relationships with people. There's so much work coming here. Any larger city and larger market you go to there's a resource, there's extra, there's E! news, there's Big Morning Buzz and you're interviewing celebrities when they're in town or as they're talking about their new movies. There's so much going on here that there was a need for entertainment and someone covering all of the entertainment news. I noticed that need, put it into action and moving forward with hopefully being the entertainment guru of the south. That'll pan out, it's a matter of building an audience over time and that's not always easy on any platform.

You have no plans to move out of Atlanta anytime soon?

I've lived in LA a couple of years, I'll never move out of Atlanta. Not for the industry unless work calls me there, unless there's an opportunity ongoing that's waiting for me, I will be here in Atlanta. It is an amazing city to live, and work, and the cost of living is so low, the value and quality of life I have here is second to none so I really wouldn't see myself leaving, especially with the market growing as much as it is. Don't do it, that's what I'm saying, don't ever leave, you'd want to come back!

How do you stay in a positive mindset?

No matter what, it's very difficult, because I have, for lack of a better way of putting it, I really have a knack for TV and film. It's a skill that I've studied for a long time that's come very naturally to me, I think I'm a good host, but I think it can be very discouraging to not be able to build your audience, for things not to move as quickly as you like, to start over, to work for free, to do it all yourself, it's very draining. I still work through my agent and book jobs - I recently went t0 4-5 auditions, five call backs, five first refusals, I was dropped from every one.

Even when you feel like you should be grateful, you still kind of beat yourself up - what am I doing wrong? The biggest way to stay positive is to prioritize - for me ,it's been trying to value the relationships in my life and not turning down the opportunity to go have a beer on a patio with somebody that's important to me. That's the best way of staying sane. So figure out what's important and don't let your work define you. Easier said than done.

What do you wish someone had told you at the beginning of your career?

Remember that nothing's a big deal. You're always going to be fine. It's never your last opportunity and it's never your last mistake, no mistake is too great to come back from. Quit giving yourself such a hard time. People are human and even if you think you're the worst or you've done the most stupid thing, casting is always the worst. There's really no reason to ever feel like you'll never work again or that you're not good enough. You're always good enough. You're the only person in the world that can be you. So quit trying to be what you think people want you to be, and do you, and love you and don't play better roles. People say play better roles but don't, do what you got to do. In a good way, not in a bad way. I've got so many pieces of advice, I could go on and on, I would tell myself a hundred different things.

129

Any final words of advice for someone starting out in Atlanta?

Don't expect anyone to do anything for you. If you want to be successful, you have to be willing to do the work. If you're not serious, just give it up. You know it's very tough. You've got to be willing to do what every other person will not do. That's how hard you've got to work.

Eric Esquer

*Born in California, and living in Atlanta since 2012. Eric is
committed to his craft and loves the art of acting. Eric's credits
include The Haves and the Have Nots and Powers. He is most
proud of his recent work in IVIDE, an Atlanta based Bollywood
film starring several major Indian stars. He is represented by
Houghton Talent in Atlanta.*

**When did you know you wanted to be an actor and how did
you go about getting started?**
I was 5-years-old, I remember looking at a program on television
and having the thought "One day I want to do that". And I
haven't looked back since. That's where it started. Why? I don't
know, but I'll never forget it.

Was there any particular TV show that you loved as a kid?
My favorite when I was a kid about that age was *Dukes of
Hazzard*. I had all their toys. I loved television as a kid but I don't

remember if that's the show that I was looking at when I had that thought of being an actor.

You went to college to study theater?
Yes, I went to college at the University of Sacramento, California and got a Bachelor of Arts in Drama.

Do you believe that the degree has been helpful?
I've talked to actors today who have very little foundation in the craft of acting. What formal training provided me was a very solid foundation. There are many different things that an actor needs to embrace early on when building their craft. For example, voice and bodywork are tremendously valuable. Not a lot of actors that I run into nowadays at on-camera classes know about how important your voice and your body is in relation to your performance and your character. The basics are important.

Also you get theatre experience. Being on stage, being in front of an audience, having people watch you, having people see you in the rehearsal, all of those things are vital and necessary to an actor. These are the sort of things you fundamentally get in any drama class or program in a college institute. So yes, it's been tremendously valuable.

After your degree you moved to LA?
I went to San Diego after living five years in Sacramento. I was in San Diego for three years and during that time, I drove up to Los Angeles as needed. So I never actually lived in Los Angeles.

After you moved there, were you trying to get agents, take more classes by well-known teachers and studios?

I found a guy named Jerry Scott. He had directed in New York City and I just happened to stumble into him in class. Through him, I managed to get an agent who did showcases for his actors. He was very much immersed in the market, both in San Diego and Los Angeles. We were all showcased to casting directors, agents, and directors. True enough, a talent agent from San Diego came there to one of the showcases and saw me. That's how I got representation in San Diego for film and television.

What prompted you to choose Atlanta after that?

Well, four letters. Love. We follow our hearts, and I fell in love with a woman who is from the south. So I packed up my bags and said goodbye to acting, and I moved east. I met her on a cruise ship out of LA and she lived in Tennessee but the cruise crossed the Bahamas and Mexico. I was followed my heart to Atlanta at the precise time it was becoming the center of all this activity. I got lucky that way.

Did you ever have any concerns about leaving the LA market because you still wanted to pursue acting full-time?

My only concerns were that I was away from my support system – my family and friends. But there was already this talk of how big the Atlanta market was going to become. That excited me. Never once were my concerns whether this was going to be a good place to be as an actor. I had to rebuild everything here. The agent was new, the casting directors were new, the people I met in the auditions and classrooms were new to me. I'm cultivating all that here. Also, unlike Los Angeles or New York, Atlanta doesn't have a very good foundation for film and TV actors. The resources are low. The industry is smaller in Atlanta.

Smaller in terms of jobs that are open to hiring actors, classes that are really good?
Yes. If you go to Los Angeles, you can walk into any place and run into somebody who will be in the industry in some capacity whether they're a writer, an actor, a producer. It's just in your face, more obvious. You feel like you're part of something. But in Atlanta, you don't feel that.

What else do you do to support yourself these days, in addition to acting?
I've always worked in the service industry, in restaurants and hotels, since college. And it became a lifestyle. I think it'll probably always be there because not only has it been there so long for me but I'm also very good at it, I enjoy it. I enjoy being of service for others. And it gives me great flexibility.

How did you go about getting an agent here?
I submitted to all the agencies here. After a year and a half, I finally got a phone call from Houghton Talent who said that they'd like to meet with me and have me read.

What else do you do to market yourself and network?
Marketing myself and networking is my largest liability as an actor at this point because of just the way I look at things in terms of the craft of acting. That being said, I managed to do something recently that sort of launched me more into the

Atlanta market than I ever could have imagined. I started my own acting group that meets up on a regular basis. I've been blessed with several people who have been speakers in the group who have reached out and marketed the group more than I ever would, making it even much larger of a success.

You meet and do exercises? You work through slides, scripts?
We do exercises and a lot of technique grounded work. We do on-camera work. We do preparations for actors who have auditions where we work the lines, do script analysis, and improvisation. We are also a support group. We all sit around and talk about who's new in town, who's the new casting director, what's the new show, who's going to audition for what? Have you met with so and so? Is there a new theatre that's coming up and doing a new show? Or someone's got a new project that's casting right now? It's very much a network of actors who are trying to support each other by really giving away information that would otherwise actually cost money to obtain.

What do you see the future of acting being in Atlanta?

Times are changing so quickly, especially with use of online casting. Now more than ever are we putting ourselves on tape and submitting to casting directors efficiently. What's happened is that now the market is not just limited to one geographical location. That's making it a little bit challenging for Atlanta actors who now compete with talent from LA and other areas as well.

But I do think that the talent in Atlanta is equally as good as that in Los Angeles, adjusted for the size difference. We obviously are a smaller, newer market. We have plenty of non-beginner, intermediate actors at this point here who are ready to take on that next level if only they're given the opportunity. After all, anybody who's anybody in Los Angeles didn't start as a veteran actor either.

I think a lot of the work will be available to intermediate actors who are going to get that opportunity. It's going to be too costly for production to hire and cast all of the roles needed out of LA while you have talent here that's ready and local and can do the job just the same. Eventually we're going to have everything just like they have in Los Angeles – a full scale setup. And you are able to do that more so in Atlanta because we have space to grow.

Do you have plans to leave Atlanta anytime soon?
Not with the way things are!

Do you have representation outside Atlanta?
Not currently. But I'm actually thinking of maybe looking into the Louisiana market because I can handle the 5-hour drive there, if I need to, if a role is sizeable enough. Lord knows they've got enough awesome productions going on there, it might just be worth my while.

How do you stay positive and motivated?
The support group I mentioned earlier has been tremendous for me, being around other people who also get hurt from

rejection. Then I don't feel alone. That's just one of the most valuable things a human being needs. When you're going through something difficult, to know that you're not alone is always one thing that gets you through it. Another thing that helps me handle rejection is putting my face into a book and reading up more about the craft and getting more into a class and doing better work. It helps me with rejection because I get this inspiration to just go in there next time and do better and better, to be so damn good that they have no excuse to say you're not good enough or you're not the right person. Also, chocolate helps. Yeah, I eat chocolate and get a good cigar. Sometimes, a massage.

Eric Goins

An accomplished actor with multiple television and film credits (http://imdb.me/ericgoins), Eric Goins is also a professional improvisational actor. He is the owner of Compass Actor Services and Yes And Films, LLC. More info can be found at http://www.ericgoins.com, http://www.compassactorservices.com and http://www.yesandfilms.com.

Where are you from and how did you get started in acting?
I am originally from Tampa, Florida. I came up to Atlanta to go to Emory University where I graduated with a Bachelor of Science in Biology. I was hoping to go to med school at the time, but circumstances changed my plan and I ended up working in the corporate world for quite a while doing all sorts of different things. I worked for marketing companies for the most part though. I ran golf tournaments for BMW. I traveled with Ringling Brothers for a year doing PR and event marketing for them. I

worked at Home Depot for a short time. I had my own business for a short time. I was an emergency medical technician for two weeks. I was a real estate agent for a couple weeks. I just couldn't find my way.

Then I walked into an improv theater for my birthday with some friends of mine. It was Whole World Improv Theater here in Atlanta, and a lightbulb went off. I thought, that looks like a lot of fun and I want to try it. At the time, I had to audition for the improv classes that they were providing. They auditioned 120 people. I'd never been to an audition before, and I just did what I thought I should do. I got chosen. And that was 16 years ago.

I've been there ever since, moved through the ranks to become a Main Stage performer and an emcee as well as one of the managers of the company. And from there, I bought into everything improv had to offer. It changed the chemistry of my brain. That's the only way I can explain it. It opened up a whole new side of me in the creative realm and the emotional realm that I didn't know I had before I started doing improv. The more I got to do it, the more I realized that I really enjoy being a part of storytelling. And the natural extension of that, for me, was to hopefully get into what was, at that time, the local commercial and industrial work that was in town. Because there wasn't a lot of television and film 15 years ago. I got a call from one of my buddies, my roommate actually, Brian Chapman, "I'm at this audition and I swear they're looking for someone just like you. Let me talk to Houghton (Talent Agency) and see if they'll send you." And so Houghton ended up sending me. I took a headshot outside where I was working. It was just a brick wall. I don't even remember what I used to take a photograph because I don't think my cell phone even had the capability at the time. I ended up getting a callback, and Houghton decided to sign me as an actor based on that experience. I've been with them ever since.

About ten years ago, I was laid off of my corporate job. I had decided that if that ever happened, that I would pursue acting full time. Before I got laid off, I had taken a year off of improv, and I found myself to be very unhappy. I told myself that if I ever had to make a decision between corporate work and what I had a passion for doing, that I would choose the passion. When I got laid off from my corporate job, I said this is God telling me something here. This is exactly what I needed to happen. And then I got a job offer at another place doing the same thing and making more money, and I actually turned it down.

The moment I made that decision, doors started opening. They weren't huge doors, but they were doors. They needed an instructor for a kids summer camp at Whole World, and then my friend got me on as a bartender at a local pub so I could pay my bills, I've never looked back. Everything just fell into place since I followed my heart and not my bank account.

Every 4-5 years in my life, I've had to make some kind of pretty substantial decision. It is to go this path or go that path, and I feel like each and every time, I've tried to follow my heart and the result is I feel like I'm where I'm supposed to be. I have no regrets, even though things could have turned out completely different in my life, I could be a doctor today, which would help me financially probably, but I don't know that I would be as fulfilled.

Do you think that the variety of jobs and gigs you did before have helped you develop the mindset of a freelancer and an entrepreneur, and does that mindset help in the acting world?
100 percent. I didn't see it at the time, but I think all those experiences I had gave me a real well-rounded view of the human experience, I've worked at the paint department at Home Depot, but I've also done CPR on a woman on the back of an ambulance for 25-30 minutes to save her life. These experiences have given me a different type of well to draw from. When I'm improvising or when I'm on set, acting has allowed me to figure out how to find the feelings that are associated with those experiences. Which is cathartic, in a way.

When you started taking classes in improv, you were not thinking really about making this a career but you just loved what you did. At some point, did you start thinking about maybe booking jobs with your acting chops?
In the beginning, I had no intention of this being a career. My friends told me I was funny, they told me I was entertaining to be around. I never had any inclination that it would be a career choice. The more I did it, the more I learned. Every time I do it, every time I have ever done improv or performed or done an audition or helped somebody else with their audition, I have personally found out something about myself that I didn't know before I did it. For me, that's what my life is all about - trying to figure out how to be the best me I can possibly be. The best version of myself, and I think by doing improv and being an

actor, that's my journey to find that. Because to do something, I have to find it within myself.

Alot of times we walk around this planet, and we're not aware of what kind of emotional depth we have, what kinds of things we can draw on. I've gone from being not so sensitive to a very sensitive man, and I think that's a really awesome thing. It's changed me dramatically. It changed my chemistry as a human being.

Did you take any other classes too after doing improv?
No, I've only been doing improv. That's it. I've taken maybe 3 or 4 weekend workshops with casting directors and done some private coaching with reputable coaches. That's been more over the last five years than anything, but I've never taken any organized long-term acting class. I think that might be atypical but I don't know. I take on a fundamental actor's approach to my improv. And I read a lot.

What do you mean by "fundamental actor's approach?"
I try to find emotional connections in all the improv work that I do. Improv, in my opinion, can be separated into two approaches. One is cerebral, so it's the very wittiest of improv. Very witty, having real quick, sharp, funny comments. And then there's also the emotional. Over my time as an improvisor, I've chosen to try to find all the emotional connections to improv that I can. Trying to look beyond what's on the surface to find the human experience that's happening on set or on stage as opposed to just the surface detail of what the audience has given.

If the audience tells us we're locked in an elevator and I'm in there with a stranger, rather than just taking that on the surface level, I try to look at it, "Well, what am I feeling towards this other person in this situation? What is the human experience?" I have an energy and they have an energy, and if they come together in this literally closed environment, what happens?

Could be because I have a science background that I think that way. Now that I'm saying it out loud. It sounds like a scientific experiment if you think about it.

Every time I'm on stage, I try to look for the human experience and I bring that to the front because I think that's what people are interested in. They're interested in how two human beings or three human beings respond to a given set of circumstances, as opposed to talking about the situation in which you find yourself.

I really dug my heels in really deep into that experience and I'm fortunate enough to have a wife that's an actor as well as an improviser. I met her at the theater. So we have in depth conversations about all these things. I get to fine-tune my philosophy and really do some deep thinking about acting and improvising. My classes have become in-depth discussions with people around me.

Do you teach improv too now?
I do. I teach improv to beginners and I also teach improv to working and student actors currently in the industry. If anybody

wants any information about my improv, the best thing to do is just send me an email at elgoins@gmail.com or I have a website, http://ericgoins.com.

You said you do continue to supplement your income with other things. You do tapings and other coaching as well?
I do. I just started a company called Compass Actor Services (www.compassactorservices.com). We do audition tapings, private coaching, demo reels, improv training and various acting workshops. My wife and I have a video production company, Yes And Films (www.yesandfilms.com), and then my wife also has two other improv-based companies. She does improv parties for kids and she does improv corporate workshops through Brain Storm CIT (www.braintormcit.com).

What do you do in terms of marketing and networking?
Never enough. I have my own personal website. I'm up on all the casting websites. I make sure my IMDB page is up to date. I'm a SAG member. The most important thing about networking for me is that my goal, my personal goal I've set up for myself, when I started doing this seriously probably about seven or eight years ago, is I made a pact with myself that my goal was to be the easiest person to work with in the industry. And that's arguably unattainable, right? But, it keeps me always being friendly, always working hard, always saying yes, always being easy to work with. Those are the kind of people that people want to work with. That's probably my best networking approach of all because I'm a big "the proof is in the pudding" guy, and so I can tell people all day and market myself as having skills, but when I get on set or I have the opportunity to be in

front of a casting director, I want to be the kind of person that people want to work with, and that's the best networking that you can do.

Every opportunity that I'm given-- an audition, a workshop, a booking-- I do not go out of my way to meet every single person on set and schmooze and make sure everybody knows what my name is. What I do is —- I have a good attitude. I do my job the best I possibly can, and then I make sure that I've exceeded the expectations that everyone had for me.

I did hire a PR person last year for *Halt and Catch Fire*, and she helped me a great deal. Made some connections in LA as well as got me some interviews with some industry people that made sense, like in the tech industry. She was great, but I had seven episodes of the show supporting that, and that's why I did it, because I wanted to leverage it as much as possible beyond what I could do. I may do that again in the near future.

What made you decide to join SAG-AFTRA?

I joined last year (2014). There are a couple reasons why I joined. Specifically, I joined because I was heading out to LA to talk to some industry representatives out there, and I thought it was important for me to be in the union when I talked to them. I also did it because when I looked back on my auditions over the last 12-18 months, there were probably close to 90 percent union auditions. I joined the union because my work history showed that I was mostly auditioning for union work.

Obviously it's a goal that every actor desires. I thought about it for a long time. I consulted with trusted mentors. I didn't do it half-assed. I did it after serious consideration and discussing it with friends and other members of SAG. What's great is that the union doesn't pressure you in any way, shape, or form to join. They just give you the details. And then there's coming off the first season of *Halt and Catch Fire*, I thought it was important to join.

I'm a big look-at-data-support for decisions, for the most part. And having a wife and kids, sometimes that does that to you. I like to have good consideration about decisions like that because once you join, for all intents and purposes, you're not supposed to go backwards. You're not supposed to drop out, so it's a big commitment, but it felt right for me and in hindsight, I think it was absolutely the right decision.

What else do you do in terms of trying to stay aware of what's shooting in town, who is casting what, industry news?
I'm pretty well dialed-in. The first thing I do is I trust my agent. I read industry newsletters. I'm on Facebook so I read all the industry updates that are up there. I belong to GPP, Georgia Production Partnership, which is a great resource for people. It meets once a month, and part of that meeting is going down a list of all the things shooting in town. I've found a really good relationship with my agent where I can have those conversations.

Now you've booked a recurring role here. Do you think it's hopefully going to lead to bigger things right here in Atlanta or do you think you might have to move out to LA to be able to get bigger roles?

In my opinion, the Atlanta market is growing as to the opportunities that are being allotted to actors here in town, and I think that will continue to grow as time goes on. We'll always have a natural tie to LA but the opportunities are rising for Atlanta actors who are really prepared and have the proper experience to have larger opportunities on set to book larger roles. That will continue. I don't see any reason why it wouldn't.

What do you think actors in Atlanta need to do to make sure they are up to the mark?

Be on a constant search for their authentic self. All of us, including myself, need to always be learning who our authentic self is and then standing by that person, making no excuses or compromises. They shouldn't change to be the character. The character should be different because they are doing it.

If I do something authentically me, it's never been done before. And it could never be duplicated because it's authentically who I am, and nobody else is me. Finding that, and having the confidence to communicate that in an audition or on set, is paramount. Because that's what people want to see. They want to see authentic human beings who are different than everybody else. Obviously, learning the technical aspects of doing an audition is critically important, but in the absence of having an agent, improv is a critical skill that everybody should have because a lot of people don't really understand what it entails. Improv is an important tool to put in your arsenal. Find that authentic self and learn to bring it to every single role you read for, to the point where you may do something different than the character description because it's the way you do things. The worst they can say is no. We all need to stop trying to fit into someone else's box.

Trust that at some point there's going to be a fit between who you are and what they're looking for, and it will work out?
One of the first things I tell people I work with on a one-on-one basis is, "You are already enough. What you have and who you are is already enough. Just show me who that is."

Do you have representation outside Atlanta?
No, I do not have official representation outside Atlanta.

How do you stay positive and motivated?
I don't hang my happiness on the amount of bookings I have or the amount of auditions I'm going to. I hang my happiness on the real relationships I have in my life, my family, my friends. That's where I hang my happiness. That's how I stay positive. And then believe it until you achieve it. Fake it until you make it. Do all the things that you know you need to do, and carry yourself as if you're successful.

I also understand that when I do an audition, my goal for the audition is to present the best version of myself. If I was in the moment, I was present, that was the best me, that was the best me I could present right now today, then I'm satisfied and I'm happy and I'm confident and I walk away and I don't worry about it. If I didn't book that one, it's not devastating because, in my opinion, this career is a marathon. It's not a sprint. Everybody has a different path to take in this career, and no one knows what their path is going to look like. I can't compare my path to someone else, because we're on different paths.

It comes down to hanging your happiness on important things that matter in life and for me that's God, family, and friends. I don't value myself based on the success or failures of my career. My value comes from the way I treat people and the love that I'm surrounded by.

Your bio says you practice hapkido?
Yeah. It's a Korean martial art. There's a lot of improvisation that comes with martial arts too.

What do you wish someone had told you at the beginning of your career, and if you had to do it all over again, would you do anything differently?
I wouldn't have done anything differently because I try to live my life without regrets, so everything that's happened to me has gotten me to where I am today. I wish that somebody, at the beginning of my career, had told me that everyone you meet in this industry, that is the decision makers in the process, all want you to succeed, and they're all on your team, and they're all rooting for you.

And there's no reason to be intimidated, scared, or have a lack of confidence when you're in front of them because they're all on your side. If you would just have some confidence in yourself, then you're going to succeed. It took me a while to develop the confidence I needed to go in there and be me in an audition or on a set. It took a while, and I wish I would've gotten to that place faster.

The casting directors want you to succeed, they want you to solve a problem. They have a problem. They need to cast this role. They want you to walk in and do it that way they can move on to the next role. The directors, they want you succeed because they want to have a great movie. Your teachers want you to succeed. Your acting coach, all the people you go work with at workshops, they want you to succeed because they want to push successful actors out into the world. Everybody wants you to succeed. And fortunately, in my circle of friends, almost all my friends are actors, and we all want each other to succeed, even if we're auditioning for the same role, we all want each other to succeed.

Eric Kan

Eric Kan's professional acting work has been featured in the New York Times and The Atlanta Journal Constitution. He regularly performs standup comedy and his work has been profiled on NPR. He has appeared in many TV series including ER, Gilmore Girls, and Days of Our Lives. He has also studied improv at Upright Citizens Brigade and Second City in Hollywood. More credits at his IMDB page:
http://www.imdb.com/name/nm1018241/?ref_=fn_al_nm_1

When did you know you wanted to be an actor and how did you get started?
It was really an accident for me. I wanted to be a doctor. At least, that's what I thought I wanted to be. But that changed in college.

Where are you from originally and where did you do to college?
I'm originally from California. But I lived in Georgia from half of middle school till college. I got a degree in Exercise Physiology from the University of Georgia. While I was there, I tried

multiple majors. I took an acting class as a requirement I needed to graduate and I really liked it a lot. I didn't know anything about acting. I started doing campus plays and talking to professors in the department, talking to anyone that knew anything about acting.

This was before the Internet was huge with all the information on it. So you had to do your own footwork and not just look it up online. It would have been easier if I had been at UCLA or University of Southern California. But I was in Athens, GA and not in LA or New York. I continued with my science major because I had completed so much course work already. Meanwhile I was also taking acting classes in Atlanta. I was traveling from Athens to Atlanta once a week for scene study classes and rehearsals. So that's how I got my start.

Did your family support you in this transition to an acting career?
In the beginning, they were not happy at all. They didn't understand what I was trying to do. It wasn't like I'd shown any desire to become an actor when I was younger. For them, the acting thing just came out of nowhere.

They also worried whether I would be able to manage financially. The moment they really started to support me was when they saw me on TV for the first time. That's when they began to come around. They saw that I was starting to be successful and do what I said I was going to do. They started supporting me more then. Being able to see it with their own eyes was a big thing for them.

When did you move to LA?
I wanted to move to LA immediately after college but from what everybody was telling me, I was under the impression that I

wasn't going to get any work in LA. California is a union state. The Georgia actors were telling me I had to get with a union like SAG or I wasn't going to get work and that I needed to start in Georgia because it would be easier. Otherwise, I would never make it in LA. I didn't know any better, so I believed what I was told.

I spent two to three years, including when I was in college, pursuing my SAG card in Atlanta, GA and in Miami, FL. I got my SAG eligibility by being an extra for one day on a set in Florida. About three or four months later, I got upgraded. I guess I made principal from the commercial when it ran for about a year. I received my SAG eligibility from that. Then I moved to Los Angeles so I've been in the union since about 2000.

When you started working in Atlanta and Florida after college, did you get an agent?
I had a lot of agents. Back then, you could have more than one agent. I had five or six agents in Atlanta working for me at any given time. I had to finally sign with one of them because he insisted on me working with him exclusively. In Florida, I had several agents in Orlando and in Miami. Nowadays though you have to choose one agent to work with exclusively.

In those days was the work mostly commercials and industrials, or was it more films and TV?
Back when I was in college and after graduation, it was probably the worst time because they had just finished running "Designing Women" and "In the Heat of the Night". "Forrest Gump" had already come and gone. By the time I really got into it, the film industry had already gone. Maybe once a while you would get a movie audition.

But they only used the southeast for environments for civil war or historical movies. There really wasn't anything for me to be in because I'm Asian. I'd see my non-Asian friends get auditions and parts. I would audition for parts like a dad, and I was fresh out of college and looked even younger than my age at that time. There was not a lot of opportunity for paying work for me. I mainly worked for free on independent and short indie films so I could at least make a reel.

I wasn't making any money as an actor. I was waiting tables to support myself and I was acting for free. That's why I moved to LA. I wasn't really in love with the idea of living in LA. I like it out here in Georgia. I was very happy here. I moved to LA out of necessity. I was looking for work. If I had gotten more paid work in Atlanta, I would have just stayed here. I don't think I would have ever moved to Los Angeles. There just wasn't any work for me then, like there is now.

I see actors like me now here but they are 10 or 15 years younger than me. There are so many different opportunities. Diversity really matters to people now. It's cool to see this happen. I wish I were younger now because I got in when the business was on the low end in Atlanta. There just really wasn't a place for me back then. All of the agencies loved me but there just wasn't anything for me to do. And the few auditions they had for me, I was totally wrong for or I just looked too young. I just kept going to class. I finally made the decision to go to the west coast to get work.

When you went to LA, was it like starting all over again?
Yeah. Atlanta is a big city but LA is even bigger. There is no real center of the city, it's all spread out and huge. When I moved to LA, I had never even visited there. I didn't know any other actors or folks in the industry there. I only knew actors in Georgia who

didn't have any plans of leaving Atlanta. I drove out there with my brother one summer, made a trip out of it.

It took about a year to get an apartment and find a job in a decent location. The first six months, I was driving from Orange County two hours each way. I lived with my cousins in Orange County because I didn't know anyone in LA. I was going to these networking events trying to talk to people. Young actors today are moving out to LA together. I think what they're doing is much smarter. They have Facebook now and other social media sites where they are able to make connections really fast. They can speak to someone in LA and get advice. They can drive there together, be roommates and save money.

Looking back, I honestly don't know how I accomplished any of that without the Internet. It wasn't as widespread and had only limited information at the time. At a certain point, I just had to go take the plunge without full information. But I'm still grateful for my experiences.

Did you go through the whole process of finding agents in LA again?
Sure, I went to class as much as I could afford to, always training and trying to meet agents and other industry folk. I was submitting my own headshots and resumes to casting directors directing commercials on TV. I was actually getting quicker results from contacting casting directors directly than I ever did with an agent or a manager.

I wish I had put more time into finding the right agent. I'd sign with people who told me they would do a lot for me and never really did much. And once electronic technology finally hit Hollywood and casting directors were taking taped audition submissions, it was difficult for actors to get in front of them. I felt if I can't get to the casting directors on my own and the agents aren't helping me then what am I doing here? I kept just getting older and not getting auditions. That was around the time that people in Georgia started talking about all this work going on here.

Was this something that you heard while in LA, that there was so much work in Georgia?
Yeah, I stayed in touch via email with people back here. And they confirmed that work had really picked back up here. Then I found out on Facebook that one of my friends had moved from LA to Atlanta. I wrote her a message asking why she was in Atlanta and she responding saying that she was finding way more work there. She said she had an agent and it was great out there. So I thought maybe I should move back to Atlanta because I actually know Georgia very well. It took me about two years after that point to finally make the move. I had to wrap my head around the idea of moving back to Georgia for acting work. Because LA is a really fun and exciting place that can make you feel like nothing else in the world exists. It's very easy to get there and stay there, it's like a bubble. Once you are in the bubble, it's very hard to imagine a life outside of it.

There's also a pride/ego component. Because there's a part of you that thinks if you leave LA, you've failed. Because it's so hard living in LA with very little money, you make a lot of friends with the same goals and you encourage each other. You become so close with these people and it's very hard to imagine leaving them. You've invested so much time and energy into LA.

You have to convince yourself that you can leave all that behind. At the end of the day, I could have stayed in LA as long as I wanted to. Nobody was forcing me to come home. But what was the point of being there if I wasn't happy and I wasn't working. I wasn't even auditioning. When I finally decided to go, a lot of the people that I was close with in LA started to leave as well. These were the lifers, the people that you never thought would leave. Some of them stated that acting wasn't for them anymore and they wanted to do something else or pursue happiness in a different way. So a lot of my core group of friends also left.

It is more important for you to be happy where you are than to try to chase down opportunities by location. I know a lot of actors who did the whole bi-coastal thing. They had an agent in New York, they had an agent in Florida and they were always traveling for auditions. They were spending four months living in LA during the pilot season. I just didn't want to do that. I was a homeowner in LA, I owned a two-bedroom condo with a roommate that was paying a nice portion of the mortgage and I said goodbye to all of that.

When I decide to do something, I do it 100%. I was not going to stop renting the condo or slide back and forth. I decided to come to Atlanta and really give it a shot. I had friends in LA that told me I could go to Atlanta, get with AMT agency, see my family, and if it doesn't work out, LA will always be there. I could always come back. So I sold all I could. I gave away a lot of really nice stuff to my friends because they needed it. I drove back cross-country. It was May 2012, so I've been back around three years now. People ask me if I miss LA and if I want to go back and I tell them, "No, I do not miss LA, and don't want to move back."

That's not to say it will never happen, but I have really no interest in moving back to Los Angeles as a no-name actor. But if I hit it big out here or a big agency or managing company says, "You're our guy and we have to move you out to LA. We're going to take care of you and groom you for something." I definitely wouldn't move back to LA to start from ground 0.

What do you believe to be the future of acting in Atlanta?
It all depends on the tax incentives. I could be wrong, but if the tax incentives stay, we got work. If they go away, we got no work. Simple as that. It's all about money. They're not coming here because they like us, they're coming here because they are saving a lot of money.

Do you see the scope of roles being offered to Atlanta actors increasing to TV series regulars and leads?
Everybody believes it's happening but I don't see it happening. I know that every once a while an Atlanta actor will become a reoccurring or guest star role. It happens but it doesn't nearly as much as I'd like to see. They look at us like day player actors, for the most part. The majority of my resume is Los Angeles TV shows and commercials because I lived and worked in Los Angeles for 12 years. And now, just because I live here in Georgia, the casting directors look at me as a local talent. It's a really weird thing.

But I do understand the producers live in Los Angeles or New York where there is a higher percentage of highly trained actors. It doesn't really make any sense for them to take a risk with us. There are really good actors here. But if you live in Los Angeles where amazing actors surround you, why would you even look at anybody here for anything major. The fact that you wouldn't have to put local actors here in a hotel and you can get back 30% of whatever you spend on them, could be a consideration. But when you are dealing with major studios, they have budgets for these kinds of things. They're already spending all of this money for the cast and crew in the local parts. They would rather not spend all this money for what maybe the wrong actor or not a good fit and go with someone who may be considered New York or LA talent.

So you believe that just being from LA provides that comfort to the studio?
Yes, I believe that's definitely true. If you were a producer, what would you think? Why would you think that someone from Georgia is a better actor or is as good as an actor from New York or LA? They spend a lot of money into these projects and spend 5 or 10 years developing a TV series, why would they go outside of so much talent in their own town to risk on someone living in Georgia- even if they are good for the part. How are you going to convince producers to get onboard with that? It's not right or wrong. It's just business.

I've told people the reason I came back here was because the work was here and that is true. But I also knew that moving from LA back to Georgia meant that I was no longer pursuing my acting career as strongly as I used to. There was a part of me that was just tired of pushing and fighting and getting very little. I wanted to start to have a life again. I wanted to have some money in the bank. I didn't want every dollar that I made to go to the rent or gas. I'd like to have something to show for my life besides just some credits on the screen. The guys and gals that move to LA and really fight, they deserve it. I was out there fighting and hustling and never got a good agent. I wasn't able to get to the next level. I tried the best I could as far as I could tell. It didn't work and I don't have the energy or the desire to do push that hard anymore.

A part of me thought that I was just coming to Georgia for a couple of years and recharge as I spend time with old friends and my family. Then maybe I'll move back to Los Angeles. But as of now, I've been back about three years and I visit LA once or twice a year just to say hi to friends and visit the place. I have no desire or pull to be back there. I am always glad to visit though. When I left LA, I was really ready to go. I thought about going back, but even none of my friends are working. One or two of them are working doing commercials but most of them are just living their lives. Working on a job or doing a web series and meeting every month to network and talk about goals. But no one is actually working. It's good to go and have drinks and catch up but when I go there, there is no real evidence that tells me I need to go back.

One of my friends in L.A who works regularly says the biggest thing is to find that job that allows you the freedom to pursue acting and not make you want to kill yourself. You have to find the right support for yourself because acting is a lifelong marathon. You're not looking for a job that makes you feel bad about yourself, doesn't pay you enough money, or stresses you out.

The biggest thing that makes a lot of actors quit acting is the inability to find that good paying job that allows you the flexibility to pursue acting. You have to find the right kind of neighborhood, job, and support. You're going to get a lot of close calls and look at the TV and think, "That could've been me." But it wasn't. You dust yourself off and keep going and hopefully you don't get a job that makes you feel bad, doesn't pay you enough money, and stresses you out because that's going to show up in your audition. You can't live your life like that. Unless you marry a rich person or you have a trust fund to live on.

What do you do in terms of marketing or networking now?
I'm a part of the SAG committee. I help out with SAG events. I go see plays. I am part of the Atlanta Film Festival. I go to the networking events. I'm with a premier talent agency, AMT. They are really taking care of me. AMT is the only agency that has produced consistently good results for me. I like it here, I miss the excitement of LA but not the stress and I have no desire to go there without a strong support team.

If you could start over and do things differently, what would you do?
I wish I didn't rush into the business so quickly. I wish I had really researched and gotten really good formal acting training for 2-3 years. It would have put me in debt but I think it's really

important to train properly. A training program where I could really build a solid foundation as an actor with good teachers.

Stop trying to be famous, just do the work. The people will be there and the role will be there when you are ready. When I was getting auditions, I was winging it because I had no foundation as an actor. I then started to find a good teacher to really learn the craft of acting. There's nothing worse than the chance of someone giving you a shot and you blow it. I called myself an actor, but I didn't understand it from a textual standpoint. It took two years for my teacher to break down my bad habits and retrain me.

Does it have to be a formal college degree program?
That's why I said a good teacher. It doesn't have to be at a formal degree program.
Unfortunately, many colleges are filled with failed actors. The universities, even the good ones, may not teach you the right information in order to do the things you should know how to do. So just because you get a degree from somewhere doesn't mean that you are a good actor. But you know if you are going to be an actor without any formal training, you should at least go away for a couple years to study with a teacher or a studio where you can submerge yourself in the technique before you start the profession. Just like a doctor, you have to go to school before you start cutting people up. You have to go to school, you have to take tests, you have to be able to understand it, and defend it. It's important to do the work.

It's hard because when you are in LA, you see all these people auditioning. But you have to be real with yourself and not compare yourself to other people. You have to be at the point where you are ready to knock it out of the park at every audition. Not rush yourself into doing things. That was the biggest mistake I made, rushing into the business. Just enjoy the process. The people will find you. There are a lot of people who are good actors that are not well trained and can't deliver when they are supposed to deliver. You have to be able to do it, when they need you to do it. That is the mark of a professional. You only get so many chances. That's my take on acting. Work on your process, the results will follow.

Gabriela Rowland

Gabriela is a bilingual actress and producer based in Atlanta. She is represented by Avery Sisters Entertainment.

Where are you from originally and how did you get into acting?

I am from Santiago, Chile. I've wanted to be an actress since I was 10-years-old. But back in Chile, the opportunities are very minimal. So when I moved to the United States, I worked for maybe 15 years in different fields but realized that I didn't want to die without trying to follow my dreams. So I quit my job and have pursued acting since.

How did you end up in Atlanta?

Because of my boyfriend at that time who is my husband today. We met in Florida and then he got a job here in Atlanta. We moved here together.

Was he supportive that you wanted to act?

Absolutely.

How did you go about starting to act?
One day I turned on the radio and heard a commercial about this company called 21st?? Century. They train you in acting and put you in a showcase in front of all the local agents. I did that and that's how I got my agent.

Have you been doing any other training since?
Yes, I've studied with Michael Cole and numerous other people in town.

Do you do anything outside acting to supplement your income?
Luckily, my husband has a great job. If not, not sure I'd have been able to pursue this career. That being said, I also landed a job as a stand-in. And I took it because I wanted to be part of the industry and learn set etiquette and all that. So I worked as a stand-in on the show *Necessary Roughness*. That way, I had a little bit extra money even though the hours were crazy. That's how I started. But I've always worked part-time. It's not like I was the main breadwinner in the family. So that was kind of lucky for me. I also joined the IATSE 479 union (for technicians and crew) and so now I work at craft services as well.

What do you do in terms of marketing and networking?
That's why I work in craft services and as a stand-in, to connect with people in the industry. Working on big sets, I meet with the producers, directors and casting directors. I'm very good friends with a lot of them. That's my way of networking.

Do you think your ethnicity is a challenge in Atlanta or does it help you find the roles easier?

Being Hispanic and speaking Spanish has been a benefit, no doubt about that. But, also it's a big challenge, because in this industry they stereotype you so much that if you don't look the way they think a Hispanic woman should look, they will not cast you. My looks are pretty much like a white person. So I have done tons of commercials with no lines because I can look like a white person. However, when I speak I do have an accent so that's a bit of a challenge for me.

Do you have any plans to move to New York or L.A.?

I have to see how things pan out. My focus is changing right now. I started as an actress and it's something I'm passionate about. But I'm also moving to producing more. I just finished producing my second project. It's a short. And we're going to turn it into a feature. So I don't think it is necessary for me at this moment to move, because things are going back and forth between acting and producing.

How do you deal with rejection? How do you stay positive and motivated?

In the beginning, when I started with the acting career, the rejection really affected me. I took it personally. I thought I did something wrong. I always blamed myself. But over time you learn it has nothing to do with you. There could be so many different reasons why they didn't choose you. And now with producing, I care even less if somebody rejects me, because I always have my own project and team I am working with.

What do you wish someone had told you at the beginning of your career?
I think the path that I'm going through right now is the path that I need to learn what I am. I do wish I had had some mentoring about what to do at every step, how to brand myself.

But that's why I'm producing right now. The idea is to do projects with a good message behind it and not just a project for me to shine in. I want others also to shine. The project has to be meaningful. You have to feel you contributed to something in society.

Jamie Moore

Jamie Moore is an actor and improv artist. His credits include Anchorman 2: The Legend Continues (2013), Identity Thief (2013) and Let's Be Cops (2014). More info at his personal website: http://www.thejamiemoore.com

Where are you from originally and when did you know you want to be an actor?

I was born and raised in Atlanta and the Atlanta metro area. I pretty much knew I wanted to be an actor as soon as I had an awareness of what an actor was. I was always a performer in my family. I was always doing skits or sketches for my family at family gatherings, and I'd play games that were actually improv games without realizing it. I just thought up these little exercises to do with my friends and things like that. So, it's just been inherent in my DNA since as far back as I can remember. Drama in high school was the first time I got to really be instructed and involved in an organized way. And then, as I got out of high school, I just started doing research on my own to find out what I needed to do to get started. Unfortunately, there was no Internet at that time. But I was fortunate enough to stumble into an opportunity to meet with an agent, and I went in there and did a monologue, and the rest is history.

Did you go to college for theater?

I was going to go to college, but this is another thing: I had no guidance at all. My mom and dad didn't encourage me to go to college. They didn't take me through any of the paces of what it took, and my school counselors too failed me in that respect I think. I had no guidance or influence to go to college. I couldn't afford or figure out a way to go to a big drama school. I didn't even know of any back then. So I just dove in headfirst into the business.

Was your family supportive once you started to pursue this more seriously, getting an agent and taking classes?

No, not at first. My mom never wanted me to be an actor. She wanted me to get a job with benefits. No one's gonna want to marry you unless you've got benefits, she'd say. My parents are very old school in their way of thinking. But I just decided that this is what I wanted to do and eventually first appeared on TV for a Georgia Lottery commercial. My mom saw me on television and that's when she was suddenly like, "Yay, you can do this!" And since then my goal has been to just work consistently doing what I love to do and I've been fortunate enough to be able do that.

Do you have other ways to supplement your income as well?

I also teach. I will also do other little side gigs. At one point I did singing telegrams. A lot of people would look at that like, "That must be so embarrassing to tell people that," but I was like, "No, I'm getting paid to perform to a captive audience." Sure there are some people who do singing telegrams that are terrible and could never make it as a film or television actor, so it gets a reputation, and I get that. But I had fun. I loved doing it. I hosted karaoke shows. I hosted trivia shows. Any outlet I had to perform, I took it. This is a nonstop learning industry. There's always something new you can learn.

So when you started, did you take any classes in town? Do you continue to train?
Yes, I took classes. I took a lot more when I was younger than I do now. Unfortunately, I don't have as much time nowadays. I think a class environment is just a great way to flex your muscles and stay on your toes regardless as to whether you're a beginner or working professional. And I also get the opportunity to learn from my students as I teach. You know, we're constantly evolving and learning together.

Where do you teach?
I'm a freelancer, but I right now teach mainly at Orbit Arts Academy in Sandy Springs.

You teach on-camera audition technique?
Yes. I teach a lot of different facets of on-camera. And I also teach improvisation because I'm a big-time improv guy.

How did you go about getting your first agent?

It was through a series of friendly connections. And I went in there and I did a monologue, and they liked me. Genesis was the agency, no longer in existence. They recommended some people I could take classes from and they signed me. If you were referred, that means somebody that they like likes you. So it's that a nice little connection. You get an instant sort of in depending on who the person is.

What do you do in terms of marketing and networking?

I am the worst at that. I don't get out as much as a lot of people do. I know a lot of people will go to every single meeting of Georgia Film whatever and this, that, and the other thing. I really should be better at it. I guess the closest thing I do to actual "marketing" is just making friends. I hate non-genuine "networking". I can't do it. Some people can get out there and they can suck up to everybody they meet and they tell them exactly what they want to hear. I can't do it. I'm terrible at it. I would rather you do your job, I'll do my job, and if we're friends, great.

You are in one of the more competitive categories as a young White male but you've done quite well for yourself. What do you think has been working in your favor?

A lot of it is about attitude. A lot of people will go into an audition nervous, for example. I never get nervous because I know that the person on the other side of the table is rooting for me. They want me to be awesome. They want me to be the one. So I never get nervous. I prepare. That's the one thing I have control over. If I'm not prepared that would be grounds for nerves, but I take care of my own business. I'm prepared.

Another thing is that I love what I do, and when you love what you do, there's not a work element to it. It's like there's no burden, ever, so I think having love for it really also can make a difference.

On a more practical side though, the idea of being a good auditioner or a bad auditioner...I think I'm a good auditioner. Auditions don't make me nervous. But I just do well in the room because I look at it like a performance for a captive audience that's rooting for me, and I get my chance to exercise my craft right here, right now, on this day. Which is a beautiful thing, right? I get to do what I love to do. I'm not getting paid for it, but it's still an outlet and I get to do it.

The other part is that a lot of people get bummed about rejection, and it can wear on them, and it can actually show itself in future auditions. They start to get stressed, try to fix something. If I can make a sports analogy, it's like a hitter who's going through a slump and then they try to adjust their grip, they do all these funky things that take them away from who they truly are and it doesn't necessarily help.

The way I look at it, I've never once been rejected. That doesn't mean I've booked every role, but I can walk out of that door and whether I book it or not, if I went in there and performed the way I wanted to perform at least once, then I have done my job. I don't worry about it again. I don't think about when does that book or when is it coming up, am I going to get it, etc. That's poison. You just do your job, and for most actors their job

172

should be auditioning. You don't get paid to do it, but it is your job.

Is this the mindset you've always had naturally or is this something you've developed over time?
It evolved over time, but it didn't take me long to figure it out. I'd always heard about how it's so competitive. Fortunately, when I came in, I didn't experience that. I experienced a helping hand. There was always somebody watching out for somebody else and so I've tried to pass that on. I've tried to always have that sort of positive mindset. If there are people that I've worked with, that I enjoyed working with, that I think are talented, I'm gonna refer them too. And if there are people I know that need help, I'm gonna help them. I'm gonna give them that advice. I'm gonna give them that nugget that I think is the difference in them continuing to pursue this career or deciding to quit. Because that's okay too.

And I have this mantra, this sort of idea of the basic ground rules of life. One of them is find something you love to do and do it passionately. And if that means you want to build things, then build things. If you want to play in the dirt, then dig in a garden, but find something you love and do it passionately. So many people lose sight of that idea and it becomes about material things or fame. But if your heart's not in it, you're destined to fail.

A lot of actors will go into an audition for a big picture with a big star and they're spending the money before they even walk in the audition door. And that is even worse than being nervous because now you're doing something else. You're trying too hard. The fact is: you are who you are. If you try to walk into an audition and push yourself beyond something that you can actually do, you're not being who you are. You're not being true to yourself. If you're truly awesome at something, then don't worry about it. You'll be awesome at it. Just be awesome.

I don't say that to say you can't work at things or you can't try to do new things. What I mean is, for example, you wouldn't walk into an audition and try to do a backflip if you can't do a backflip. You'll just look like a person who can't do a backflip and probably hurt yourself. You have to know your own limitations as well as where to stretch, and that's what classes are for. You go take classes to learn new techniques and ways of expressing yourself or ways to do things you can or can't do. That's where the evolution never stops.

That's one of the reasons I love improv as well is because improv teaches the idea that taking giant risks to risk failure can ultimately lead to success. In that classroom environment, you get to learn that and you get to learn how to harness that, how to take a big risk in an improv and to fail. Then when you go into an audition, you know where your limits are. It's a two-sided coin. Don't make yourself look like an idiot, but at the same time don't be afraid to look like an idiot! There's a distinction there, and it takes a while to learn.

What do you see as the future of acting being in Atlanta? Do you see the opportunity to book bigger roles here?

The idea that has been around for so long has been that New York and L.A. are where all the talented people are. But I have learned that Atlanta is such a wonderfully powerful market, and there are other markets that are producing wonderful talent as well, like Chicago, for example. But, unfortunately, right now, most of the productions that come into town are still holding onto that regional bias for New York and L.A. So a lot of the Atlanta talent right now are reading for the same old tiny faceless nameless parts, such as Man at Bar or Attendant #1.

My hope is that as the industry becomes more entrenched in Atlanta, more opportunities will arise and they will start to see that there is some talent here that can hold up with anybody from anywhere. Hopefully it will lead to that. Change is happening, but it's very slow. I hope in maybe ten years, we'll start to see leads and series regulars on a bigger basis booked out of Atlanta. I think it's just a matter of time.

What do you think Atlanta actors need to do to step up their game?
I think that everybody needs to train, and a lot of people are training. They've been told by their mom and their grandma that "oh, baby, you're so talented," that kind of thing, and they might do some high school drama or what not and then they think they're ready to just jump in full force. They forget to continue to train. Whether you go to theater school or just take classes and pursue it, whatever, everyone should train. Training is one of the elements that American actors are just missing generally.

That's probably why so many British and Australian actors booking lead roles in the US now, right?
Yeah, I think that's probably a big reason for it.

Do you have representation outside Atlanta?
I don't have anybody on the west coast. I've had flirtations with representation in New Orleans, but I haven't had a need. I might stoke those fires again someday, but for right now it's local.

Any plans in the near future to move to L.A?
At one point that was my plan, but then as John Lennon so brilliantly stated, "Life is what happens when you are busy making plans." That's exactly what happened to me. A life event occurred, and I put that on hold, and at this point I don't know when or if I would go, but it's never off the table.

What do you wish someone had told you at the beginning of your career? Or if you had to redo your career all over again, what would you do differently?
There are some things I would do differently. One is I would have taken some classes in business and economics because the economics of being an independent contractor are so very different than the way you work on a salary W-2 sort of thing. So I wish I would have had someone to advise me in money because I've had to learn the hard way as I went along. If I had to advise anybody, it would be learn about business and finance, because the truth is, it's show business. But there's a lot more business than show. Not only do you have to hone your craft as an actor, you have to hone your craft as a business owner. That's what you are. You're a business owner. When you

go into the acting world, you are running your own small business, and that's you. So I just wish that little nugget had been passed onto me. I would say maybe take a small business class. There are things like that available at online schools and community colleges. The information is out there.

Jessica Leigh Smith

Jessica is represented by J Pervis Talent Agency in Atlanta, Georgia. More information, including reels, can be found on her website: www.JessicaLeighSmith.com.

When did you know you wanted to be an actor, and how did you go about starting it?

I don't know when I really knew for sure I wanted to be an actor, I know that it was something that was part of me my whole life, and if I could have dreamed big, I would have when I was little. But it never occurred to me that it was okay to dream that way. I grew up in a small town in Georgia and at that point, we didn't have the industry. We didn't have the Internet so you couldn't go research how to get involved in it; it was more difficult that way to know about it. I did all the church plays, a couple of them every year, big productions and I had a lot of the lead roles, and I did a couple plays in high school and had a wonderful time doing it, and even had my high school drama teacher encourage me to get involved with the community theater near my college where I was going. It was the Rome community theater, a really good community theater, but I didn't know it then, and then I went to college, and every year said to myself, "This is the year that I audition for a play" and then I just never did. I was pursuing another line of work, so I was more concerned with getting the classes and the internships done for broadcast journalism than I was for being an actress.

What did you study in college?
I was studying Broadcast Journalism and Spanish. The plan was to be a newscaster, I wanted to be a news reporter. That was more of a viable option for me than the crazy world of acting. But by the time I graduated college, I didn't want to do that anymore, and I wanted to go, I always wanted to change the world, save the world and try to figure out what God wanted me to do, and I ended up being a missionary. Well, first I thought I was going to be a teacher, so I started pursuing my masters, and then decided to go to Honduras, and I spent a year in Honduras teaching English at a Christian school, thinking that I would stay there and I was going to be an English teacher, or come back home and be a Spanish teacher, and that was going to be my life.

But over time and just spending some time with God and prayer, I decided I wanted to be an actress. So I came back from Honduras in my mid-twenties thinking I would be an actress. But then I was on my own and I was single. I had to have multiple jobs to pay the rent; I ended up getting busy. I still didn't do it, and it wasn't until my late twenties when I was working a job. I was working a non-profit and on the board of this non-profit was a woman named Eaddy Mays who is an actress. She and her then husband were running a community theater and they were doing a play. They needed an 18-year-old blonde girl. At the time, I looked 18 and had blonde hair. They cast me in the part.

When I did the play was when I realized this is what I wanted to do, this is what I was going to do. I didn't even tell Eaddy I wanted it, Eaddy is just the kind of personality that pushes. Within a couple months, Eaddy had me my first headshots, a commercial and an agent lined up.

That's really how it started, I got thrown into it, but it was always what I had wanted, I just didn't know it until it happened. Part of it is that I never believed that I had any real talent. I thought that I could do a church play, I can do a school play, I can do a community play, but I can't compete with Los Angeles actors. It never really occurred to me that I could until it happened and then I just started doing it.

And you happened to live in the Atlanta area?
Yes, I grew up in Georgia, I grew up in metro Atlanta, lived here my whole life. It was right before the Atlanta area started hitting pretty big in the market, too. I started acting right around the time that the Atlanta industry was starting to boom. It all lined up together at the same time, which meant I didn't have any reason to go to L.A., because it was starting to happen here, and since I was just starting out learning, I needed to learn things here first and then everything just started happening.

Your family was supportive?
My husband, who had just proposed to me right before all this happened, was very supportive. We were recently engaged but he was a 100% on board. And he always has been, he's never wavered in that. I couldn't do it without my husband. Not only because of time, because of our daughters and things like that, but I don't think I could have confidence enough in myself without him sitting there telling me, yes you can do this. The rest of my family, I really didn't tell anybody for a long time. It was a secret, I wasn't living with anybody so I didn't have to tell

people where I was going and what I was doing. I never really had a family that told me good things, that complimented me. So I was never told good things about myself, and I was never really encouraged. It was probably at least a year, maybe longer, before I said out loud to my family that I was pursuing this career. They're mostly supportive now.

Did you take any classes around town?
I do believe heavily in classes, and I believe in admitting when you don't know something you know. I can readily admit that I wasn't the greatest actress and I needed help so I signed up at YourAct. I first did their on-camera prep class, around where auditions were and getting some exposure on-camera. I had done a couple of sessions with YourAct in 2008 when I decided that I didn't have enough of a foundation, because I hadn't studied it in college.

My biggest regret is that I had not had that type of education and the conservatory training. I wish I could have had that. So I ended up going to Los Angeles for a couple of weeks in 2008 and working with some teachers out there privately. They gave me a great foundation, taught me how to get in your character, how to live in it, all the things you're supposed to be thinking of and doing when you're prepping a scene, when you're prepping a play.

When I came back from LA, I was talking to Vince Pisani at Houghton and found out he does private coaching. He has a Meisner background, so I started training privately with Vince for a while. He gave me an even deeper foundation. Shortly after that, in 2010, is when I found The Company Acting Studio and I started working in Lisina Stoneburner's Master Class there. She has an Adler background. I was with her for four years and where all my training has been, with Lisina mostly, and help from some teachers in LA.

What made you want to go to LA for a couple of weeks and how did you find the teachers there?
I jfelt like the training in Atlanta, especially at that time, to me, was mostly focused on on-camera technique, or audition technique, and I wanted to learn how to act. I was doing fine in auditions, I could go get call backs all day long, at a commercial audition, at least. I wasn't having trouble with that. I wanted to learn how to act, and I wasn't finding anybody that was teaching. At the time, I hadn't heard of Lisina Stoneburner. Had I, I probably would have already been in her class.

At first, I thought how am I going to get out to Los Angeles where all the great teachers are? But then I realized, there's no reason I can't just go out there for a short amount of time. I did some research, got online, Google searches, who's the best backstage actor teacher for this or who was rated the best in LA in 2007 for this, then I went to the teacher's website and learned about who they were. I ended up finding a woman named Janice Kent who's a very successful actress and teaches comedy. I wanted to learn some comedy. I really wish we had that in Atlanta. I also worked with Margie Haber. I ended up working with two former teachers from Margie's studio. One of them taught me the mechanics, how to find your beats, your moment, your goals and your obstacles. The other one taught me how to just sit and use my imagination. How to sit with a scene and imagine the whole thing, and I put those two things together. I was able to put her imagination work along with the other work, and come up with my own craft.

Do you think the quality of training has since then at least caught up in Atlanta, or do you think that there are still some differences?

It's definitely gotten a lot better but it hasn't caught up to New York or LA. Because of the industry booming, we have more people coming here from LA who've had great training backgrounds. They are bringing it here and I think it's wonderful. I had not heard of Lisina Stoneburner in 2010 but once I found her, I loved what I got in her class. She was trained in New York, her family is a famous theatrical family and she grew up in the industry, so her training is amazing.

I don't know Rob Mello, I've never trained with him, but I've searched a little bit of what he's doing, and I like it because he's bringing a technique to Atlanta. We're definitely seeing more technique come to Atlanta, which is what we needed. We're overrun with workshops. We're overrun with on-camera techniques and what I don't like about it is that it tells new actors this is all you need. If you just go do a little bit of on-camera technique, and then you go to a casting director workshop, you'll be fine. I wish we didn't give off that impression.

We also don't have the commitment level here that some people in L.A. have. Maybe it's just a percentage because I'm sure some people in L.A. aren't really committed either. I wish we had a conservatory in Atlanta. A 2-year conservatory would do well here. It would be incredible. I would have done it.

In terms of training, what do you think are the top three kinds of classes that an actor needs?

Every actor needs a technique of acting class. It doesn't matter which philosophy you follow. In my opinion, when you boil them all down, they're all very similar, they use different lingo for different stuff. I believe that every actor, if you really truly want to be an actor, and you don't just want to try to be famous, must have a technique class. You cannot book the big roles without a technique. You'll get lucky once in a while, but the truth is that you still need to go exercise those talents and make them stronger. On-camera classes, in my opinion, depend on you. Some people do need to get comfortable with that and therefore they need some on-camera classes.

Improv is immensely important. You will learn to listen to your scene partner when you're doing improv. It loosens up your body and makes you feel a little bit like you can flow into the scene. You gotta use your entire body. Actors need to be taking care of their entire instrument which is your voice, doing vocal training multiple times a week. Working on your posture, standing up straight. Staying in physical shape so that you can breathe well when you're talking. All of those things are important to learn if you really and truly want to master this as a job and a career.

What have your survival jobs been? Has your husband also been providing financial support?
I didn't have to worry about that too much because I got married. I was working for this non-profit when it all happened. I ended up working a customer service job at a company but it wasn't a big deal. It was a stopgap to be able to save some money and pay my rent, but I had a few health problems and actually can't work full-time. I can only really do part-time. Because of that my husband, my then fiancé, and I decided that I would stop working full-time and go part-time. I worked a motivational speaking job for Monster. I got lucky my husband was able to pay our bills. I didn't have to stress over that. And then when we had a child I decided I would stay home with her.

So right now you basically take care of your kids and pursue acting full time on top of that?
Yep! That's it. It's definitely not easy.

It's a tough profession. How do you stay positive?
Because I have two really small children, I don't have time for that. It's really, really hard to be a parent and have a career. I work out a lot, which is important for the career and my health. I run a lot and try to do races with my husband.

So basically having a strong family life provides a core that lets you not get consumed by the acting career.
That would be a good way to put it because I've been going through that a lot lately. That's been a big issue for me, how easy it is to be consumed by this career, probably because we love it and it's such a challenging one. Because you can't really have control over where it goes. You can do all the best stuff but you're still not going to get booked if they don't want to book you, and it's just a weird thing. It's so different from other careers and we can get obsessed with that. I've had my moments when I've been obsessed with it.

I've been going through a thing in the past year of learning how to let go and get rid of that, stop working so hard. Realizing that my girls are way more important than the career will ever be because they're human beings and I can't ignore their tiny human hearts, they need their mommy. And so I've been working on focusing on them more and I find when I do that and when I'm focusing on them more, I don't really care about the industry, I love it and I'm still doing it, and I'm producing a movie now and a web series, but I don't really care as much as I used to about whether or not it succeeds. But I'm just going to do whatever, I'm going to throw it out there, and see if it sticks.

And if it doesn't, I've still got two gorgeous little girls at home to play in the yard with.

Because you can only control your actions, not the outcomes?
Yes and it's really hard because, in a lot of other careers, you can control the outcome with the action but you cannot do that in acting. It's hard for someone like me, I've always been able to do great things. If I could just do what I wanted to do, things would happen for me, but not necessarily. So I've been letting go a lot. If people can find those outlets outside of acting, it makes you a more whole human being which in turn makes you a better actor. If you're volunteering in the homeless streets of Atlanta once a week, then you're a much more compassionate, caring person who can then become a more compassionate, caring actor.

You believe that self-producing, learning to produce and write is an important skill also for an actor?
There are a few things that I get out of it personally. I believe wholeheartedly in it for one reason--how can I possibly sit around and complain about not working when it's so easy for me to do something on my own. My philosophy has become - if no one else will hire me, I will hire myself. And that's what I'm trying to do these days. I just premiered my own web series. And I created it around my life and what I know. I'm producing an inspirational, faith-based movie that I'm very excited about.

When you are self-producing, you are doing these things for yourself. That goes back to having something outside of your career. It's another way of not sitting around and wallowing in your self-pity. If you're busy then you don't have time to worry about that commercial you didn't get because you're too busy producing something.

What else do you do in terms of marketing and staying informed about what's happening in the industry?
I never know how I'm doing in the industry. Ever since the beginning I've done the mailings, I do the postcards regularly, only every couple times a year, nothing major, but I've always done the postcards and sent them out to all the casting directors locally. I just recently started doing the quarterly email blast, so instead of doing the postcard mailing, for people whose email address I have, I now send them a newsletter kind of thing. Which is really better because a postcard is sometimes hard—such little space to write in. If I haven't spoken with you in six months, I have a lot to write on that postcard and that's really crowded and not well done. I like the email because I can add pictures on there and video to it and links. I believe in trying to stay on the radar the best you can but authentically, it's got to be done in your own voice. I'm a southern-grown woman. Writing thank you cards and personal notes is part of who I am.

It's completely authentic for me to send a casting director a thank you card for an audition. It might be weird for somebody's brand who is maybe a body guard. Or some big, huge, biker dude sending a thank you note might come off as a little bit weird. You find what works with your brand that way. I don't spend a whole lot of time on Twitter or Facebook marketing, but I do believe in it. I do have a Twitter account, I just don't do it very well. I do believe that you can have some success by reaching out to a director on Twitter. It's happened, we've seen some stories of people who have reached out to their favorite director and they got an audition and even a part in his movie. It happens once in a while, so I believe in that, but again it has to be authentic. You can't use Twitter and beg for an audition. You have to use it to create a relationship and build a friendship with that person.

Are you trying to get representation outside Atlanta?
Not yet and not heavily. I was going to and then I realized how much time this movie is going to take up. So I think instead of trying to force it, I'm going to try to let it happen naturally. They used to book the Atlanta actors more here but they aren't doing that as much anymore. Most of my TV auditions last year were large roles, and they all went to LA actors every time. So they're willing to bring them here, and some of them are willing to fly themselves here and be local.

What do you see as the future of acting being in Atlanta?
I have a long answer to this. I'm trying to be optimistic, but cautiously so. I've believed since 2010 that we were going to get large roles opportunities in Atlanta. In 2015, we're seeing that. A lot of Atlanta actors get a lot of opportunities that they couldn't get even five years ago. I do believe that since it has changed in that direction, it can change even more. If we can get enough Melissa McBrides jumping out there, they're going to give us some opportunities. I love the fact that LA actors are coming here because that makes us up our game. I had a call back for a movie in 2010, and every other girl had flown in that morning from LA. At first, I was a little bit territorial, that this is an Atlanta job, it should go to all of us. But then I realized if they were coming here, that just meant that we had to work harder, which would only make us better.

If Atlantans continue to work smarter, better, harder then the industry will continue to grow. We've got a lot of good production companies who are starting training centers for crew, which is important, and more people are moving here. We have great things to offer if we will continue to train ourselves to be great actors, we will get bigger parts and we will see series regulars come out of Atlanta, definitely.

No plans to move to LA in the near future?

No plans. I'm not opposed to it, I'll never say I never will but all the grandparents are here and the aunts and uncles and cousins are here. We don't want to take our family to LA. My husband has a very steady job. It's a huge risk to move. If something were to happen for me or if my girls wanted to act, and it ended up being their future, then we're not going to say no to it. But it's not in the plans.

Are you SAG?

I'm not yet SAG. I've decided for now I am not joining. If I join SAG, I can't do non-Union commercials, but I can stay non-Union and do SAG jobs, so I can do both if I stay non-Union. One of the biggest arguments people say is that non-Union commercials are terrible and you shouldn't do them, you don't make as much money. The truth is, I've done nine, only one or two have been SAG and I make just as much money on the non-Union ones as I have on the SAG ones. I've been treated wonderfully on non-Union commercials. There are very few SAG commercials in Atlanta. Extremely few Union commercials are shot here. Which means if you are a Union actor, you have just cut yourself down from a ton of commercial opportunities to very few. So you may not make any money in commercials if you are a SAG actor because you are only competing for a couple of jobs. If you are non-Union then you can work in commercials and industrials all year long.

As far as the shows are concerned, I've only had two co-star roles so it's not been a demand that I have to join. They are not marching down my door yet, saying we won't let you work anymore. I don't need or want the medical insurance, but I know you can get it even non-Union if you make enough money. But it hasn't been an issue for me. I know people say that they give preference to those that are in the Union, but the truth is when TV shows are being booked, the producers don't look at your resume, they look at your tape. They can't look at the tape and know that you're SAG or not.

What do you wish someone had told you at the beginning of your career and what mistakes did you make?
I wish someone had told me what to do, which Eaddy kind of did, I suppose. I like to educate myself and I like to know what I'm doing before I go do it. It's nice for actors who have been there and done that to help younger actors and tell them to beware of this or do it this way, don't do it that way. Sometimes you run into a lot of actors who have been in it for a while, who are stingy with their knowledge and they are fearful of sharing their knowledge with newer actors, because when that person comes up they will take their jobs.

That's such a fearful way of living, I much prefer to help people so anytime I see someone who is starting out, I tell them what I wish people had told me which is here's how to get your headshots, here are options for class, here are some good agents. I tell them everything that they want to know so they don't have to learn by trial and error. It can save people three years of heartache by being with the wrong agent when they didn't know that that agent wasn't getting auditions. I try to help people out in the beginning, and I've done that many times with many actors, spend that time with them. I don't do everything for them, I say here's my resume, and you can use it to format yours, I'm not going to create the resume for them, but at least keep them from being overwhelmed. If they get overwhelmed by the industry then they just may not ever start. I don't want someone to not do it because they felt overwhelmed by what they didn't know. I wish people would be more open with their knowledge and maybe even have a way for older actors ready to mentor new ones.

And the other biggest thing is don't try to get in front of any casting directors until you know for certain you're ready. A lot of people want to just jump in and go get in front of someone like Mark Fincannon before they've had training, and know what they're doing. What you should do is go get your training, go work on your craft, don't be too stressed about it not happening fast enough. Just go do the things, get in class where you will meet other actors and they'll help you learn things, and then when you're ready then go.

Finding mentors is an authentic thing that sometimes just has to happen naturally. I'll ask actors oftentimes, how did you get started and how long have you been doing it. They are very cagey and don't want to share their answers. Sometimes they'll just outright lie. They don't want me to know that they've trained to become a good actor, they want me to think they were just naturally talented and gifted.

When I started to produce this movie that I'm producing, I've never produced a movie, and this is a big one. I started researching how could I do it and I found a producer who has a very long resume, very successful producer who's had movies in theaters and TV and I didn't know him from Adam, but I emailed him requesting five minutes to ask a couple of questions, and he said yes. That turned into a mentor, he is helping me do this movie. He's not a producer on it but he's just telling me what to do, and giving me the advice.

Jyn Hall

Jyn Hall is a SAG-e, Atlanta-based actress signed with People Store talent agency. www.jynhall.com. She is also a writer and producer, and has her own educational webseries, The Dinner Project, which guest stars casting directors from all over the Southeast. www.thedinnerprojectshow.com.

When did you know you wanted to be an actor and how did you get started?

I started acting on stage when I was 6-years-old. My mom always knew that I was going to be an actor. When I was in high school, I took a career class -- the test came up that I should be an entertainer. My mom said, "See, I told you, you'll be great." I don't know if it was the combination of just being a rebellious teenager and not wanting adults telling me this is what I was going to do. Or, at 16, most kids think they know everything. I thought, "A career in acting -- that's not conducive to a family lifestyle." I really wish I'd listened to my mom. There, mom, I said it. I didn't know really what I wanted to do -- I had so many passions and interests -- but I didn't pursue acting. In college, I started as a Psych major and ended with a degree in Elementary Education. I thought I might teach, possibly all over the world. I went back for a Masters in English Lit and Drama, when I realized I was pursuing a career I didn't want. So I entered the business world. And then I just really missed acting.

When I moved to Atlanta in '97, I started acting in community theatre -- just as a hobby -- never even considering it as a viable career option. But it just kind of snowballed. I was asked to audition for more theatre and an improv troupe, and then I did the Unifieds in Atlanta. From the Unifieds, I was contacted by 13 theatre companies, and one of them was The Academy Theatre. The Academy Theatre was the oldest professional theatre company in Atlanta and founded/directed by Frank Wittow, considered by most to be the Grandfather of theatre in Atlanta. It's my understanding that The Woodruff Arts Center and 14th Street Playhouse was built for him and The Academy Theatre. I accepted a position as one of the four actors in a traveling troupe performing social issue-based plays to elementary schools/high schools throughout the Southeast. We had six plays covering different things like bullying, teen pregnancy, issues like that.

Before and after The Academy Theatre, I started studying all over Atlanta. I'd figured out this really was what I wanted to do for a career, as crazy as it was. I was engaged at the time to my now-husband, Steve, and he knew that's where I was headed. I didn't want to work in a cubicle anymore. Right before The

Academy Theatre hired me, I decided I'm quitting everything. I'm doing this full time. I haven't looked back since.

Are you originally from Atlanta? Where were you brought up?
I was born in San Diego but lived all over the west coast, in California and Oregon, and moved to Atlanta in '97.

You'd done some theatre in school? What gave you the confidence to go for the Unifieds?
I did do theatre all throughout my school years and was on a sketch team in college. The Unifieds was a scary set up. At that point, I was still only doing theatre and hadn't branched over to on-camera work yet. A lot of my friends were participating in the Unifieds and said this is a great thing, you have to do it.

The Unifieds is where all the theatre companies come and audition talent in one location?
Yes. They divide you into union and non-union actors. When it's your turn to perform -- in front of about 50 Atlanta area and regional theatre companies -- you have two minutes to do two contrasting monologues. And sing 16 bars of a song, if you want. And I think I remember bringing a ton of headshots too so every company gets a headshot package.

Did you have to sing also?
If you want to. Oddly enough, I can't remember if I chose to sing or not. It was a while ago...Probably not. I was nervous enough as it was for my first time.

When you decided that you were going to go into this full time, what kind of jobs were you working on at the time?

Before acting, I was working 60-80 hours a week at a leadership development company. I was so burned out. I didn't want to be in a cubicle anymore and under florescent lighting. I felt the life was being sucked out of me. I was in my early 20s and I was dying. I couldn't do it anymore. I remember one time, it was 2 am in the morning and I was the only one in the building. I kept hearing a noise in the conference room. I thought, "I can't just sit here scared all night -- I'm going to confront whatever it is." So I took a pair of scissors to defend myself and walked into the room. And of course it was nothing. But it was a turning point for me. I was done. I was done working 60-80 hours a week at a job that I disliked, with a boss that kept responding to my request to hire an assistant to help with my workload with: "Work smarter, not harder." I'd wanted to leave the company and pursue an acting career full-time, but I was scared to take the leap. This deserted conference room night was the kickoff, the lift that I needed to do it. So I put in my two-week notice. After I left the company, they hired 13 people to replace me...

Eventually I joined The Academy Theatre, which was a full-time job rehearsing and then traveling. After my year with The Academy Theatre, I didn't want to travel because I was a newlywed. I continued to pursue acting full-time. But it takes a while to build up momentum and I didn't realize that at first. I think I just thought I'm going to head out and it's all going to happen the way that it should. I felt that this was what I was really supposed to do.

I just didn't realize how long the process would take. In fact, it took me three years to get in with People Store! I kept submitting to top agencies in Atlanta and I kept getting their rejection postcards (or silence) --"Thank you so much, we have too many of your type, keep checking back in." So I did. I was persistent. I kept checking back in. And finally, after about three years, I got an audition with People Store and got in with them. So then I thought, "This is it, my career is finally taking off." I didn't realize that it takes a while for you to get to know your agent, your agent to get to know you, and keep submitting you and then the casting directors have to get to know you and want to call you in.

I started temping. Most actors in Atlanta have a part-time job, but temping wasn't it for me because you're expected to commit to job for a day or a week or so. But in our industry, we have to be able to drop things at a moment's notice to go to an audition. I needed to find a flexible, part-time job.

Your husband, or your fiancé at the time, was supportive of your decision to go do this full time?
He was. And if he wasn't, we probably wouldn't have gotten married. He's the one who puts me on tape now that we do self-taped auditions. And he takes up the slack with family, our slightly needy rescue dog, friends, etc. when I have to be at a rehearsal or I'm on a 16-hour shoot.

Although, even after knowing him for about 14 years, as a businessman, sometimes he still doesn't understand how we in the industry can still be so underpaid. I don't act for free anymore, even for a great project, but I still might act in an ultra low project. And now that I'm also producing, there was a lot I did for free. I've gotten to the point where I need to draw some lines, but then another friend approaches me about a project and I think, "Ok, this will be the last freebie." I really do need to draw better lines.

Regarding getting a good agent, basically its persistence that really paid off?

For me it did. It is interesting, as far as submitting to agents. For some people it may be easy for them to get an agent. Some people, it may not be. It's important to understand how to submit. Some new actors ask me if they can just drop by an agency. No, that's not how it works. Follow the agency's instructions. It used to be you mail in your headshots, many now accept submissions via their website or via a certain email. And then they'll eventually, hopefully, call you in to audition.

My agency, People Store, was very good about sending out rejection postcards. With other agencies, for me, it was crickets. I appreciated that about my agency. And I actually saved those rejection postcards. I taped one to my wall to motivate me. "I hear your rejection, but I refuse to accept that as the final word." Because I'm one of those people, and I have lots of stories, that if someone tells me "no," or "not now," and it feels like they're discouraging me -- there's part of your soul that gets discouraged -- but usually I try to get past it -- to prove that I can do something in spite of the odds. I decided, a little bit ironically, that I'm going to overcome this. And People Store was the only agency I got a rejection postcard from, so they're

197

the agency I want to get into. And I finally did. Persistence did pay off.

Every no we get in this industry -- it's not a rejection of us. That's an important concept to understand. It's not a rejection of me personally. It's more about maybe this isn't the time or this isn't the agency or this isn't the role for you. It's not a rejection of us. And I think when actors get burned out and quit, it's when -- this is probably one of the industries where we get the most no's -- we just have to realize that it's not a rejection of us.

Did you do any more training after you decided to get into this full-time?
I've taken a lot of classes in Atlanta. Atlanta doesn't have, unfortunately, what LA has in classes, but I have tried to take advantage of what classes there are. There are positives and negatives about a lot of classes in Atlanta. One of the dangers in Atlanta is that actors can pop around to workshops, like a day workshop or a weekend workshop and think that they're studying when that's more repeating of knowledge or meeting people. It's important for people to get in and almost always be studying somewhere. I've been taking a study break lately for time and financial reasons. I am looking for my next serious class; I'm not sure where that will be yet.

You mentioned something about it not being like what's available in LA. What are we lacking?
There's a bit of discontent here in Atlanta with what we can study under and whom. We have some teachers who are no

longer acting and that maybe puts them a little out of touch in an industry that is rapidly changing. There are more people moving from LA -- teachers that look at Atlanta as this place that's ripe for growth. Or people coming that say that they're from LA but they don't really have a big resume either teaching or acting. That's a little scary to me. So actors just need to do research before getting into a class.

Do you do anything else outside of acting for extra income?
At this point, I am fortunate that I do not have another non-industry job. After I traveled with The Academy Theatre, I was hustling with low-paying industry jobs and promotional modeling. But after we were married for a couple years, my husband said, "I support your acting, but what do you think about a flexible, part-time job?" So I looked for a long time for the perfect part-time job. And again, I tried temp work, but again, it wasn't flexible. I finally landed on this personal assistant job where I worked 20-25 hours a week. They were pretty understanding about auditions. This was around 2004/2005. I worked there for about five years. At that time, actors were still going in person to all of our auditions -- before self-taping. As the industry started to pick up -- which is phenomenal and I really hope that this growth keeps happening -- even my part-time job was too difficult to manage with so many auditions. So I left that job around 2009.

Since then, I have not had a non-industry job, but I have expanded to casting, writing, and producing too. A couple years ago I optioned a non-fiction book written by a U.S. prosecutor. I spent almost a year writing and rewriting my screenplay. It was a huge creative outlet and I loved pouring everything I had into it. My first screenplay was a finalist in the Oscar-qualifying Atlanta Film Festival screenplay competition!

If I ever end up making it, I'll probably shoot it in Morocco. I have a couple friends in the industry there and it would be the perfect place to shoot it. I'm also open to selling it. I had my first pitch meeting in L.A. with a major production company. I'm not going to name them but you would totally recognize the production company. It was a good meeting. The screenplay is very political and because of the scary international political climate, I'm letting the screenplay rest for now. I backed off of that, but it was such a fantastic creative endeavor.

And you've done some casting too?
Yes. I sort of fell into that because being in the industry for so long, you meet people and filmmaker friends ask, "Hey, do you know an actor like this, do you know an actor like that?" Absolutely. I love networking and connecting people. And now I get paid to cast industrials, short films, and independent films.

Then there's the producing. That all started a few years ago with a fellow actress friend, Elisabeth Andre, who was an incredible go-getter. She started Off Off Peachtree Theatre. She and I would have long talks about how I was thinking about getting production experience too. Maybe something with a little more creative control than most actresses are afforded. She talked to me about directing and producing film. Now I'd directed stage plays, but not films. And at the time, I'm not sure if I was too nervous or too busy -- or a combo of both -- to take the jump.

But Elisabeth kept encouraging me. Tragically, she ended up with cancer that eventually took her life, way too young. But before she died, I was over at her house and she said, "Jyn, I really think you should start producing. I'm going to connect you with a friend of mine. We're working on a project together." A couple of weeks later, she passed away, and I didn't really think about that part of the conversation anymore.

Then a few months later, her friend contacted me and said, "Elisabeth said that I should contact you about being the producer for this short film. Do you want to go to lunch?" So we went to lunch. I told him that I was "very interested, but I have to be honest with you, I don't know a thing about producing." He said that was okay -- that he'd walk me through it. And he did. So Elisabeth, from beyond the grave, gave me that boost that I needed -- someone to empower me, to believe in me for half a second that I could do it.

After that, I started producing with writer/director Vandon Gibbs. I've produced a few projects with him, including the award-winning feature film 'Solace," which was an incredible experience. Working with Van greatly increased my confidence. Now I produce my own educational web series called "The Dinner Project." [http://www.thedinnerprojectshow.com] We interview Southeast casting directors about the industry. It's a great little show. I am also a contract producer working for Amber Sky Records producing music videos and I love, love, love it.

Doing all this keeps you sharp. And just seeing things from different perspectives, does it make you a better actor too in the long run?

Yes, absolutely. It would be fantastic if every actor could be a casting director at least once. Actors tend to get really down on themselves about not booking an audition. I can't tell you how many times I've heard friends say, "I felt like I did such a great audition, why didn't I book it? Aren't I good enough?" And it goes back to what I said about the rejection of a booking not being a rejection of you as a person.

One of the things I learned in the early stages of casting when I brought in talented friends and acquaintances -- I know them and their work, and I know I could cast any of them without an audition and the director would've been happy. But how well do people work for this project -- how do they fit together as a family, as a couple? I was bringing in all these people who I felt would be right for the part, and are truly great people to work with, responsible actors and work on their craft and show up on time. But there's only one person per role that's going to be cast and you look at all these people that could be cast. And again it's not a rejection of them. It's just how they fit the role, who is the best for the role. And so getting to see that and even having some of my friends ask, "Why didn't you cast me?" We could've cast any of them and it would've been a good project, and a different project. It helps me as an actor to let it go just a little bit more when I don't book a job. I think most actors understand that in their heads, but not in their hearts.

What else do you do outside of the industry itself just to keep your sanity?

I love to read. It's one of the ways that I calm down or let the world go. I read about 50-100 books/year. I also love, of course, seeing movies and theatre. And I'm a big outdoors person. I love white water rafting, horseback riding, hiking, scuba diving, traveling.

What do you do for marketing and networking?

That's such a big undertaking. The industry is changing so much. Sometimes, my friends and I talk about how it's harder and easier to be an actor in these times. And one of the harder things is we're not just actors anymore. We are actors, but we are also our own PR and social media managers, our own audition tapers, our own managers, sometimes our own agents. There's just so much to keep up with in this digital age with everything changing. So many casting websites we have to pay for and continually update. I have to say, I'm not as good with marketing as I would like to be. But who has the time?

I originally got on Facebook for two reasons. First, to keep up with some young friends in Morocco who didn't email. And the other reason was everyone at that time -- 2008 -- was pressuring me that you have to get on Facebook to do your marketing, for acting. And so I did. But I don't know how effective social media really is for that. I can say maybe I've gotten two jobs from things that I've posted. I don't have a fan page, just my personal page. I try not to be too crazy about posting industry stuff or too obnoxious about multi-posting about one job, if that makes sense. I feel other actors don't want to hear about auditions and callbacks, etc. -- that looks desperate -- we all have auditions and callbacks. Why post those? And then, you have casting directors, like one in town I know of that never ever wants you to post about any job that you're on that you book through her. In fact, she's said that if she ever sees you post anything about any job that she casts you for, she will never bring you back in again. So we have to manage our social media carefully. And then there are other things, like being on set and taking selfies or photos with famous actors. That's a huge topic actors are discussing now because what we've heard from bicoastal actors is that it makes Atlanta actors look green--- it makes us look unprofessional.

On the other hand, you have most of the Atlanta actors doing that. I personally don't. I have one picture of me with a producer and Burt Reynolds but that was at a read-through that included a meet-and-greet and Mr. Reynolds was encouraging us to take photos with him. That's the only photo I have of me with someone famous – who's not already a friend -- because I'm not the type to go on set and start snapping away on my iPhone. I don't want to come off as green and unprofessional. But it comes at a price, because I do miss having photos of me with all the famous people I've been on set with. But there are respected Atlanta actors much farther along in their career than I, booking more, at a different level and some of them still do it, so...

Back to marketing, part of that is a relationship with your agent. People Store says to feel free to check in once a week. I don't check in that frequently, but if it's been a couple weeks since

I've had an audition, I will check in and see what projects might have a role for me. Or I send them a copy of recent work that they haven't seen yet. One friend suggested -- and I've done it a couple times -- to take the types that you frequently book and ask if there are any of those roles in breakdowns – like: "Are there any mom, teacher, nurse roles this week?" Sometimes that's gotten me an immediate audition and other times they say no, but they've been submitting me and I'm on their minds. Which is still nice to hear. Did I mention I love my agents?

Do you go to any events around town?
Yeah, I do try to go to industry events. There's not one that I attend regularly. But I do try to sometimes hit GPP [Georgia Production Partnership]; WIFTA [Women in Film & Television]; Film Bar Mondays; Eat, Drink, and Be Indie; ATLFF events. If my agency has a mixer, I'll definitely attend that and I try to see plays too, as well as local film screenings. I like to be around and be involved. I enjoy networking on both sides of the camera and I feel that in an industry where it's so hard to stand out, relationships are paramount. Sometimes just being present in the community and building relationships is what eventually works.

Which reminds me -- back to social media -- one of my friends says that on Twitter, for every tweet you tweet about yourself, you should tweet three or four about other people and give them shout outs. Another actress friend, Samantha Worthen -- in Banshee -- she's great at this. She shouts out and celebrates people all the time. I learned from her and I try to do that. If I see a friend on a TV show or in a film, I will post on Facebook, maybe even take a screenshot, "Hey, I saw you, great job." I always try to shout out people in the community because I think trying to promote yourself on social media can be a tricky thing because you don't want to come off as too braggy but you also don't want to come off as fake humble. If you praise other people and draw positive attention to them, celebrating other people's successes, it's a huge thing. I posted a meme recently about there being enough success for all of us to go around. I really believe that. And so I try to celebrate other people as much as possible. I find when I do that, people also shout me out and celebrate me. It's that whole "A rising tide lifts all the boats" -- which is The Dinner Project's motto -- and it's the same thing that you're doing with this e-book. We're all trying to contribute to this rising tide in Georgia, so we appear more professional and projects will cast bigger roles in Atlanta because we're rising to a higher level.

What do you see the future of acting being in Atlanta?
I hear actors who've been in the biz in Georgia longer than I have talk about "In the Heat of the Night" and about how there were a few great things being filmed here and everyone was very positive about it. But then it just kind of dried up for a long time. I've heard there are a couple reasons for that. But I just hope lessons were learned and that all the work is here to stay. I'm grateful for the people who were very active in campaigning for more projects to come here and campaigning for the tax incentives. I joined many industry people in the march on the Capitol when a senator was trying to remove our new tax incentives. We all need to be active and proactive about keeping projects here. I hope that this isn't some kind of flash in the pan

thing. It's been going great for several years and it keeps growing, so that does make me hopeful. It's not just one or two TV shows here. There's a lot of TV and film and they keep building new studios all over town.

You don't anticipate a move out of Atlanta any time soon for yourself?

I don't, and if I do move, it will not be for acting. Steve and I, in the back of our minds, we always talk about moving back to San Diego to be near my family and the ocean. Also, Steve and I thought very seriously about moving to Morocco last year. We both had job offers. And if I did that, it's possible I could get my film made there. My screenplay is set in Saudi Arabia, but I'd never be allowed to film there. Morocco's a good stand in for KSA. But Steve got a great new job in Atlanta at the same time I started producing for Amber Sky Records. And again, with the political climate and everything, I don't think I'm going to make that film in the near future. But every once in a while, we do think we could pick up and move anywhere. Where do you want to live? Anywhere in the world. The sky's the limit for creative people.

What do you wish someone had told you at the beginning of your career?

People don't really talk about how hard an acting career is, but you can't really know how hard it is until you get in. I'm not sure I wish I'd known that because maybe I would have never pursued acting.

People get very emotional talking about following their dreams. I was like that in the beginning. But this industry is less about dreams and, like other industries, is about hard work. And it's less about the actual craft and acting and mostly about the business side. That's another thing I wished I'd known. Or maybe not. Maybe I wouldn't be here doing this interview about acting, if I'd known that actual acting is about 1% of being in the business. It's definitely a journey, not a destination. In most other industries, the way that you move is up — up to the next level, to the next position, to the next title. It's not always that way in acting. There might be different stages, different levels, but I feel that with so many hurdles, when you hit a hurdle, you feel like this is it, now my career is going to take off. But there are always more hurdles. My first hurdle was getting an agent. But then I soon realized I wanted a top agent --another hurdle I spent three years getting over. When I finally got in with one of Atlanta's best agency, I thought, "My career's going to take off!" But then it took about a year to even get casting directors to see me. And when they did see me, another year or so for them to trust me and ask for me. It's a much longer process than I ever expected. Now I know there are some actors who are young enough, unique enough, and gorgeous enough that they just ride that shooting star up. But that's just not normal. For the most of us, that's not reality. It's much more of a daily grind and bettering ourselves and our craft. I wish I would've known that. Because after I booked my first TV show, after I booked my first movie, even earlier after I booked my first industrial, commercial and voice-over before movies and TV shows. After each one I thought, "This is it. It's all up from here." But it doesn't always work that way -- for some it does -- for me and others, we can book a great role in a great show and then...crickets. It's just not a straight up trajectory and I wish I had understood that in the beginning so maybe I'd experienced a little less discouragement.

I wish I would've known in the beginning what I know now about how it's not a rejection of me. I wish I could've understood that concept at the very beginning. But I think no matter how you say that to people without being in the industry, they won't understand it. It's a tough concept to get.

My first piece of advice to people who want to pursue acting used to be: Get in a great acting class. Now my first piece of advice to people is: If there is anything else that you are passionate about in life, pursue that first. Because you will probably be happier doing that and probably be more successful. If there's nothing else -- you still come back to acting, then that's when you pursue it. When I say this now, people look at me like I'm jaded or cynical. No, I'm not jaded. I'm just being realistic. If there's anything else you're passionate about, do that. But if you still want -- need -- to act, then jump in and give it your all, but be ready for a tough ride. If being a storyteller -- and that's what acting is, storytelling -- is where you will find your passion and your creativity, then pursue it wholeheartedly.

Kara Michele Wilder

Born and raised in Lyons, Kansas, Kara grew up an athlete, an artist, and a serious tomboy. Her credits include a recurring role on The Red Road, Ivide (a Bollywood film) and Let's Be Cops. She is represented by AMT Agency in Atlanta. More info at her IMDB page: http://imdb.me/karamichelewilder.
(Rafiq's note – Kara and I worked together in the play "It's a Wonderful Life". I also helped cast her in IVIDE, the Bollywood film that was set and shot in Atlanta.)

When did you know you wanted to be an actor and how did you go about getting started?

I started acting when I was in 8th grade in a small town in Kansas. I watched a movie called 'Who I am' and it was about slam poetry and it starred Saul Williams, a well-known spoken word poet. I'd never seen anything like that. I started writing poetry, just for myself. And in high school, a friend of mine got me to join the Debate and Speech team. So freshman year, 14-years-old, I started doing competitive speech and drama, which is really like acting with poetry and prose. I did that my entire high school. And I knew then: Wow, I wanna be an actor.

Did you pursue it?
No. Not beyond doing the competitive national tournaments. I would travel all over the United States competing on the national scale of a high schooler. That was awesome. I did a little bit of theater and spoken word in college too. But I lived in Kansas. There wasn't really an opportunity to pursue it and I didn't really believe in myself in that stage. I should've done what my friends did. Move to New York.

How did the switch happen that you decided you want to pursue this more professionally and why Atlanta?
I moved to Atlanta after dropping out of college in Kansas City for personal reasons. My sister lived here with her three kids who I'm very close to. Moved here, finished my degree and then decided to go to Law School. That was a disaster. Every minute of it. I reached a point where I woke up 6 am journaling and asking myself this question: What do I love? What do I want to do? And I was making a list. I love art. I love children. I love animals. I love acting. The next thing that I did was write down the one thing that I could do, that took me less than 5 minutes, to propel me towards that. And I did that. I asked a friend for some headshot help but he said, "... if you are looking for an acting class, speak to Michael Cole." From there, it spiraled. Within a matter of a week, I was the lead in a play at a community theater. It all happened really fast.

Had you dropped out of law school by that time?

No. I was taking a hiatus from law school. All this happened in
October 2012. I took the hiatus after the end of that semester,
in December 2012. But I was still working full-time in a law firm
as a law clerk and pursuing acting. It wasn't until February 2013
that I signed with my agency and summer 2013 I started
working full-time in a restaurant.

So you quit your law firm job?
Yes. I was no longer employed by them.

**Then you started working in the restaurant industry and had
time to pursue acting?**
I did. I did lots. The restaurant industry is actually very
demanding. Most people think that working in a restaurant is
flexible. To a degree, it is. Because you're working shifts and
people cover your shifts. But if you aren't at a restaurant that
actually understands and supports you, it's tough to get a lot of
time off. Its an ongoing struggle.

**You continue to work in the restaurant and pursue acting right
now?**
I continued to work at the restaurant until the day that I got
fired. It was a Monday. And the same day I booked a
commercial, got a call back and I was shooting that Thursday
and Friday. I had a call back in North Carolina on Tuesday. There
would have been no way I could have made that work if I was at
my job. Sometimes you get pushed in the direction you need to
go. Since that day, I haven't had a day job.

How did you get your agent?

I was not one of those lucky ones. I got some headshots by Barbara Beneville and created a resume out of no experience, just followed the format. I made a list of seven agencies, got all my stuff together and sent out headshots. I submitted to AMT three times before they called me. Houghton called me once but it took them six months to call me. J Pervis straight up denied me since I didn't have enough credits. And I don't think I ever heard back from People Store. Another agency offered me a contract but I declined it. AMT is a big regional agency. If you are in a category that's mostly young and white, then good luck because it's such a competitive category.

What's your training like? You studied with Michael Cole. Are you doing any classes, have you taken anything else?
I have. But Michael Cole's class is like: "Introduction to the film and television industry 101" and it's so crucial to have that. Most recently I trained with Drama Inc., with Jerri Tubbs doing the Chubbuck method. That, plus the book, The Power of the Actor, is what I'm using currently. It's a practical guide, full of information. I met this guy from L.A. who had trained with Ivana Chubbuck, the author of that book. He trained with her 15 years ago for about 10 years. And he started a class last year in Marietta. We start training next week and I'm excited about that. I did improv at Village Theater and Auditioning by Heart with Crystal Carson. That class was huge for me. It just depends on what you want during your journey. If you feel like you want to be better in auditioning that class is the one to take. If you feel like you want to get better in acting that class isn't the one to take.

You've been focusing pretty much on acting only. No side job?
Right. I do have one little pay. Remember how I mentioned
speech and drama in high school? I was looking toward it as a
survival job, and started judging tournaments for American
schools. Then I started coaching for a private school in Atlanta.
And I just came back from a national tournament with them. So
next year we're gonna bring it on to coaching here, just teach
acting basically, but it has a beat of its own. This is like the
perfect deal, right?

How do you maintain a positive attitude in this industry?
One of the most important things, not just for an actor, but for a
person in this world who's actively seeking a life better than
what they have or pursuing their dream, is to manage their
stress. It's a journey. But for me, it's a combination of
eliminating things around me that are unhealthy – bad
relationships and bad habits. This year I stopped drinking liquor.
And then cut out negative thoughts too. Instead of waking up
every day thinking of what you're not doing and what you don't
look like, doing daily affirmation. I spend most of my free time
focusing on just improving myself. So diet is really important to
me. I have this app on my phone called Day One. And it's
awesome because it's a journaling app. It takes all sorts of data,
like where you are and what you're doing and it saves that. And
you can open up a journal and you can hashtag it, so you can
come back and read something, you can take notes on it.
Journaling is very therapeutic for me.

What do you do in terms of marketing and networking?

Not very much. I'm figuring out the marketing thing for myself right now. There's lots of stuff about what one should do. I find that a lot of it seems just foreign to my character. I'm not opposed to celebrating my successes. But I am really not the person constantly bragging, "I booked a commercial, I had an audition." So I have an alternative figured out. I have some ideas about what I wanna do. Sending postcards is very simple. That is something that older actors told me is a must. Especially if you're not being seen by a casting director, you gotta send them a card. I'm on Facebook, of course. Instagram, and then Twitter. I recently got on Twitter. And somebody contacted my agent and asked if I would live tweet during the airing of one of my episodes on *The Red Road*. Another actor and I were tweeting about everything that happened in the episode. And I went from 15 Twitter followers to a 130. So cool.

Do you plan to move out of Atlanta anytime soon?
I don't know. Last Fall, I was having an existential crisis about myself as an actor, like where I was headed and what I'm doing in terms of proving. I was going to move to New York but booked a big job so I'm gonna stay for now, I don't have any plans to move.

Atlanta is booming right now. Hollywood is coming calling with momentum. When the whole industry is moving towards where I am it seems like the dumbest thing to go against that and go in a different direction. However, I wouldn't be opposed to it if Hollywood or New York starts calling. Isn't that a dream? If they're calling, I'm going.

One of the big reasons why I wanted to leave was because I felt I wasn't getting the quality training. There's a mindset in Atlanta, in a regional market, people here don't think that training is important. I don't know why, what kind of cultural thing that is, if it's because the market is still evolving. Actors here are planning to make a living off a U5 ("under 5 lines" roles). So that's another reason why I considered moving. Move for 3-5 months, go live some place, couch surf, whatever, get the training and come back. A few months ago, I looked up every single acting coach in L.A. and in New York. I'm going to save my money, so I can go and get trained in one of those places. Maybe do a workshop or a weeklong program. If I could afford it, I would go. That's still an option for me. Once I can afford it.

What do you think Atlanta holds in the future for the actor?
From what I've heard talking to Craig Fincannon and different acting coaches and my agency, it is only going to get better, as far as the amount of work that's coming here. For the actor, it's very neat. We're going to continue to get the run off. We're going to continue to get more day player roles. And that's more opportunity to be on set, get credit for work...an opportunity that actors in New York and L.A. just don't get.

For a new actor, this is the best place you can possibly be, because they are looking at new people. There are more opportunities now to get guest star roles than when I started. And I was fortunate enough to fall into a recurring role. But I don't know. It could go either way. They can continue to book out of L.A. or all the L.A. actors are going to come here. I know the big talent agencies: CAA, William Morris are all setting up offices in Atlanta as we speak. If that's the case, that means they can get easy access to the talent on the market and maybe recruit local talents. But that's going to shift the entire industry for actors in a way I can't predict. One thing I'm still afraid of, as an actor, is when larger agencies come in, there's going to be an immediate interest from every actor in town trying to get into them. But that's the wrong move. One of our agents at AMT, a former manager in LA, says: The biggest downfall in being with some of the big agencies is getting lost, because you're just a number. They don't care about you. But I walk into a smaller agency and they talk to me. They take their time out of their busy day, whether you are booking or not.

Do you have representation outside Atlanta?

I don't have any...I don't plan on it, because I was looking into it. Maybe getting represented in New Orleans and L.A. I talked to a few actors who do have representation in other markets. They said if you have the means to get between these locations, do it. If you can afford a plane ticket to get to a call back to LA in 2 days, do it. But only if you are willing to spend the money to go. It's going to cost you. Getting representation in New Orleans is totally doable. I know people who've done that. But I also know that New Orleans is very big on in-person auditions. And I know actors that drive 10 hours for one under-5 audition. Its not just resources in the traditional sense, but how much emotional patience do you have? How much do you want to spend? Of your time and energy and all the effort it takes you to be a good person and to be a good actor. Just to do a 20-hour drive for a one liner. How many times can you do that before you just give up.

Are you SAG?
SAG eligible of course. But I'm considering becoming SAG. First, I am also a stuntwoman. And most of the stunt coordinators will not work with you, unless you are in the Union. And some work pays the same amount day rate as an actor. So good money, it's fun. It's hard to get into. But unless you join the Union you're not getting a whole lot of money. So I've done a bit of stunt work outside of my regular acting work.

So there's potential for me to make more money doing stunts. And whatever reason it is, the Union is being real flexible with their rules. I make my money mostly through non-union industrials. Not even through my agency, it's all based on relationships. The Union is now allowing Union members to do industrials that are non-union based upon a Union contract.

And you have those relationships with directors and producers and all that. I don't think it's that difficult to say: Hey guys, you know, I joined the Union, I can still work for you the same, but you know, you're going to be paying me a little less potentially or you're going to pay me a little bit more. And for me, to be a member of the Union, is you get all the benefits of the pension and the health care and it's almost worth it if you can work it.

How did you get into being able to do stunts?
I was on a film called *'Let's Be Cops'* and I started a conversation with the writer on how do you sustain yourself? He suggested

stunt work given my athletic build. He even put me in contact with a stunt coordinator on that film. She told me where this stunt gym is here. Believe it or not, that's how you get into the stunt industry. You go to the gymnastics style gym and you meet people. You put together a headshot and resume, which is way less professional than acting. Then let's say you find out a production is shooting at Screen Gem Studios. You take your headshot and your resume, go to Screen Gem and ask for the stunt coordinator. Former military people do really well. Former SWAT team members and former gymnasts do really well, for tumbling, flipping, and having awareness.

Any mistakes you've made that others should avoid?
One of the mistakes I made was in believing that I needed to be connected to those in higher positions than me to get work. Having relationships with producers, directors, writers, famous actors, that's not going get you work. And nepotism is not as big a part of the industry the way most people think it is.

The other big mistake that I made was not being myself. I didn't give much thought about who I am. My first year, professionally, I was trying to fit in this mold of...the first job I ever got was the role of Gorgeous Woman. I tried to fit that mold. I pulled my hair straight. I would wear lots of make up to every audition. All my headshots portrayed somebody like that. And it didn't get me any more work. I ruined my hair. I had to cut my hair off to get my curls to come back. And ultimately it was hard to be motivated to work towards your goal when you're being somebody else. Authenticity is so important. I'm at least

219

comfortable with knowing what I'm not. You should stay true to who you are in the core.

Karen Ceesay

Karen Ceesay is an actor, writer, wife and mom. She may be seen in the films, "The Internship" & "Last Vegas" and has had recurring roles on ABC's "Resurrection" and USA's "Satisfaction." In 2008, she was a guest on "The Oprah Winfrey Show" after a ratings busting appearance on ABC's controversial "Primetime Live: What Would You Do?"
IMDB:
http://m.imdb.com/name/nm1957798/filmotype?ref_=m_nm_fl mg
Twitter & IG: @karenceesay

Where are you from?
Philadelphia, PA

When did you know you wanted to become an actor?
Out the womb. It found me.

How did you go about starting your acting career? Was your family supportive?

I started taking classes and performing when I was 10-years-old. My family has always been very supportive.

What was your training like? Do you have a formal degree in theater?

As a kid I studied all forms of acting as well as dance at Freedom Theatre. Throughout high school, I took on-camera classes at Weist Barron. Went to Spelman College to get my degree in engineering, but the theater department pulled me into its web and I graduated with my BA in theater... and a minor in math.

What made you choose Atlanta?

Spelman College.

How did you get your first agent?

Traditional way - submitted headshot and resume, got called in for an interview. That was about 1999/2000-ish.

How did you support yourself when you started out? What were your survival jobs? Do you do anything else to supplement your income today?

In the early days it didn't get in the way of my hotel audio visual job as bookings were few and far between. It also helps to be married to someone with a "real" job. Coaching/teaching has been a good outlet. But I just started back at my old job in audio-visual - they're very supportive at my day job.

What do you do for marketing and networking?

I have a publicist, Christa Shreck, who is in LA. We work together as needed when I have something coming up. She also gets me in on various events around town where I take pretty pictures with pretty people that end up online. Social media is essential though. I've built up more fans/followers live tweeting while shows air. People want more access these days.

How do you stay aware of industry news? Read any specific websites/newsletters?
I read the online versions of the trade magazines – *Variety, Backstage, Entertainment Weekly,* plus anything I find on my Facebook and Twitter feeds, especially as they relate to Georgia specifically.

What do you see the future of acting being in Atlanta? Do you see series regular roles coming here?
The series regular roles are already here. A number of local actors are now booking jobs we never would've been up for just a few years ago. We are experiencing a time of great opportunity. Finally.

What can actors in Atlanta do to step up their game, to be worthy of the bigger roles and to stand out from the increasing competition?
How do you get to Carnegie Hall? Practice, practice, practice. You need the training and techniques from an on-camera class (and to actually see yourself) but you have to be able to stay open and take direction easily. Nothing helps more with that than improv. Plus people need to be better prepared for auditions. Have those lines memorized, have different creative

options to work with. We need to own our accomplishments and not look at ourselves as some sort of step child of Hollywood. Be proud of where we are and not where we think we should be.

What would you like to see happen in Atlanta to grow the film business/opportunities for actors?
It's going to take time. LA casting directors don't know us yet. As more of the local folks get hired and do great work, the opportunities will increase.

What about roles for your ethnicity? Is it a limiting factor?
Yes and no. There are limits to the number of roles offered to people of color in general. The friends who are in my category and I joke about how we probably won't ever get to work together because two black women won't be cast in the same scene. But we're allowed to audition for a wider variety of roles and not stuck in just one category.

Are you SAG? If not, why?
Not yet but that won't be for much longer. Early on the work here didn't justify joining. And then it was just financial.

Do you have representation outside Atlanta?
I did years ago, but wasn't able to stay with them. Now, to regularly go up for the bigger stuff, outside representation is essential. It is an immediate goal for me.

Do you plan to move to LA/NY in the future?

I've done the pilot season thing a few times, but no interest to move. There's no need now. Here I'm big fish in a small pond. There I'd be a piece of plankton on the back of the tiniest fish.

How do you handle rejection? Do you ever feel like giving up?
I've felt like giving up plenty of times. To get through this long term, you need to surround yourself with good people who support you. The absolute best thing about working in this market is the support we give each other. People who are my "competition" are also my very good friends. The mindset as a whole is, "What's mine is mine, what's yours is yours." No one can take anyone else's job. Also, I look at bookings as a numbers game. It takes ten No's to get to a Yes. Another No just gets you to your Yes faster. As you get better, your booking ratio will improve.

If you had to redo something in your career again, would you do anything differently?
Not to wait to have a family. I have one son who showed up just as we were getting ready to move to LA ten years ago. You can't put your life on hold for this business. It will always be here. Always. Regardless of age, gender, ethnicity or body type, there will be some place for you to fit into someone's project at some point in time.

Kristen Shaw

Kristen Shaw is an actor and teacher in Atlanta. She has appeared in over - dozen Film and Television projects, including 2 Series Regular roles, multiple pilots, as well as over 25 National Commercials. She is represented by People Store in Atlanta. More info at: http://kristenshawactingstudio.com/kristen-shaw

Where are you from and when did you know you wanted to be an actor?

I always knew that for some reason. I was a very shy kid and I didn't talk much, I was not very bold. But I just felt very compelled to do acting and my parents didn't understand it. I don't know where it came from and I started taking class in 3rd grade at the community theater up in North Carolina. I did that up until high school. Then in high school I started with high school acting classes and then I did get a degree. I ended up graduating from Wake Forest University, also in North Carolina. I went out to LA about 6 months after I got my degree - after I had earned some money waiting tables. All the jobs we all do to be able to make it to Los Angeles. And I had researched the market and I had a couple of other friends. I moved to LA when I was 23 and I stayed out there for 15 years. I had a lot of bad actor habits, I had not much of a real look or I didn't have a very obvious fit in the business. So once I was out there, Ireally soaked up all I could...I took a lot of classes about a lot of different aspects of the business. My philosophy was, and I encourage other actors to do so as well, just to find a really sound expert in each area and I soaked up what I could get from them.

Once I found somebody who I believed in and who I understood, who I felt had been in a place I wanted to go and had a perspective, I stayed in that class and absorbed what they were teaching. I ended up working with my acting coach for 13 years for Strasberg Method Acting. That's the core of what I have as an actor. You never stop having that next level of training. Once I got to the place where I was on a TV show and I started working with a stylist, I started working with a publicist and a publicity coach that would help coach me through interviews. How to talk about your character, how it began, answer questions for people in a way that still promotes you as an actor. I went from really working just to be a decent actor, to a place where I had a stylist, a makeup artist and publicity help. I had someone to teach me how to do it, every step of the way. There are experts in everything.

Was this something you did because you felt that it would help you create a certain brand and a type? At what level should actors consider doing this?

There are aspects of it at all levels. The first piece of it for me was really trying to understand: Who am I? What do I have to offer? Where is the category for me as an actor and how do I get really good? I figured out very quickly I'm not really a particular look or a type. I better be the best actor because I can stay more in control of that. First, I really wanted to get good as an actor, and then I also started to notice there were some parts where I felt that I have something to offer naturally. A lot of times, as actors, we want to play what I would call 'the better sides of ourselves'. I realized very early on that I have more to offer playing the parts of myself that I had a harder time accepting or putting out there authentically. I played a lot of women who other people consider very bitchy or harsh. I got comfortable doing that and was able to bring something authentic, that a lot of people don't want other people to see in them.

At some point, did you decide that you wanted to move to Atlanta? Did you decide to become a coach here?
Like acting decided to pick me, Atlanta seemed to pick me as well. I got to a place in my career where I was working as an actress for many years and that's all I did. That was my main means of making income. I also had a lot of time, but not a lot of money usually. My actor friends and I supported and coached each other. We helped each other with projects and auditions. I found along the way that I was really good at coaching people for their auditions. I did a little bit of teaching. In Los Angeles, you either teach or you're an actor. There's not a whole lot of working actors who also teach, so I was doing some of that, but I did not have an identity out there as a coach. I just coached the

actors I knew and they coached me. My agent would send a lot of people to me to give them tips.

It was that "destiny" thing. I loved being in Los Angeles for about 13 years. In the 14th year, I was out there, I was feeling the pull, I don't know if I want to continue with this. And then the last year, I felt very compelled to live in Atlanta. It wasn't like I decided to move and then I picked Atlanta. When you're an actor, you develop instincts, you develop a toolset of knowing and trusting sort of an external process or force out there. I felt a very strong pull to move here. I didn't know why or how I was going to do that. I packed up and moved myself here, decided I'd figure it out when I got here. I started coaching and haven't looked back. It has worked easily and naturally, and I've jgone full force. I find in my business coaching actors, I'm using all those aspects of me that I honed as an actor. Coaching uses so much more of my skills and my natural abilities.

Had you visited Atlanta in the past?
No. My sister lives here with her husband and three kids. I knew of Atlanta. I grew up in North Carolina and I always had relatives here. I've been to Atlanta a couple of times.

The fact that Atlanta was beginning to see so much work was not really a factor when you moved here?
I had no idea. But it ties to the power of trusting and knowing that instinct. I thought there was some business here. But I figured if it doesn't work out, I'll do something else. I tell my students all the time, I don't have a fear of failing. If you fail, it's fine, just get up. My only fear would be standing still or getting

stuck. I remember hustling and getting out there in LA, and seeing all levels of the game. I'm happy that I was trained in LA.

It's good to see that people like yourself having such exposure and skills offering that level of coaching here now.
It's invaluable. As an actor, you need a home, a safe place, to make mistakes. The creative process is not always pretty and there's a reason we do multiple takes. This business is completely illogical in many ways. It's not a linear process. You can't just be a good actor and keep working in bigger and bigger roles. Why are we in it? And what do we need out of it? When I'm in class, when I was an actor in class, even when my career was going nowhere I knew I was an actor and at the very least, I could work on my craft today. I was so lucky to be doing it. I always tell people the cure for your career stalling or not going anywhere, is that you always just do your work as an artist. Do your work to the point that you know that you have something to offer -- always.

They understand that in Los Angeles because they're so big and there are so many casting directors. Their West coast mentality is a little different from here in the South. Here the mentality is, you're never going make it if everyone doesn't like you. But there, all of them liking you, that's never gonna happen. Too many people. So the mentality in a big city like LA is there's no hard right and wrong way of doing things, people are not too worried about breaking the rules, or pissing someone off. They are more concerned that you don't know them. They're willing to do it - what does it take for me to get you to notice me, to know me, or see my work? Not: how/what are the rules and how do I make sure I don't break them? That's a very different mentality for us in the South.

How did you go about setting up your acting studio in Atlanta and getting students?
It was a gamble. Success is always when opportunity comes to those who are prepared, right? I was talking about moving here. I had a friend, one of the actors that I also coached, he's a big star in Ireland now. He introduced me to an actress from Atlanta. We talked on the phone. This ties into marketing for actors too – one of the things I teach in my marketing class and I believe in is you always offer what you have to offer. You don't ask for things, because people don't like when you start to take from them.

I offered her classes once I got set up. She offered to share my information with her agency. She was with People Store and they called me when I first moved here. I had one meeting and they signed me.

What do you see for the future of acting in Atlanta?
The fact that they are building all these permanent stages that are just here for movies and TV is tremendous. This is the best place for an actor starting out. On average, once a month, I have an actor show up in a class that just moved here from L.A. The bar is going up in terms of what we need to be able to do to provide and our skill level, and though that seems threatening to some actors, it's absolutely a benefit for all of us. If casting directors only have five actors they know that are skilled, maybe one of the five will get it. But if we have 10, then the business

gets more and more comfortable with us, as a location that consistently offers people who are capable of providing, at the level they need to provide.

Why do you say that this is the best place for a starting actor?
People will probably not like hearing this and I know it does not feel like this, but it's so easy here, right now, to get started. The competition is less, it's smaller, there's a window of opportunity happening here. I have coached 8-10 actors who moved here from Los Angeles for the last 3-4 years. They signed with top-notch agents and get auditions. Back in LA, they had no agent. They say, "I am getting better coaching here, I am getting better auditions and I am getting a whole lot more since I moved here." I've never had an L.A. actor say it's not working for me in Atlanta. I'm not saying it has not happened, I'm sure it has. But I've not heard of it.

What should actors in Atlanta do to step up their game?
Start with a head game or mindset. You have a very important choice to make early on in their career. That is going to define the path you're on. Many of us don't think about it or don't do it thoroughly enough. The question you ask yourself is: Am I in this for a job or am I in this for a career? Because I will sacrifice the job to help my career.

What I mean by that is if I get called in on something that's not right for me, because my casting directors don't know me yet, the mind-set in the south is very much play-it-safe, make sure you don't upset them, make sure you follow the rules and don't take any risks. Because they might not like you. Well, that doesn't work. You can't play it safe. You have to be willing to say: I'm not getting this job, because this is not my job, this is not right for me. But I'm gonna go in there and then show who I am and they're gonna get a good sense of me and they're gonna realize how I can be cast.

When I first moved here I got, through my agent, called in for a lot of housewife roles. And there are far better actresses here for housewives. I don't have a whole lot to offer in that department that's interesting or unique. So I brought myself to those roles, I still did a good job. But you know, I made sure my personality was in there. I was probably not the best choice for a lot of those jobs. And they figured that out. By the time I'd been here a year, I had fewer auditions, but they were better suited for me. Quirky, bossy, complicated women with an acerbic sense of humor. More 'bitchy', less 'wife-y'.

We really need to decide early on: I am in this for a career and this is about me helping. I have something to offer the business and also allow the business to understand how to best utilize me. All casting directors will say the number one thing they want in actors is confidence. And you can't fake it. What gives you confidence? Be damn good. So good you know it. I'm good at what I do, I'm highly skilled and I'm willing to go in there and show you what I've got.

It's not a make or break for each audition, right?
Right. It is for the ego. It is for our sense of we're in this, because you need to get the job. Whether you get that role or not is not up to you and it's not always about your work. If

233

you're waiting to book a job to know if you did a good audition or not, you're never gonna get very far in this business. Because there are a hell of a lot people doing great auditions that don't book it. Your job is to be on that short list. Your job is to be one of the few actors in town that the Casting Directors know – I can call this person and they come through for me every single part. That's how you build a career. This is an art. We go and we paint our painting, because we're painters. Not because we need permission. If they want to buy our paintings, that's great. But if they don't buy your painting, are you less of a painter?

What are your thoughts on how actors can do their networking and marketing in Atlanta?
I teach marketing from a way that I believe in it. Because I'm a natural introvert, which is not the case for all actors. I do not go to networking events, I don't like to smile and shake hands and I feel uncomfortable and out of place. It's torture for me. I don't like to feel like I'm trying to push or be fancy. I teach a way of marketing that I have experienced and learned, done for myself, which is about thinking like what I call "the other of the table", or thinking like the people who are hiring us.

Put yourself in their shoes, allow them to be real people, allowing us to make an offer. Actors would tell me all the time: I don't want to be pushy and I don't wanna just walk into people's offices.' Well, have you ever offered to be a reader for a casting director for free? Do you not think it would help? Why do you not offer to come in and help them file headshots? Who is going to say: "No! Take you and your free labor and your time and get out of here!" That's just ridiculous. We get so lost in our head with what we want that we don't get outside of it. So I believe in marketing from a place of authenticity. A place of genuine connection and a place of offering, not trying to take.

That's how I see it and it's always interesting to me because the way an actor markets himself to me is the way he markets himself to others. When actors are gracious and appreciative, I feel compelled to help them because I like them, believe in their talent and I want to do what's right.

You have The Actors Way or some class related to acting career advice offered in your studio?
I do. I believe in what I'm gonna call the "Three-pronged Approach" and this is what I discovered for myself that works the best for me. On one side of the triangle is the acting. You have to get good as an actor, it's a necessity. Another side of it is the marketing. You have to know who you are, understand your business. You have to be able to get out there in a way that feels good to you and to those who are on the receiving end of it. The third piece of this is what I call the personal. That is the part that we understand who we are and how we behave. Part of why I got good at marketing myself was that I knew I was too shy to do it the other way very well. So I had to work within my own personal parameters. I'm good in connecting one on one and I'm good at speaking at events, but I don't like going out there and having to shake hands and talk to people. I had to adjust based on what I knew of myself. That is uncomfortable. We don't like to change habits, we don't like to do things differently, we don't like to grow, it doesn't feel good. But if you don't do that part, you can't succeed. If you're not growing,

you're dying. In order to *have* more you have to *be* more. You don't have to be better, you have to be more of you. You have to be more capable, you have to be more present, you have to be more willing. You gotta expand into a bigger version of you that's capable of living a bigger life. And I don't think it's more difficult for anybody than it has been for me. Because none of what I do came naturally.

It seems so hard to believe because you do it so well. But that's just an indication of how much you've practiced doing that. How much effort you put into it.
And how long I've been doing it. When I first started teaching, I liked people to be happy and liked them to feel good, liked to help them find what they're looking for. I had a very hard time allowing people to be in a place where they were unhappy with me, or the work, or where they were. I was out there and I realized after a while, I'm draining myself trying to want it more for them than they want it for themselves and sometimes I have to trust the process for them, too.

That's just an example of me, 40-years-old, having to grow into a bigger version of myself. I didn't want to make a website. I don't know how to do that. It overwhelmed me, it's scary, I thought it was gonna be really hard and I just said to myself: No, I love this business and this studio and it's my obligation to have a website that represents this studio in an authentic way. So I have to grow in to a person who can handle this. It's a never-ending process. I always tell people we have to be willing to get comfortable being uncomfortable, if we're going to be artists. Even to be decent people in our lives.

236

If you had to redo your acting career would you do anything differently?

The one thing I wish I could have done differently that I didn't really get until really, really far into it is...I don't know how possible it is, you have to put your whole heart into it but not your feelings. We gotta not take the business personally. Get your guard completely down when it comes to work. Beginners mind at all times. When it comes to the business, treat it as a business. It's not personal. They're not thinking about you, nobody is worried about your audition except you. Just get out there and be willing to learn and grow and know that you're gonna make mistakes. It's less about every little potential opportunity and more about the big picture. Make your career more about who you are and how you show up. Care more about your work, your art, your craft -- and less about other people's opinion of it. That's the key to success, from my vantage point.

Lee Armstrong

Lee Armstrong is a SAG-AFTRA actor who has worked in Los Angeles and the Southeast. He currently resides in North Carolina and is represented by STW Talent (stwtalent@me.com). (Rafiq's note – I've worked with Lee when I was casting an Indian feature film, IVIDE, that was set and shot in Atlanta.)

Where are you from originally and when did you know you wanted to be an actor? How did you go about pursuing it?
My father was in the military. I'm one of those kids who moved from base to base so I lived in a number of different places when I was growing up. Usually the new kid in school, so you learned to adapt pretty rapidly. I was 7-years-old when I decided I wanted to be an actor. It wasn't a big glory kind of thing. I thought I could be good at it. But you know what? It was only girls that were involved in the theater classes. Who wants to be the only guy in a bunch of girls at that age?I had to mature past that. The first acting-related thing I did was in third grade; and then about eighth grade. I started doing plays, I went out and auditioned. I wound up with the lead.

It was an interesting experience and I started in theater. I went to Illinois State University to get my Bachelors. Turns out it was kind of a golden era, there were so many working actors that are out there now that were my classmates when I went to Illinois State. After that I went to University of Iowa and got my Master's Degree; and from there I headed to Los Angeles.

Your Bachelors and Masters degrees were in fine arts and acting?
Right, so I'm educated. But it was mostly in theater, and there wasn't a lot of film. I knew that I was interested in film. My thought was, if you could make it in film, then probably you could get a job in the theater pretty much wherever you wanted to go. I went to Los Angeles from '79 to '91. I worked two or three times a year. I had a fairly good resume by the time that I left; it was a family thing.

I had a small child and Los Angeles was just not that kid-friendly. You were living in cramped little spaces that you could afford. For quality of life, I moved to North Carolina. There wasn't a lot going on in the early 90s. Some production in Wilmington, but it really was with the advent of the digital camera about 2000/ 2001 when people could afford not to have the big Hollywood cameras to work exclusively in film. They could record on digital video, and suddenly, production started springing up all over the place. Once that started happening out here, you could do a whole lot of work. So at this point, I've acted in 96 films, done 15 or so television projects. I've worked a lot and enjoy that regularity of being able to work frequently.

By the time you left LA, you had done some work and you were already a SAG member?
Yes. Joined SAG in 1983. I left LA in '91.

Why North Carolina?

We had friends, my wife's job brought us here. And really it was because of being a dad. My child was 2-years-old when we left. The cost of living was not all that higher. The one single thing that was extremely higher was housing. When we lived in LA, we lived in a one-bedroom apartment in Burbank. When we moved to North Carolina, we bought a three-bedroom house. Our mortgage was $50 a month less than our rent was in LA for our one-bedroom apartment.

When you have kids, with my priorities, God is first, family is second and career was third. I was clear on what my priorities were so it was a sacrifice I made without even thinking about it. But the Southeast has certain advantages in that there are a lot more opportunities that you can get that you didn't have back there. I worked a lot more each year than I ever did when I was in Los Angeles. But a lot of the bigger projects are shot there. Casting people still have a prejudice that the good actors -- the really good actors -- are from New York or Los Angeles.

I even tell them to come to Atlanta, its such a big center now. But frequently, the lead roles are cast on the coast and the smaller supporting roles, or under-fives even, are what's available to actors that are being cast locally. Because I lived in Los Angeles for 11 years, I really have no fear of those actors. I don't put them on any pedestals. I have a high regard for talent, and there are many talented actors that are based out there and live out there.

In the 21st century, we have airplanes. All it takes is to get on an airplane and go someplace in order to be able to work. I've got a series that's gonna shoot in August in St. Louis; it'll be my first time shooting there and I'm looking forward to that experience.

Even actors from LA or NY, they have to travel to Atlanta to shoot there; why doesn't it work the same way? Nobody's asking for priority to be cast, but the thing is just opportunity.

What do you think of Atlanta's growth? Is it something that's going to continue to grow overtime and maybe, hopefully change overtime, the perception that there is a depth of talent available in the Southeast?
To some extent, it is changing a little bit already and what we have to figure out is if the Atlanta boom is here to stay or is it simply the new hot spot? A few years before Atlanta, it was New Orleans, a few years before that it was Vancouver, and then somewhere sandwiched in between there it was in Michigan because of the great rates and incentives.

Politically, here in North Carolina, we elected a state government that totally got rid of the incentive programs. So much of the production that we had in North Carolina -- there was a lot -- *Iron Man* shot here, a huge number of large films have shot here, but because of the incentives they are moving elsewhere. Even South Carolina has work. You know they are shooting the *Vice Principals* down there with the people who were on *Eastbound and Down* that I was on. There's a lot of work, but producers are going to go where the incentives are.

Atlanta kind of boomed, you got some really big producers down there -- you got Tyler Perry, you got the Pinewood Studios that's going on, and they're building a lot of infrastructure and facility so I would think that there was a really good likelihood that Atlanta is here to stay, I know so many people are thinking about moving to Atlanta from this area.

To answer your question specifically about Atlanta, the jury is still out. I wonder if decades down the road this is gonna still be

241

the hot spot. But certainly it is at the moment. And because of the infrastructure that they're creating there, that looks good, politically, it seems like the government has realized that there is a lot to bring to the state because of film, and so they seem to be supportive of it. But you know you could have another administration that changes things, the legislature, that could change overnight like it did in here in North Carolina. And so you know there's no crystal ball on politics.

Do you have representation outside North Carolina?
My agent is based in Wilmington, but she does have an office in Atlanta as well. I don't know if she's currently getting work down in Los Angeles. I submitted out there, I had a call back for a series last weekend for Los Angeles and I self-submitted it by Skype. I can't remember exactly which site it was on but everyday I'm looking, I submit, and so I don't usually remember exactly where it was I found the audition. I keep working and of course it's not the bigger stuff, but you never know who you're gonna meet and one of my good friends that's a casting director says "work begets work."

You don't have an agent in New Orleans, LA or New York?
My agent does submit to New Orleans and part of the Southeast, when they're sending out the breakdown. She submitted me to Texas, as far away as Kentucky. She does know her clients, who's willing to travel and who's not. Most actors in the Southeast also have additional sources of income. Day jobs, or whatever else you do. I work three jobs. I am a professional actor. Some years acting is my second, and some years it's my third, but you look for flexibility. People that you can work for that allow you to, at a moment's notice, take the morning off; to go take the audition.

The biggest challenge of the older actor is the technology, I am just not good with the tech. I know how to use the computer. But to shoot it, have the lighting right, to have a reader, I really appreciate a service that does that for me. And does it at a reasonable rate. There are some people in Wilmington that are just great. [Actors Arsenal -- shameless plug] Looking through the Screen Actor's Guild is also another way to access and find who is casting and projects that are being cast.

You're a SAG actor in a right-to-work state and mostly right-to-work area, has that been a hindrance in any way?
Yeah, it's a big issue. I am in the position of acting as a union advocate to some independent producers who think of SAG-AFTRA as some really difficult organization to work with, and actually the opposite is true. From student films, to short films, to all of the low budgets, to the new media that's out there for television, the internet distribution, for all of those levels, the signatory agreement, and there is paperwork involved and you need a producer to fill out some forms but that's part of the business.

If you're not professional enough to fill out some forms, do I really want to waste my time with you? I hate to put it like that, but really it's not that big of a deal anymore; and so I am still working, I think last year I hit my goal, which was twelve projects to film during the year. So I hit my goal that I set at the beginning of the year; that's gonna be twelve film and television projects, and I did that. And it's still my same set goal for this year, I'm at three right now.

But the right to work thing is difficult from the standpoint that you've just got to explain it to some producers. And I've certainly have lost jobs because I'm in SAG. And the global rule one if you're a Union actor -- you don't work on non-union sets. It was an issue with an independent feature I did recently too.

They said SAG when they invited me down to audition. After the call back, they said would you work non-union. "No!" It's a potential $5,000 fine or boot out of the union if you do that. To work for $100 a day to torpedo a career, am I going to do that? No. And the other issue with the right-to-work state is the SAG-AFTRA eligible actors. These are the actors that have done enough work that they are able to join the union. But some don't. I worked with one guy recently who was in his 50s who became SAG eligible as a child actor. He was still SAG-AFTRA eligible. I have some actors, because I teach acting as well at the college level, it's one of my three jobs. I try to tell young actors, if you're SAG-AFTRA eligible, people understand if you just became eligible within a year and you want to accrue a few more credits before you go professional, they get that. It's not a big deal. But when you walk on a set with actors and you tell them proudly that you're SAG-AFTRA eligible, and then they ask you how long you've been SAG-AFTRA eligible, oh for 13 years; and I've done three network series with recurring roles as a SAG actor. It's like you're able to work for Union wages, get Union residuals all because of Union actors like me who pay the dues to enable you to do that. If there weren't union actors, there wouldn't be a union.

If you're gonna regard this as a profession that you're really serious about pursuing, there comes a point where you need to just step up and become a professional. I can't tell you how many productions have done SAG signatory agreements because they wanted me on the show. It's usually five a year or something like that. The strategy we have as SAG actors is simply that if there are more SAG actors out there, producers are going to realize that if they really want talented people on the screen, they need to be able to access union talent.

What else is it you do to supplement your income?
I work in human resources for a manufacturing company. That's the job that gets me my benefits. They're very nice to me. I've been with them for over 20 years.

They know about your acting career?
Yes. I don't push it in people's faces because there are a number of people that are also interested in it. There's one woman that I work with that this year became a television producer. She produced an Internet soap opera. I work for a very good company and they give me the flexibility that I need to be able to get off most of the time. Now if there were some business need, and it hasn't quite come up yet, I'm usually able to juggle things. But if there was some business need that came up and they say, look you need to be here or you're gone, well I have to figure out, what do I want, a job that pays me over $60,000 a year or to work for $100 a day at some other place.

Does this HR job require you to be in the office, but then you just have to notify your manager when you want to take off?
Yes, there are jobs like sales or something where you might be out on the road. My job is in human resources, I do work out of an office. And so if I'm not there, I do have to get notification and permission to be able to go, but after 20 years, I've liberal vacation benefits; so it's good. When I was in Los Angeles, I had four jobs at once. I had a 2-year-old and a wife, and I was trying to be an actor; and I didn't have a huge corporate job then at the time. I worked for a mannequin manufacturer at one point, I taught English as a second language. Unless your dad is a major director or star, you must claw your way into this business.

Has the formal training been helpful to you in the course of your career? Do you think haven gotten the exposure to the highest level of acting in LA helped you book more jobs in the Southeast?

Training doesn't ever end. So the fact that I have college degrees in theater, theater acting and film acting are certainly related in this craft, but they are very different just like commercial acting is different from film acting and film acting even is a little bit different from television acting in terms of the technical things that you have to learn. So your education doesn't end. I take classes in Wilmington; there's a good studio down there that I work with, and it's basically audition technique that I do and I've been doing that for about two years now.

The training that I found in Los Angeles, I've worked with a number of different teachers that were out there and did so many workshops. Some of them were meet and greet. The training really has helped me. I don't know if it's the big calling card out here, because I really think that people are not looking for what you used to do, they are looking for what you could do now. And they are not looking for who you were in the eighties they are looking for who you are in 2015. So, the nice thing about being an unknown actor is that directors tend to see you in terms of what their needs are.

You mentioned some particular training that raised your game, you were booking four times what you were booking before, what was the training?

Jeremiah Comey is his name. He's an acting teacher in Los Angeles. He's got a book out "Film Acting for Actors and Directors" and his studio is large enough in Los Angeles, certainly there are a lot of really talented teachers out there. But his is invitation only, so that you have to be invited to be able to pay money to take his classes, that kind of echelon. He's got other people that have been students for a number of times that also teach, in his studio during the times that he's not up and teaching, so some people can enter in one of the subordinates classes or something and they kind of move up. It wasn't invitation only when I started. It's Meisner based.

But unlike Meisner, it's a lot more, it's the best system that I have to get actors looking good quickly. If you have a film with any kind of depth to it, any kind of emotional depth, learning how to work off the other actor, being unpredictable, not just for the sake of being weird, but, because you're in the moment, you're working off the other actor, you don't want all of your takes to be exactly the same. It's the sign of a mediocre actor. You want to be in the moment, the takes will be similar, but then it gives your director choices in the editing room.

Actors all work differently, but to be able to have that unpredictability, do a scene brilliantly once, and them being able to catch it and for it to be in the can and make a great movie. Actors like Jack Nicholson, you never know what that heck is gonna go on with him. And that translates into Oscars and a great career.

What do you think you would do differently if you had to do your career all over again?
There are a lot of people that become successful in this business out of celebrity, rather than ability; and celebrity can open a door and get you into the industry; but it's only talent that's gonna keep you there. So you've got some crossover, people who are stars, like Kris Kristofferson. I was watching him in a movie the other night who become known as a singer, and then moved from music into film; there are people that; there are some reality stars that have had doors and opportunities that

have opened to them, into the industry. There are certainly a number of stand-up comics who have been able to translate their stand-up comedy into an acting career as well.

And improv is another one, there are a lot of people that become known in the world of improv who then are able to piggyback usually into commercials first and then from commercials into an acting career; so there are a number of avenues into this. When I was younger, I was totally focused on acting as the technique and the spirit of acting and really trying to give good performance. And while that may make for a good performance, it doesn't always translate exactly into the biggest job offers. I wish I had thought, what are the other passages into the business in addition to just being good at what you do? Does that sound crass? I don't know? But if I had to do anything differently, I'd just consider that. You had some people that were like sports stars that become known as actors. So there's just not necessarily one hat that somebody can wear; so you just got to try and figure out, well, how do I do this?

What's been keeping you motivated all these years to keep you driving eight hours for one call back to Atlanta for working multiple jobs and pursuing this? What keeps you going?
I love to do it, and it's not that I have an incomplete life when I'm not acting; I enjoy many aspects in my life, but there's just nothing quite as fun for me as being able to do this. I like my work and I like what I do. My favorite thing about acting is when you walk onto a set, nobody knows who you are. And then suddenly they see what you can do, and then all of a sudden, you have a whole room full of new best friends. That, to me, is conquering spirit. It's just a priceless experience, being able to do that.

With this field, you have to be really passionate about it. I do know some actors that are trying to do it because they think they can make money out of it. Money is a good thing and in this field it's a good thing because usually the more you're paid, the larger the visibility of the project is; therefore the more people that are going to see it. I still work, I work on student films, because you can get some good film in it, but also that is where the next generation of directors and actors are gonna come from other than in the film schools. So for me it's part of giving back to the career and the profession, to make time to work with the young directors, because they need to know what it's like to work with an actor, when they ask them to do something, they can actually do it. Rather than taking 14 takes to get them do something right.

Mark Ashworth

Your IMDB page talks about you having come over from UK and having worked some odd jobs and then moving to Atlanta. Tell me about your journey from UK to Atlanta.

Well, my parents bought a business in Tennessee in 1992. It wasn't really a business move for my Dad. Rather I'd say It was more of a lifestyle change that he wanted to give us, because in the UK me and my brother were getting into trouble. So we visited Tennessee on vacation and just fell in love with it. It's a different way of living than Manchester which is where I was brought up. It's like a concrete jungle in Manchester you know.

In Tennessee, it was more of the beauty of the countryside. The people were so nice. And you know, we were horse-riding where we lived, down at the lake, waterskiing on the weekends, just a completely different way of life. A few years after our initial visits, my dad bought a business, an auto part business, something he had never done in England, just kind of a means to a way of being over here. And he did that for a few years. And then he got, he kind of got put out of business by Walmart, and then he got back into doing kitchens which is what he used to do in England so it's kind of full circle for him. His journey really was inspirational to me, to this day.

I made the move to Atlanta in 1997. I'd lived in Tennessee at that point for fours years and I think I was about 20. And I saw Atlanta as holding the most promise to me at that time you know. It's the closest big city to Tennessee and it was affordable and it just seemed like a great move at the time. So I came here in 97. I never said that I would stay but here we are in 2015 and I'm still here you know. It's a great city to be in. The people are really friendly. And you kind of get the best of both worlds. It's cosmopolitan and country.

Yes, it's an awesome city.
I never thought that all the present industry work would be going on, all the film work and such. It turned just to be a real blessing that I ended up being here at this present moment.

So when you moved to Atlanta you didn't think about acting?
No. Not necessarily I didn't although acting was something for me that I've always been interested in . Acting was something that I always felt like I would like to have a go at one day you know, I guess I was always under the impression that you had to go and be enrolled in a dramatic arts school, that you had to go to the big schools.

And it was something that at my age, at that time and doing it by myself, I just couldn't afford. So I was in my twenties just doing things the kids in their twenties do, you know. And before I knew it, I was in my thirties. And then, I had a friend of mine who was going out with this girl and she told me about this acting class in town. It was Nick Conti's place. She told me about that and she explained to me that it was like "You can go there at once." There are beginners and intermediate all the way through to advanced classes and that you could go and drop in take a class without the monetary investment I had been afraid of. I went with her along to her class there and I just fell in love with the nuances of the craft. They had numerous teachers at the studio, but I really kind of gelled with my now mentor and actor here in town, Michael Cole. I enrolled in his classes and just began to appreciate everything that he was teaching. Within the first year that I was there, I was able to get an agent and start getting on some big, meatier auditions. I've been at it now for probably about 9 years.

You're kind of a veteran at this.
Well, I've got my share of experiences in class and on set, and in the business itself. But I feel as though I'm still kind of getting to know myself and getting to know the craft. It's an ongoing journey. If you want to be an actor, it's a whole lifestyle and a journey that you should commit to. So, I feel as though, I have got a little bit of experience and I'm somewhat cautious but I wouldn't consider myself to be a veteran, or anything yet, you know.

How did you get your agent?

I'm with J Pervis Agency. I got with them right up after Joy came back from LA . She was a talent scout with The Osbrink Agency previously. At that time J Pervis were up in Lawrenceville and were expanding their adult division. I remember going up there, we used to have to drive up to the auditions and they put us on tape there. And then they moved into town. They've been in town now for the last 5, 6 years I think.

And how did you go about submitting? Did you submit to all agencies?

Well, you know, there's no better place for networking with fellow actors and filmmakers than in the class room. So I went to a lot of classes and workshops. I did a lot of Southern Casting calls. It seems like it has turned into a page for hiring extras now but, you used to, you could find good roles on there you know. Student films, I would do a bunch of that stuff, so I kind of built my resume single-handedly to the point where I felt like it showed that I did have some experience. When I was in class I learned how to properly do a cover letter, how to submit without coming across as needy. Focusing on the fact that I'm trying to better their business at the same time. It's a business, we work together. As much as it should be, you both need each other.

Absolutely, it's a partnership.

So I guess I just submitted. I submitted to the top tier agencies, the top five. After a while, I was with Real People for a little while and had some really good success with them doing commercials. I just felt that they didn't really have at the time as much as film and television. I felt like that's really what I wanted to be doing, more film and television. Then I went over to J Pervis and asked them if they would represent me. But you know I think I submitted a good cover letter, just short, sweet, to the point, telling them who you are, why you are drawn to their agency, what you think you could book with them. Just something real short, and real sweet. What I did as well when I submitted my headshot and resume was put them in a clear headshot envelope.

It's just the small little things like the clear headshot envelope. I think it tells the agency that you care about their time. They don't have to open the envelope if they don't want to in order to see the head shot. It kind of makes them want to open the headshot envelope up.

That's a really good tip.
Yeah, so many people submit all the time and sometimes peoples' headshots are done by on a phone or done by somebody who has no idea what they're shooting. You know I've noticed my headshots over the years have improved just because of my vulnerability to the camera. It's not about just point and shoot and me smiling. There has to be something going on there in the eye that the camera has to capture.

Do you think you're getting the auditions for meaty roles with all the big projects in town, as many as you are fit for?
Yes. I think so but as an aspiring actor it's never enough! I wish I could have more meatier auditions but I think I'm getting my fair shake of the stick, I don't ever complain. I think complaining

just opens up a whole world of negativity that you don't need. I think the way that you think, the way that you project, enables you as a person. Do I wish I was auditioning more? Of course I do. I wish I had auditions every week but I don't. It's up to me in my downtime to be proactive and to do things that I need to do for me, whether it be going in front of class, working out with a teammate, with a fellow actor, and being put in on-camera. Just doing something that keeps my hands dirty, that keeps the muscles moving, keeps the universe working for me and in the direction that I want to go.

How do you continue to train and take classes and what else do you do outside of acting?
I'm currently in class over at the Rob Mello studio with a fellow actor, Jayson Warner Smith. I just thought I'd do his class because he's somebody that I respect as a fellow actor, somebody that is working. So yeah, I think it's important to go and get different teachers' perspectives on the craft. There's so many different methods that you can pick up along the way and there's not one specific one that is right for you, you know. You may take a piece of one person's thoughts. You may take another person's thoughts as well. There's not one special thing. We're all so different you know so it's important to get a good grasp of what everybody has to say.

And coming back to Michael Cole. One of the things I really like about Michael Cole, and I stay in his classes too. He does a really really good 'On-camera audition technique class' in town. It's over by the Renaissance Project on the east side of town. It's an ongoing workshop. It's for the working actor and when I say the working actor it could be just even the one-liner. When I say working I mean auditioning, because that is the real work, when you're auditioning, you're working. That's the work. When you're on set you play. So I always go to Michael's classes over at Nick Conti's. I always kind of gravitate back to him. He's just somebody that I have a special connection with.

I'll take workshops that come up in town. I think if I want to be seen specifically by casting directors that I have not been seen by, I'll take a workshop because those things work, they do. They can't take your headshots at the end of the workshop anymore. It gives false hope I guess. But they will remember your name and you know, I think I've done probably like five of those workshops and each and every time I've been called in for an audition by some. They do work for me. As long as the casting director is working in your region then you're in good shape.

So workshops do work.
Yeah, yeah. I think so. You have to go in there specifically with a plan of attack. What do you want? You've got to know. You want to go in there to get an audition hopefully. You want to go in there to impress. I think, with workshops too you have to be very diligent with your time over. If it's like a two day workshop a lot of times they'll give you a lot of home work to do that night. So it's important that you're fully focused on that homework during that time so you can go and give the best impression possible to the Casting Director or agent or whoever is leading the workshop. You got to put your right foot forward

and if you don't put your right foot forward, there's no point of even going.

Absolutely. You don't just go, waste time sitting there.
Yeah. You can't want to go to a workshop to spend all that money just to get feedback on a headshot. You can ask your industry friends, or somebody you respect and admire, somebody who does have experience with those things, for that kind of feedback. But that's not the right reason to go to a workshop. You want to go there to knock somebody's socks off so they got no choice but to call you in for the scene, for the audition.

And about what I do outside of acting...I just got a baby girl about ten months ago.

Congratulations!
Thanks mate. Yeah I'm so in love. I'm hooked. I'm hooked on my own daughter. She's the most beautiful little thing. I'm so happy. That's my best work! I have my wife. I'm happily married, living over at East Lake. I wait tables as my consistent work. I find it's important to have a consistent job, for me right now, anyway. Until such time as I've been booking richer roles and series regulars. It's important to me to have another source of income.

It's one of those "farm-to-table" restaurants in town. I work with one of my best friends who happens to be my boss now. He's been my boss for about fifteen years and he knows where my heart is. He knows where my passion is and he does everything he can to help. When I need to get off of work, he'll let me take off when I book something. You have to be adaptable in this industry because they're not going to wait around on you. You have to be ready to go at the drop of a hat. Whether it be auditioning, whether it be booking, whatever it is you just got to be ready to go. In order to deal and get ready to go, and be updated you got to, you go to have updated headshots. That's important too. There's a lot of cost involved. There's a lot of investment involved but you know, you're investing in yourself so it's important, it's good.

And it's the holy grail, isn't it? To find a job that you can support yourself and your family with while having the flexibility.
Oh man. Absolutely. That's one of my short term goals, is to be able to act and just to be able to support my family by doing that. I'm getting warmer. I'm in year 2 of a 5 year plan and I'm really focusing on my vision. Last year I made more money acting than I did at the restaurants so that's a real step in the right direction.

That's great man.
Yeah, I was really shocked to get that news from when I did my taxes the other day.

Your family, your wife and parents supportive in this career?
Yeah absolutely, everybody's been just so good. My mom and dad love it. I'd like to credit my mom for giving me the inspiration to actually get off my ass and do something about it. We sat down one day over cups of tea and we were talking

about dreams and aspirations. And she said "You know how many people have dreams to do something. 75% of the people do, they're fortunate thinkers. People that have the ability to be able to think, and to aspire to achieve." But she said "Do you know the amount, the actual percentage of people who act on those dreams? Less than 5%, jump in and take action." I don't know actually where she got those numbers from but it was enough and what I needed, enough for me to get up off my bum and stay up off my bum. It's not going to drop in your lap. You have to go out, seize the day.

If it was easy, everybody would be doing it right? For you though it has been a bit of a niche here, in terms of your British background. Do you think that it helped you?
I think it helps as much as it hinders, you know. It's nicely thought of when specific roles come through but here in Atlanta, I'll probably only ever have 3 or 4 auditions for a Brit. I think the casting directors can look beyond my accent, and now that I can do my American accent, with a little bit of work.

I think my beard, as much as anything, got me a lot of work. You know how it's so funny about that. I've got my beard now for a while so it's like I get those specific roles like some crazy man, nervous guy, biker, bartender, crazy guy, homeless guy. Get a load of the homeless guy, roles you know. Which is good. I don't care what. I don't care how you think of me, just me.

You just gotta get the work.
Yeah, put me to work. But yeah I think it's a blessing as much as, well it's not a curse. Sometimes people that know my work, but

don't know I'm British would call me in for a Southern role, which I love doing, I love Southern. I lived in Tennessee for a few years. I think the English accent's not too far from the Southern just cause it's got so much pitch. So up and down you know. So is ours.

So you are able to turn it on off as needed?
You got to have it, when you need it. But you got to be able to lose it when they ask you to, you know.

What else do you do in terms of marketing? Do you do any mailers, any emails, etc.?
Yeah I do a little bit of digital marketing you know. I do a little bit of flyers. When we do the work we hope that people will see it. Part of the payment of being an actor is having people put their eyes on it. So I try to let people know via my social media platforms you know, that I've got something coming up. I usually give a little flyer of the season of the episode, or whatever, of the show that I'm on. And then I put my name with my agency on there and I just send it out across social media. I used to send postcards. I've kind of gotten away from that. I've met a few people telling that they just go straight to the bin. I think digital is kind of the way to go. It seems like everything's kind of leaning in that direction.

I'll get on IMDB. I'll get on twitter and I'll try and connect the dots between pre-production stuff and stuff that's in production, and just try and put myself in their mind. If I can find out who the casting director is, I'll shoot them a tweet and I'll say "Hey I hope pre-productions' going good for ....project," and just leave it at that. "Hope to see breakdown soon. @JPervisTalent". So I'm just going to try and connect the dots, as far as that goes.

That's a really smart way to do it.
Yeah. It's just one of the ways to be proactive you know. Rather than just sitting around waiting for a door to open you got to just knock on a door and see if they open. They're not going to open if they don't hear you knocking. And if they do, don't leave it. They're not going to stop to talk to you if you already left.

Do you think that there's a chance that they might start booking series regulars out of Atlanta?
Yeah, I definitely do. Things are changing rapidly here. And I've noticed the difference in the last couple of years. I've had more season regular auditions this year than I have in the last nine years put together. It's constantly changing because the work is here. I think there are a lot of people who are moving here for work. There's people moving into our market which strengthens the talent pool locally. So these production companies, they've got no problem with looking for local actors here. I think the stereotype of there only being seven actors here is not the case anymore. There are people from all over the place. They're here and they know that the market is hot.

Do you compete with the actors from LA? Do you see that happening?
Oh yeah. I was at a callback for a PlayStation show. And there were a few actors that were in the callbacks from LA. And it was so funny because they're from Atlanta but they moved out to LA

and here they are now back in Atlanta. For the callbacks for the show that's going to shoot in Atlanta. It's kind of funny to see that happen. But yeah, I felt great for that.

Do you think you might consider or want to move to LA or is this where it's going to be at for the next couple of years?
Yeah. I'm staying put. I'm not going to go. There's no reason to go anywhere. With so much stuff coming here, I'd be foolish, it'd be like losing the last 9 years of networking that I've done here locally. I might have to just start again you know, which I'm not against doing. But I'm not going to go out there to do that. It's not that I'm afraid of the work. I would go out there if I was offered work you know. But I'm not going to go out there to look for work.

Right. You've got good momentum here.
Yeah. I recently have been repped management wise by Gail Tassell. And one of the reasons why, because I feel as though, with a manager it can be a little bit more focused as far as getting work outside of my region, something that my agency can't or don't do that much. For the people at my level anyway. I'm happy to work outside of my region as a local which is what it would take to book a role.

Do you have agencies representing you in New Orleans or North Carolina or LA?
Yeah. I'm with Joe Chavez at 'Bold Agency', down in Louisiana. They've got an office down there. There's a lot of stuff that goes on in Louisiana too. They've got great structures. And they've got great infrastructure. You know, there's a lot of stuff going on

there, always has been really. But most of the work is right here though, for sure. That's really the short term goal, is to be auditioning regularly for things outside of my market. I'd love to travel, see the world. As an actor it would be great.

Are you SAG?

Nope. I'm not SAG. I'm SAG eligible. Here in Atlanta I'm afraid of becoming SAG right now because it's so up and down for me. If I could consistently book studio work. I love doing indies. They keep me busy, they keep me focused. They keep me working my muscles. If I didn't have indies, I'd be just running around in circles and just go crazy. There's so much opportunity to learn and to delve into character. Like an opportunity to create a character that I just wouldn't be able to do on big budgets. Not for a long time yet. Character arcs. Stories. Play the lead. Get a feature.

Have you ever been through phases when you've been facing a lot of rejection and you feel like "what am I doing?". Are you going to think of giving up? Has it ever happened?

Yeah. Of course man. It happens everyday, you kidding me? In one respect or another, of course it does. We face up to rejection square in the face every time we go to an audition. There are many things that I go through. It may be slow, maybe no auditions. And I'm second-guessing myself. But like I said before, it's those times that you really need to start bunkering down and be doing some more work. You can't say "I've got no audition, it's my agents fault." No it's not. It's not my agent's fault. It comes down to you and your work ethic, at that point to just dig in.

But yeah of course I think every actor gets down because the highs are so high, you know. The highs are so high that when you come down, it makes the lows even lower. All it takes is just going for a barren two weeks. No audition and then not shooting anything in a month it's like…"What's going on?", And then of course self-doubt creeps in. There's the importance to be in classes ongoing. Because that keeps you focused. It keeps you in front of a camera.

One of my short term goals was to be in front of a camera twice a week. In whatever respect that is, whether it be the classroom, whether it be an audition, whether it be helping a friend out. Just putting yourself in the creative mold that you want to form. Doing it, doing work. I've been released from four projects back to back pretty much. And this was going on about a month or two ago. Yeah I just go so frustrated. I think I posted something online about it. I was like "Got released today, fourth time, it's a joke". My agent said "Oh you're on hold." I was like "Really?" I said "How long do we have before they relieve me?" It's kind of funny to me but in a sad kind of way. It's great to know that you're on hold. Albeit you're first refusal, that's great. But when you get relieved, and you're not booked, it doesn't feel great.

It's the booking that you want. It's just a part of what we do man. Once you get that call they say you're on first refusal, it's like yes, that's great. They check your schedule, ask if you can shave your beard, and you get up because you've got something there. There's something! And then sure enough you get relieved it's like "God..... Rejection. AGAIN, I'm not good enough, I should have don't this or that differently, I'm not worthy. I knew I should've done a different bow in the end of the audition. Maybe it was too much. Was it too much?" And then, you know finally you just have to let it go, learn something, always learn something from rejection and you're winning.... You just got to stay focused man, Stay on the path. You just have to have faith.

Any final thoughts?

The one thing that I want to say is don't complain as an actor. Don't complain. And if you hear somebody complaining, walk away. Not necessarily in a rude way but just you know, don't entertain their thought. If you're upset, don't talk shit about anybody. Don't complain that you're tired. Don't do anything negative, just be there and be grateful for what you are, for who you are, for who you are and what you've got, the blessing to be able to do. There are those people on set that work twice as hard as you behind the scene and don't get to sit in a trailer and have a doze. Don't complain about hours. Don't complain about anything. Just enjoy the journey, and show up to set with great work ethic and a great attitude. Make it to where people enjoy working with you because of how you don't complain, you work hard and are always open to just creating. Be that person and you'll go far in this industry.

Matt Cornwell

Matthew was born in Palm Beach Gardens, Florida. After living four years in Huntsville, Alabama, he moved back to Florida and went to high school in Tampa. He graduated from Duke University with a Bachelor's Degree in Mechanical Engineering in 2000. He received his Masters Degree in Mechanical Engineering from Georgia Tech in December, 2001. After working 2 years as an Acoustical Consultant, he quit to become a full-time actor. He has been a working actor in Atlanta since January, 2003. He and his wife, Brooke Jaye Taylor, a fellow actor, also have a hilarious, popular web series about acting in Atlanta: http://www.beckyandbarry.com. They also run an audition taping service: http://www.get-taped.com

When did you know you wanted to become an actor? Did you do any acting in school or college?

Sitting alone in a movie theater watching Ace Ventura when I was 14, I decided that being like Jim Carrey would be the coolest thing ever. I didn't start acting until I was a junior in high school, and even then my main focus was still on my studies. I went to Duke for Mechanical Engineering, and took several acting classes there, but it was still a "dream", not a viable career. Then I came to Georgia Tech to get my Masters in Mech. Eng., and got involved immediately in their theatre, DramaTech. It wasn't until sometime in 2002 that I decided it was my career.

How did you go about starting your acting career? Was your family supportive?

I didn't consciously "start" my career. I eased into it. I started with classes, then started doing independent projects, then got an agent, and suddenly I realized that I was an actor. My parents were always supportive, though I'm sure they were skeptical during those first several years.

What made you choose Atlanta?

I came here for Graduate School, and then discovered that there was a great market here.

What was your first paid gig?

After I signed with Houghton Talent in May 2002, I immediately had an audition for a Zocor Commercial. It was actually an extra role, but they needed football players, so they held a formal audition. Melissa McBride (Carol on The Walking Dead) was the casting director at that time, and I got cast in this national SAG commercial on my first audition.

How did you get your first agent?

By being in class. After 8 months or so of training, a classmate came up to me one day and said "Don't tell anyone, but I work for Houghton and I think you'd be great for us. Do you have headshots?" I said "No, but I will by next week." So I made an appointment with a photographer, and just like that I had an agent.

What was your training like? How do you keep your instrument sharp between projects (if you have the time)?

In college I got exposed to a variety of philosophies, but most of my training has been influenced by Meisner. I took classes every week for the first 10 years or so of my career. I transitioned into teaching classes, and still teach today. Even though I don't actively take any classes currently (though I plan to in the near future), teaching keeps me sharp. Also, running a taping service for actors is the best cold-reading training around. I cold read DOZENS of scripts a week (for over 5 years straight), and can honestly say I'm an expert at it.

Are you SAG? If not, why not?

No, but this is the first year I'm seriously considering making the jump. I've been eligible since 2003, but non-union work has been my bread and butter all these years. However, since the tax incentive has brought so much work to town, I've been booking more and more union work, so I'm almost to the point where I can safely leave the non-union work behind.

How did you support yourself when you started out? What were your survival jobs?

At first I was stuck in the corporate job. Less than a year later, I quit that job and starting doing substitute teaching for middle school and high school. I also did freelance editing and web design. Let's just say I was very poor the first 5 or so years of my career, BUT I was very happy.

Do you do anything else to supplement your income today?
I teach 3 classes a week, and I co-own Get Taped

What do you do outside acting (family, hobbies etc.)?
Ha. I don't have much else on my plate right now. I used to be big into sports (mainly soccer), and I also used to draw and paint a lot. I still do some art occasionally.

What are some ways you stay on the industry radar? How do you make your mailings stand out?
Get Taped definitely helps us stay connected to all the major players in the industry, but honestly, kicking butt in all your auditions is the best way. I've never sent postcards, and don't do any other marketing for myself. I received a piece of advice from an improv teacher years ago that has become my philosophy: "Be the actor that everyone else wants to be in a scene with." That keeps me on the radar.

What do you see the future of acting being in Atlanta? What would you like to see happen in Atlanta to grow the film business/opportunities for actors? Do you see series regular roles coming here?
I think the size of the roles offered here will gradually increase over the next 5-10 years, but let's be real; lead roles require

actors who are proven moneymakers. So until celebrities start making Atlanta home, LA will always be the hub for the leads in TV/Film. I do think series regulars would be an eventual possibility.

Do you have representation outside Atlanta?
No.

Do you plan to move to LA/NYC in next five years?
No.

How do you handle rejection? Do you ever feel like giving up?
Each year I'll go through at least 1 or 2 dry spells that last anywhere from 1-6 months. Those are the toughest times. No amount of positive thinking seems to help. BUT what I did discover several years ago was that producing your own content is the cure. When we started our web series, Becky & Barry, it took all the focus off of the roles that we had no control over, and gave us creative freedom to do something that has been truly fulfilling. So when times are tough, we just focus on that.

What do you wish someone had told you at the beginning of your career? What mistakes have you made, if any?
I am not someone who looks back at what I should've done. Just like in an improv scene, you just need to focus on the moment and build from there. Every decision I've made, and everything that has happened to me has brought me to this point, and I'm very happy with where I'm at...so no regrets :)

What advice would you give to an actor starting out?

Stop. Turn around. Find something else that will make you happy. Because if there is anything else in life that will bring you fulfillment, you should do that. This business is hard. Nearly impossible. It will chew you up and spit you out over and over again. You have to be all in to even have the slightest chance in this business, and too many people try to only put one foot in, and they wonder why they don't make progress. And if you ever get to the point where you ask the question "How do I know if it's time to quit?", then you don't have what it takes.

Michael Cole

Michael is a successful working film, TV & stage actor as well as acting teacher & on-set acting coach. In the 2002 edition of Who's Who of American Teachers, Michael was honored for his work. He is the Artistic Director of The Renaissance Project theatre co w/ dozens of stage credits & directed over 30 productions. His aggressive teaching style is driven by his passionate belief that every actor deserves a chance. He is represented by Houghton Talent in Atlanta.

When did you know you wanted to be an actor?

I stumbled into it. I did grow up around it, in the business, with my uncle who was in a television show called *The Mob Squad*. He played Pete Cochran. He's also my namesake. He's Michael Charles Cole. I'm Michael Highland Cole. As a kid, I was not that taken up with going to work in Hollywood and seeing him shoot. It was very boring and it took an awful lot of time to record very little stuff. My uncle was not supportive or encouraging me to be a television actor. A lot of it was because of the bad experiences that he had. However, the first time I did something on stage, I was 12 or 13-years-old, I really liked it. Within a year or two of that, I started doing it more and more. Anywhere I could find opportunities to do stuff on stage, I would do it. And that went on for a while.

Was all this in California?
No. Some of it was in LA. Most of it was actually here in Atlanta. And some of it was up in the New England area. A friend in Atlanta said, "Hey, I've got this agent that represents me here in Atlanta. And I think you're really good for this audition for a Rhodes Furniture pirate". So the agent sent me the information. I went to the audition. And the very first thing I did, I booked. Then the next four things I auditioned for, I booked each one of them. And I went, this is easy. How little I knew. I had a bit of a falling out with that agent. It was about 17 years ago, that I was approached again. Somebody saw stuff that I was doing and said, "I would really love for you to audition for a part." It was a different agent, and I did, and for the last 15 years now, it's been a major part of my income.

You were not actively pursuing acting when you got that invite 17 years ago?
I was, but on stage, not in film and television. When I had that bad experience with that first agent, I didn't want to mess this. It wasn't until about 17 years ago that I was approached yet again, and got involved. Within a couple of years, I found I was able to make pretty good money doing it. Not completely, but enough to supplement my income quite well.

Were your parents or siblings also supportive of this career?

Yes. There was never any "Aw man, that's so stupid. Why are you doing this?" My uncle said, "Okay Mike, I know it sought you out. Let me give you some red flags to watch for." He didn't hide it, and when he saw one of the things I did, he was very supportive and has always been supportive.

When you were starting 17 years ago, Atlanta was not the hotspot it is today?

Oh no.

So when you started getting work, you decided to continue working here. Never thought of moving out?

No. I lived in LA, San Francisco, Sacramento, Atlanta. But I'm now an adult, with children, and the cost of living was so high out there. I was doing stage, and teaching for extra income. But what I was really doing well in was commercials. The film work here and the television weren't until 2007 when the tax incentives first were in place for a full 12 months. And after 2008, it went crazy.

Have you been with the same agency all these years?

I am with Houghton Talent. Came to Houghton in 2004 or 2005. They were my third or fourth agent.

A lot of new actors want to know how to get an agent. But in your case, you'd been doing work. You were approached by your first agent. And then you built enough work that you didn't have a problem in being able to switch to Houghton?

Houghton knew that I was with an agent called CodeTalent. It was my second or third agent. That agent was just a one-person agency. They had a close relationship with Mystie (at Houghton). I had a contractual job as the voice of this animated talking deer head for a company called Tinks. CodeTalent handed the contract over to Houghton, so I scheduled a meeting with Mystie. I'd never met her before. I walked into the office and the very first thing I said was, "I'm here to make you money. Give me that chance." She smiled and said, "I like the way you think." And it's been that way ever since.

That's definitely an unusual path. Most actors don't get in that way.

It was a lot easier for me getting an agent. It's a lot harder right now to get top tier agencies because the agencies can be picky. You have to realize that the bread and butter for the agencies still is not film and television. It's the commercials and industrials because it requires them to do a lot less work to get those bookings. And the chances of their actors booking them are a lot higher. Also their commission is higher. So the agencies primarily did film and television to appease their actors. Now that there's a lot of film and television work, the bigger agencies are able to make a commission. They're only getting 10% of off this. So what they want is bookers with their agency because they've got to pay their staff, put gas in their car, and put braces in their kid's teeth.

What kind of training have you had, and how do you keep your instruments sharp between projects?

When I started, I did the school of hard knocks, and if I wanted to act, I created my opportunity through stage to do it. Even writing plays and helping others out. On my own. I just wanted to act. I loved getting in front of people. I love affecting people and changing them, and making them aware of whether there are social issues or personal issues.

I did some classes in college, and I found them to be very boring. My degree is in graphic design. It's not as an actor. When I left college, I earned a living while I was doing stage. I headed up a studio that was creating animatronics for a children's television show, where I would do sculpting and clay, and create molds, and do illustrations and paint them. I had a crew of five people under me. I loved doing that. I love working with my hands, which is why I like theatre, because I could build and design the sets.

So everything was giving me an opportunity. Whether I was in it, or I was directing it, or I was facilitating it, I loved doing theatre. As a director, or as an actor, or just as the artistic director helping people, I loved knowing that I'm beyond the scenes and helping a play go up that really touches people's lives. That was my school of hard knocks. It wasn't until about 1999 or 2000, just prior to me getting more into film and television, that I started at Professional Actor's Studio. I enjoyed Nick (the owner of the Studio), but most of my instructions came from working with the other actors that were there, that became long-term friends with me. What I found was that Nick can only challenge the students so much, but the students had to challenge themselves.

I was always making myself do things that pushed the envelope on what I was doing. It wasn't because I wanted to become a better actor. It's because I was bored if I didn't do it. If I'm going to do a scene, I want to do a scene where I have to be a convincingly gay man. In dealing with subject matter, I want to do a scene where I'm crying about something that people don't cry about. Because I enjoyed it. It was entertaining to me. It's like a big scene I did.

One of the last scenes at the Professional Actor's Studio was called "The Pilot House Scene" from *Jaws*. I hand selected Tom Thon and Vince Pisani. I said, we're all going to do this together, and I'm going to put the script together because it's the scene where Shaw, who played Quinn, and Brody, who was the sheriff and Richard Dreyfus' character, were in the small boat at night in the pilot's cabin. They were showing off their battle wounds.

I did Clint, and the reason I wanted to do Clint was because I added in this kind of strange accent. I had to come in singing and also be a little inebriated but not stone-faced drunk. I did it because it was fun, not because it was developing my talent. Everything for me has been based on me enjoying it. If I went to a seminar, went to a workshop, if I was bored within the first 15 or 20 minutes, whoever was talking, I'd leave.

I love being around people who are challenging. I love casting actors that I love hanging with because it's fun to hang with me. They become good friends to me. I love doing the creative process together. Why? It's fun. I'm self-taught in Meisner Technique now. I was drawn to it because it's fun.

Do you think theatre is one way to keep your instruments sharp, to keep be in touch with yourself and know you have the commitment to do this?

Yes. There are people who are going to argue with that, being on the other side of that, and point out successful actors. I like looking at it this way. If you were to list the top two dozen A-list actors in Atlanta, they're the ones who are usually booked. Every one of them, if it's not theatre, it's performance improv or sketch comedy. And many of the A-list actors are Equity (the Theater Actors Union) as well. Once they book a lot of film and television they can't do much of it.

But when they're not doing film and television, they're doing theatre or they're doing improv shows. Why? Because it's the nature of them, to just perform. And if none of that's happening, they get a video camera and they click record and talk. That's why they're A-list actors. I love Chase Paris, before he left Houghton to become a casting director. He's very successful at that of course. About a year after he was doing casting, I asked, "So what's the big thing? I know you've got a lot of revelations from going, from being a talent agent to casting." And he said the biggest revelation to him is that more than three quarters of the actors that he sees, do this as a hobby, and he feels it. They're not really committed. And then you have these actors that come in the room, and they own the room. They want to be there because they've got an audience. And if you walk into an audition with the intent that "I'm here to book" you're going to live in a different planet all your life. That's always one thing I can guarantee you. When you walk into an audition that's live, or you're being put on tape by somebody, you have an audience, what are you going to give them?

You had periods where you struggled and faced rejection. And you've wondered what am I doing?
When I was struggling, it was not related to acting itself. I was struggling with whether I wanted to put up with the crap of this film and television industry. I was never struggling with the craft of acting. But this business is a pain in the ass.

Can you give some examples here? Some things to be careful about first for new actors, any issues or vices?
If you want to get taught by somebody, the best choice is to make it a current working actor who auditions and books. The reason for that is this industry is changing so rapidly, so quickly, that you've got to have current insight. It's what this person is experiencing. Are there other instructors that you can go to that used to teach, and are still reliable? Sure, but they're usually very expensive and none of them are here.

What you really need is to get with a current instructor whether it's Matt Cornwell, everyone at Drama Inc., Mike Pinewski, Shannon Eubanks, Greg Allen Williams, Vince Pisani, Clayton Landey, Crystal Carson, Steve Coulter, Eric Goins, Rob Pralgo, to name a few. I want to hear from them. I want to know their experiences. I want to know what they dealt with just last week. It makes me feel current with stuff. That's my very first thing.

Find the actors that you can form a relationship with, or attend their Q&As on panels, or attend their workshops. That's the biggest piece of advice to start with.

You can do private coaching with a bunch of them. I find that most of the time I learn more by sitting and listening to them. Not necessarily performing because all I'm going to do is to get a critique from them. But what I love is to glean knowledge and motivation from these people. And most of them I can call a friend.

What do you outside of acting? How do you support yourself?
The only other main thing I do is I teach on-camera. I do that because I love teaching. I love working with students. I love giving the knowledge that I get, to them. And I love seeing them succeed. Or seeing them realize that this isn't what they should be doing. I do occasionally tape people. I don't do it full-time. I may go through weeks and never have anybody to do. And then all of a sudden I'll do 4-5 a week. I mean it's $20 or $25. It's not a lot of money. I do it because I like doing it. I like helping people, giving everybody a chance at this. I love the creative process of being in a taping session, and helping the actors see the script, and see what it can provide to them. But then again, it's a small amount of money and the money I do teaching on-camera supplements my income when I don't book. I can go through long periods without booking.

What do you do for marketing and networking? Do you do any mailings to casting directors?

Once I started in my second season with *Being Mary Jane* (TV Show), I secured a publicist who I pay on an event basis. Christa Scherck has been with me for a year and a half now, and I really like her. She helps me get interviews. She communicates with BET (the TV Network) to let them know what I'm doing. I also have a Twitter account. My Facebook page is just about my acting. I've never done mailings. I've attended workshops. I've attended a couple of events. But I don't really focus on those. The events that I do attend are the ones that my publicist arranged for me to go to. If I do an event, it's usually because I'm being asked to come and speak. There's a level of networking with that. I make sure that my IMDB page is current so that if somebody looks at me they can see what I'm doing currently. And for me, that's more than adequate.

You never felt the need for a personal website?
I've made so many attempts to start a website. Let's talk about it from the point of view of practical and applied. I have people who eat, sleep, and breath, and drink, on websites, which is great. If it works for them, great. But I wanted to look at it from a standpoint of "Okay let's get specifics with how is it going to benefit me?" So I get an audition. Do I get an audition because somebody went to my website and said they want to see me for something? No. If a production company wants to see me, they go to breakdown services. And they want to go to Actors Access and they might cross reference with my IMDB page. I've got my reels on Actors Access. I've got my reels on 800casting. If they want to see my profile, they can go to these sites and they can see. And I've got a resume on IMDB as well. So I've got those three sites that are heavily covering what I do. And I have yet to

ever have somebody say to me "Oh if you had just had a website that repeated everything you had on IMDB, that would've been the lynchpin for me." So I've seen a lot of people go to this great length to do something that they think because it's out there, that Steven Spielberg is going to Google your name. In websites they lie. You can put everything on there that you want. IMDB doesn't. It's linked to the production company. And so the one piece of advice that Chase said to me before he left Houghton: "Mike I want you on Twitter. I want you on Facebook. I want you to get current with your IMDB page." And he said "I want you to take off anything that is on your resume that is not on IMDB, except food commercials." And so now if you look at my resume, my resume is consistent with the three sites I've referred to. And so I have found, for me that works great. I would love to encounter an actor who says, "My career really took off with me starting a website, and so many people were driven to my website that they just wanted to ask me for auditions and booking." Do you see where I'm coming from?

Does this mean I'm not going to do a website? No I'm probably going to do a website, but it's not critical for me. The only reason why I'm probably going to do a website is so that I can also link it to my theatre, and I can have something on there about my classes. So it's like a business card about my classes and how I can help actors. They can go to my website and they can look up a lot of information. I'm going to use more as a site to help people than it is necessarily about promoting me because I'm already being promoted.

What do you see the future of acting being in Atlanta? Do you think casting and producers will start to see this talent pool here being more reliable and maybe even start to offer some series regular roles here?

The talent here is already reliable. The production stuff that we have is already reliable. It's the perception that we aren't reliable as much as they are in LA – that's the problem we're facing. I will say that I agree with them that there's a very good chance that the pool of A-list actors is higher in LA. But the problem is, I have a lot of friends that are there now, and they're telling me that pool is shrinking because they're leaving. I'm so glad that Georgia decided to table the religious freedom law that was passed in Indiana because that would have had a massive impact on our film and television industry. Things like that are what we have to fight because we can lose our tax incentives and it doesn't take much. We've got to make sure that's still in place. It's probably only on two hands and one foot with toes that can I name the actors that are making a pretty decent living doing this here. And it's not because we don't have talent here, it's somebody perceiving that they want to give you the opportunity. It's really that simple. California's broke and scared of us. They're throwing everything they can do to move the industry back. But the fact that is there are so many venues to air stuff on cable networks. The pilot season used to be end of January to end of April. Now in Georgia, pilot season is all year long. Everything's changing. You can drop a pilot in December. The nature of how the business is functioning is changing... and LA is slow to change. Georgia is very slowly whittling away at that perception. Every year that we stay in the game and do more and more work, the better it gets. There is going to come a breaking point where the industry is going to realize we have the talent pool, both as actors and as production. What I say to actors here in Atlanta and production crew: Get training. Be positioned. Do the acting. Stay in the business. Be in here for the long haul.

Luck is when opportunity meets preparations.
Absolutely. Thus you hear the phrase "a lucky break."

So no plans to move to LA?
No. I don't really have a financial motive to go there. I'm here, unless something yanks me. And then, at this point, it's only going to yank me for a period of time.

Do you have agents in the other places?
I have one in New Orleans, and one here in Atlanta - Houghton, representing me for the entire southeast. The only reason they don't represent me for Louisiana is that Louisiana no longer sends work here because they have residency restrictions. The actors in Atlanta don't want to go there for a U5 (Under 5 lines) scene and then have to do a callback, except no hotel and no travel. They're willing to accept that here. I have an agent that represents me in Louisiana, and only in Louisiana. And it's for when there are big projects where I'm in a big role that they want to see me for that I could do at least three days of work on.

You're willing to work there as a local hire in that case?
In that case, because then it's financially equitable for me.

And what about Texas, or LA, or New York?

Those auditions don't come in our way. And if it did, I'd probably do it through Houghton.

Are you SAG?

I joined last December. I believed that with the number of credits that I had now and the work that I'm doing, that I was getting ready to run into an interference issue of perception about why Mike is not in the union. And the union also changed its rules regarding industrial work, which I also like to book and make money at under a provision called an OPO – "One performance only". They now allow me to audition for projects like that. As a matter of fact, I have a job coming up that's non-union and it's an industrial. And the union is allowing me to do it through an OPO. That helped tipp the scale for me to join.

And you get the perception value now, by being SAG?

Yeah, that I'm a professional actor. People perceive me as an actor but I just didn't want, with the number of production companies that are coming from LA, for them to see me and see my resume and not understand why I wasn't SAG yet.

But you don't suggest that for somebody who's new, starting out their careers?

No. I have my three boys who also act and I'm telling them I don't want them to join the union right now even though they're SAG eligible.

What do you wish somebody told you when you started your career or what would you give as advice to somebody starting out at Atlanta?

Sustainability. And what I mean by that is, this is a very hard path that I don't wish upon anybody. Film and TV are filled with rejection. It's filled with very little money. You have to be able to be doing something that you also enjoy, that allows you to sustain yourself financially, that doesn't bring you fear. And if you can find that, I can guarantee you 10 years from now you're still going to be acting. But I hear a number of actors that find jobs that completely inhibit them from doing any acting. Or they do jobs they hate, and don't really pay that much. They're starving in the process. They don't think about being here for the long haul. If you're here for the long haul, you'll get the training. You'll build relationships. You'll be known by the casting directors. 20 years... This is what you're going to do. It's not just financially, but relationships too. Don't put off, if you find somebody who loves you, marrying them. That's part of sustainability because it's really easy to get isolated - To work your job and never be around anyone. Do yourself taping at home and never be seen. And you're cut off. So if you can sustain yourself financially and emotionally, you'll do it. You just need someone to share these experiences with. Now you don't want to deal with somebody who's going to hate you and badger the whole time you're doing it. Somebody who supports you.

Mike Pniewski

Mike Pniewski is a SAG-AFTRA actor based out of Atlanta. More information including demos, credits and link to his IMDB page can be found at http://www.mikepniewski.com.

When did you know that you wanted to be an actor and how did you go about pursuing that?

When I was a senior in High School, I was fortunate enough to get cast as a lead in our Senior musical *Fiddler on the Roof*. It was a huge success and I had a wonderful time but I never thought of it as anything to pursue as a career. I had a scholarship at UCLA to study sports medicine. So that was going to be my path - I was going to do some form of sports medicine which, in the late 70s when I graduated from High School, was a really hot field. But I started having a hard time in school and was doing really bad, got assigned a counselor to try to help me out. Looking at the courses that I would have to take to figure out my four years to get a degree, I discovered that I had to take a lab where I had to dissect human cadavers. I decided that it really probably wasn't for me. That drove me to do a lot of soul searching - about the fact that I was at a great school, which is where I wanted to be, how could I make this work. I wanted to find that thing that I was passionate about studying to take advantage of the opportunity and to help pull myself out of the hole that I had dug for myself. After talking to a lot of people and really digging and searching, what it came back to was that experience of acting in high school. Not only was it fun and successful, but it was profound and the first thing that I'd ever done in my life where I was completely one hundred percent self-motivated. Nobody had to tell me to do anything. In fact, there were days where I was pushing harder in rehearsal or staying longer than anybody else. It's the first thing that actually drove me like that and I felt like it meant something. I gave up my scholarship, which was big and scared my parents to death. I walked out of the training room at the end of my sophomore year and by the end of my junior year, I was on the dean's list. I had pulled myself out and I never looked back, I found my niche.

You are originally from California?

Yes, born and raised in California. I was born in Los Angeles and I grew up down in Southern California.

After UCLA, you stayed in LA looking for work?

Once I graduated, I stayed out there for ten years and started looking for work. When I got out of school, I had to get a job. I was a runner at a modeling agency, a job that probably doesn't exist much anymore. I was doing deliveries and driving little 18-year-old girls around town. It was a great gig then because I was out of the office quite a bit, doing errands and delivering model books and pictures. If I had an audition I could go do it, nobody would ever notice. And if I got a job, I'd just call in sick. I did that job for probably two and a half years before I started working enough where I didn't need the job anymore. What made the difference for me is when I started doing commercials. Because commercial residuals can be really nice. And once you have that residual stream come through, that really made a difference in allowing me not to need that day job.

Has getting an undergraduate degree in theater been worthwhile for your career?
Absolutely. And I qualify this all the time by saying that this is my experience, I understand that there's more than one way to do this. But in my experience, I developed a real, I believe, understanding and appreciation of the fundamentals of basic acting techniques. I still had to study once I got out of school because I had to learn how to get a job. But UCLA really taught me how to act. I also made some great friends there. And was lucky enough to be in that department with people that are now, 30 years later, significant in the industry. Those relationships are priceless, and have been over the years, not just as friends but a lot of those relationships I've been able to turn into work, over the years, which has been nice.

Also the college experience of being in that kind of environment as a student, where you experience different cultures, different points of view, meet friends that are different majors, it gives you a world view which is helpful as an actor. Some actors make the mistake of studying in places that are too solitary and just the acting program without exposing themselves to lots of other things, which eventually feed characters that they play. I enjoyed the social experience, of college, I enjoyed the friends I made, I enjoyed the place and the location and all of that it afforded me through those years. It's made a gigantic difference in what I've been able to do in my career.

Being in Los Angeles probably made a huge difference?
Yes. Los Angeles, where you're right down the street from the industry. We had some industry people take part in the department back then, nowadays there are more people involved than there were back when I was there. We had some showcase events where they would come. But surprisingly, back then in the late 70s, early 80s, there weren't that many. But you were close enough that you still had access to information and knowledge and certain things that were helpful.

Did you take any classes after you graduated?
I took some classes outside of college. I took improv with the Groundlings, which was a great experience. I studied out there for a number of years from a fellow name Brian Reese, who did scene study and cold reading, from a real practical perspective of "how to get a job" point of view. I always tell people, UCLA taught me how to act and Brian told me how to get a job. He's still a great friend to this day but I learned so much from him about how to approach the business, how to brand yourself, how to market yourself, how to go into the room and command attention in a productive and creative way. A lot of working people over the years have studied with him. Clooney's been there. Mike Dorn from *Star Trek*. Jim Hanks, Tom Hanks' brother. Numerous actors who have worked and are very

successful in the business. It was a great place to study and learn how to be a working actor.

What made you move to Atlanta?
I met a southern girl. Going to Atlanta was never a business decision. When I got married, and we'd visit here very often, we saw another way. We decided once we got married that we didn't want to raise kids in LA. We just thought it was best for us. I was also at a point in my career where I was craving something different. It all came together after the earthquake of 1994. It was not a career choice, it was a life choice. It was about my family and their quality of life. And that has worked out fabulously. But with tax incentives now the work's here, which is even better.

One of the things that attracted me to moving here was that there was a pretty good regional business in Georgia. There were two series shooting here - *In The Heat of the Night* and *I'll Fly Away*. Then there were a number of movies of the week and feature films that would come and shoot on location. It was a pretty decent regional market. Not to mention the whole southeast, North Carolina, Florida - there was a good amount of work.

When you moved to Atlanta, were you still focused fully on acting or did you have to look for other ways to support yourself and your family?
I knew moving to Atlanta that I would not necessarily be making the same kind of money or have the same kind of exposure. Soon as I moved to Atlanta, I opened up a place and started

teaching classes. I taught class for probably eight years, the first eight years or so that we were here. An ongoing class was very similar to what I learned from Brian in Los Angeles. And I had one or two and sometimes three classes a week; it was ongoing so I was always teaching. And that combined with the acting work that I did get. My wife still worked, she does hair and makeup, we did OK.

Did you have an agent in LA that you continued to be represented by after you moved to Atlanta?

I did. And a couple of people over time, one was my agent and then she decided to go into casting and then I got somebody else. So yeah I always kept my toes in the water out there. I always tried to spend some time out there when I could.

How did you get your Atlanta agent?

I had already gotten connected with Atlanta Models and Talent agency on a business trip before we moved so I already got them to represent me once I moved.

And you were already SAG?

Oh yeah, I was already SAG and AFTRA at that point.

How do you stay positive and keep your mind in the game?

That's work and it's changed over the years. Its evolved with the times so one of the things you gotta try do with your work is keep it fresh. Your prospective about the work and the business has to stay fresh so it evolves over time. I've always been pretty driven and very motivated. I always keep my ear to the ground about what's going on. I get breakdowns every day, I keep up with certain places where you can find information on what's going on. It's different now. 30 years in the business, it's a little different. I have a little bit of a reputation for myself and I don't have to do that as much as I used to. I have a great family, which keeps everything in perspective for me, and I try to take care of myself, exercise, taking care of the instrument, that kind of thing. Stay busy with productive things whether it's related to the industry or not. The worst thing you can do as an actor is to sit and wait for the email to come or the phone to ring. You gotta keep your mind active and busy. Age and experience makes you more secure. You're never gonna work as much as you want to, that's the nature of the business but I learned it was really only one time that I ever really started to wonder if that was ever going to happen again and I was almost ready to take another job but fortunately changed my mind.

Was that was when you were still in LA?
No, it was when I was here in Atlanta, it had gotten to a point where it was really stressful with money. And I started to think that maybe this isn't really working out. I'm also a first-born, hyper responsible, and I take that responsibility very seriously. I was sick and stressed myself. I had a friend who was in financial services and he turned me on to an opportunity doing presentations to retirees that was potentially very lucrative. But after another round of soul-searching, I realized that if I were to do that, I would really just be doing it for the money. And I don't ever think that's a good reason to ever do a job. Especially if you're gonna make a big career change like I was going to make, I couldn't just do it for the money, I'd be miserable. So that just set me on a path of reinvention and rethinking the way I did the

293

business. I got an agent in New York and opened up more opportunities. It's never gonna be exactly how you want it.

Do you have any specific tips you can give to other actors about how to stay on top of what's happening in the industry, what to do in terms of marketing and networking?

The number one rule is don't isolate yourself. You gotta be out there. Whether it's taking class or going to industry events. Or creating your own work. Whatever, you got to keep yourself out there in the business, spinning in the circle. That's absolutely essential. You don't just sit at home and call yourself an actor. You gotta be out there doing it. One of the cool things about where we are today is that it is so much easier for an actor to showcase themself and build an audience for their work than it was when I started. For little to no money, you can create a product and put it up on the web and have worldwide distribution, start to build an audience for yourself, start to build your brand, hone your craft in a way that will potentially get people's attention and open doors for you.

It's exciting but it does level the playing field, it does mean that anybody can do that so it does make it more competitive. But the fact that the access is so easy and so affordable, there's no excuse whether you have to write it or you find someone else to write it.

The worst thing actors do a lot of times is that they isolate themselves. Whether it's a social thing or actually creative productive thing, you've got to be out there spinning the wheels and creating opportunity. There's no excuse. It's too easy and it's too cheap.

What about attending GPP or other events, is that something that you think has value for actors?
I definitely think it does. It's about building relationships. Until you have a body of work that's speaking for you, you've got to get out and meet people and build relationships. And even if it means you volunteer for a committee, help out at an event, in one of their fundraisers or whatever, just because you'll get to meet a bunch of people in doing that. And you'll probably meet casting directors, agents, whoever, people who could potentially open doors for you.

One of the things actors underestimate about a group like that, is you got a lot of independent filmmakers that are in that, who are making their own stuff. By building those relationships, they might not even hire a casting person. They go by the people that they know and if they meet you, to be a part of that organization, there's an opportunity where at the very least you get some footage that you can use to showcase yourself. If not, some really great work that gets seen and noticed maybe.

What about mailing lists or sending out postcards, do you think those still have value?
I'm not sure about the physical postcards anymore. I don't know to what extent people really read those. I know, in the Southeast, for example, all of the local casting people are on Facebook. And there's no reason why an actor A) Shouldn't be on Facebook and B) Shouldn't be getting connected with the

casting people. Most of them are pretty good about if somebody sends them a friend request as an actor, they usually don't turn them down.

The electronic social media space is probably the place where the actors want to focus their energies now. Most auditions don't even ask for a printed headshot and resume anymore. Everything is primarily electronic. Casting people are used to working in that space, whether they're younger or older, because that's where all the casting and submission process is now, is electronically. I focus on Facebook, Twitter, but Facebook primarily because I know that casting people use that and casting folks from the Southeast are all there.

Everybody's so panicked these days about releasing information ahead of time about certain projects. Don't take pictures of the set and put them on Facebook. Don't take pictures of your dressing room door with the character's name on it.

You've been in the Atlanta industry for 21 years now. There's a lot of talk within Atlanta of Atlanta being this hotspot. Is there a bit of an echo chamber effect going on here or is this something you see as real, that Atlanta is really coming up as a viable production center for the long term and potentially then hiring actors for bigger roles?

\The hiring actors for bigger roles is something that we're gonna need to continue to fight for and hopefully can do it with a unified front with the agents and casting people. For the long-term success in the business, I continue to point to the fact that they are not building new facilities in New York and Los Angeles, that they're pouring concrete on new studios in Atlanta. They don't do that unless they see long-term viability. That's really significant that that's happening here and it indicates that they're confident that the tax incentives are secure, and they're confident that the market can handle it, and they're confident that this place has viability. The long-term prospects – 10-15 years out are very good.

Do you think this separates Atlanta from other markets that were hot in the past, for example, Vancouver, or North Carolina? They built studios there too but then the industry there becomes less hot overtime as other locations offer better incentives.

Right, they've had Screen Gems in Wilmington, which obviously was there for a long time, they built that quite a long time ago, I know that they built a lot of space in Louisiana. That's primarily driven by the fact that their tax incentives are still very viable and even in New Mexico, they've had some pretty significant building. But right now, with all of those places, economically, we're attracting more business than they are. We're the #3 production market in the country. And a lot of that has to do with all of those things that we've been talking about. The talent, the space, the airport, the accessibility. The fact that we have crew here and we have a variety of locations - we have a lot of things going for us. We have tax incentives, which are viable, which have a good long-term structure to them. We have the support of the state government. All things pointing forward are looking good. We just went through a process in SAG-AFTRA interviewing all our local agents about the industry and how we can help each other out. One of the things that we're talking about is the idea of actors getting access to the larger roles. A lot of times agents don't have access to the complete breakdown for the entire project because all they get is the local breakdown, whereas if they got all of it they could possibly see a couple of larger roles, supporting roles, that they could and they would have submitted people in the Southeast for consideration.

What do you wish someone had told you at the beginning of your career?

I'm not one that looks backwards like that. I got a lot of great support and help from a lot of wonderful people including my family. I was always pretty realistic about everything. I knew I wasn't Tom Cruise. And that's fine. I am who I am. And from the very beginning people always told me that the best years are 10-15 years down the road. They were right - I'm a character guy and it's just gonna get better as you get older. I feel like I'm finally growing into my niche. Which has been great, it's just been very good to me.

Omer Mughal

Omer Mughal is represented by Houghton Talent in Atlanta. More information can be found at his IMDB page, http://imdb.me/omermughal, and at his personal website, http://omermughal.com. He also runs an audition taping service: http://www.actorstapingactors.com

When did you decide you wanted to be an actor and was your family supportive?

I had no idea growing up that I wanted to do this specifically, but mid 2009 I made a decision to quit my corporate job and do something meaningful to me. I knew I wanted to do something artistic and creative. I never thought I could pursue this as a career unless you moved out West. But after college, I was working an office job for too long, and was burned out on the job. I went on Craigslist looking for gigs and I was trying to find something that was fun to do that might bring me back to life. I came across a post - Extras needed for a Zombie movie. I said I'm going to do it. A few days later, I got a call to audition. Turns out the movie was *Zombieland*. In hindsight, it wasn't like a normal extra gig. I actually had to audition, not just submit a current photo. They gave me a breakdown of what they were looking for. With no expectations, no training, I gave it a shot.

A couple of days later, I got a phone call saying, "Hey, they want to book you. Are you still available?" Yes! And that was my first opportunity to get on a real film set. I went through two and a half hours of makeup and I worked for one day but I got to see how the business worked. That was my foot in - getting on a professional set. I gained an understanding of how the job worked. The bug bit me, and I decided to start taking classes right away.

Where did you start classes?
I started training at The Company Acting Studio mainly because they are the only nationally recognized acting school in the Southeast. They've been around the longest, they have a full curriculum, and I wanted the full training. I jumped in their level one class and audited a couple other places to learn. I also became a full-time extra. I quit my day job. I did that for about 8 to 10 months. I was just taking classes and I was working on set as much as I could as background. And then, I got a stand-in gig. I got asked to be a PA (Production Assistant), and then I got asked to work as a camera PA. So all these opportunities essentially came from just being on set and trying to work and learn as much as I could. That was my internship. I'm not making a lot of money, but I'm learning how this works, what the expectations are, what people want from you and what's the job. Knowing your job and what the other jobs are, when to do your job and when to get out of the way so other people can do their jobs. Then I got an agent, started auditioning, and here we are.

You knew you weren't happy in your corporate job but what made you think of acting? Have you done any acting at all in school or done anything related to this?

No. In middle school, I did a play and I was in chorus. I took a class in college. But I'm left-handed, I'm artistic and creative. I was looking for a job that was creative. There was a hole in my heart that I couldn't fill with my current job. But you've got to make a living. You have to support yourself somehow. That's why it's tough to live as an actor, especially an untrained one! So I focused on training. I streamlined my expenses. I moved in with my sister and her husband. I was basically living rent-free for two years, and that allowed me to stay in class full time, learn as much as I can. Not having that burden of paying rent was a huge thing for me. I could focus on training without totally struggling, even though I was still waiting tables. And I still had to do that in between gigs for a few years, a couple nights a week, to supplement my income.

Your family overall has been supportive in this?

Oh yeah. I could not have done this without them. I think a lot of people don't really understand how it works. It's not the normal 9-5 job. But overall, yeah, my parents were cool with it. My parents were strict growing up - you need a normal regular job and blah blah blah, I did get a little bit of that. At the same time, I was trying to figure out who I am. I was doing whatever I was doing previously just to make other people happy. But you have to make yourself happy first before you can do that for other people. My sister obviously was supportive, letting me live with them when I was in a bind and I needed money. I couldn't have stayed in class without them. I was always independent. I paid my way through college. So for me, it's hard to ask because it's just not something I do - borrow money for whatever reason.

What else do you do outside of acting right now?
I like working out, playing golf, eating, watching movies, and hanging out with friends and family. I am always up to try something new and fun.

What about staying positive? How do you handle rejection or the stress in trying to be in this business?
When dealing with constant rejection, you have to change the way you look at it. A lot of people approach the whole process of auditioning the wrong way. If you've worked in sales, that's kind of the way that I approach it. I know it's a numbers game, and if I go on 25 auditions I'll probably book 1 out of 25, if I keep doing good, consistently better, work. You have to have a life outside of acting. This will allow you to do better work. Yoga or a good workout does it for me. Find something you enjoy and are good at. This will build confidence and keep you grounded as well. It's a numbers game. I know that I'm probably not going to get this, but it's one step closer to the one I will get. You do your homework and put in your best effort every time. And if you just go in there and not approach it as an audition, but approach it like you're going to set to shoot, you need to be ready to shoot, right now.

That's what they want to see. And that's the level of professionalism that they expect. One of my friends will treat himself after every audition. He'll buy a milkshake or beer, and that keeps him in a positive mind state. And there's always another audition coming. It's not the end of the world if you don't book this one.

What do you think is most important in terms of marketing?
Actors Access, Casting Networks and other actor sites. They are your marketing materials. That's how casting directors find you. If you already have an agent, that's how they're seeing you. So

stay on top of it. Make sure your headshots and resume are current. I try to go in every month and tweak. Every time you book a job, go in and update. You have to keep that stuff current. I think Facebook and Twitter are great places to market. Social media is great for all that stuff right now. And even doing YouTube videos. People watch that stuff. If you ever shoot a short or skit, post it to your YouTube page. Share the link on social media.

You mean just create your own work and put it out there?
Absolutely. Anything you can do. There are so many people that are doing little videos on YouTube and they've been approached to do their own show. Most of them are just doing it for fun. You have to take action essentially. You can't just wait around for things to happen.

What do you see the future of acting being in Atlanta? Do you think the opportunity for bigger roles and leading roles are going to eventually come to Atlanta?
Absolutely. I don't see how it cannot. More and more productions are shooting here. There are big studios in the works right now. And they're not small time things. They're big deals like Pinewood that make the James Bond and Harry Potter franchise. I'm getting opportunities to read for bigger things every year I do this. And I'm assuming that it's just going to continue to happen. It's just the way the market is going. It's young and new. We, as talent here, have to step up our game. It's no longer I'm an actor on the side. It's a full-time gig and there are people that are working full-time, booking work all the time. It's because they've been in the market for 20 something years. They're trustworthy, and have proven themselves. They can do the job. They can handle the work.

Are you planning any move right now out of Atlanta?

I don't have any desire to move to LA or New York. I'm getting really great opportunities here. If I move, I will have to start over from square one. There's still that stigma of Atlanta not being up to par with LA or New York but that's not true. It's just a bad generalization. One bad apple spoils the bunch. But now that wall is crumbling because people are doing the work. People are getting bigger opportunities, they're meeting expectations. They're doing what they're trained to do.

Do you have representation outside Atlanta?
I don't at the moment.

What would you give as advice to somebody starting on a career in Atlanta?
Take your training seriously. A lot of people think they can just wing it, because anyone technically can get in. But you're not going to get the bigger jobs just winging it. I say get in class and learn the craft until you have a solid foundation of technique. And then you can continue to grow but you must get your basics right. The biggest mistake people make is just waiting for an audition. They're not reading anything in between. They're not working on anything in between. It's your job to read. Pick up a newspaper, book, script, anything. You have to find a way to practice and get in the acting gym, work out those muscles.

What about investing in marketing material or not being willing to?
Some people overdo it. You must have patience and moderation. Don't blast everyone everyday with your marketing stuff. Eventually you'll just turn people off if you do that. For example, I have an actor friend who sends out a monthly or bi-monthly email. It's not that often that I'm annoyed about it, and I want to read it because it's an update about her. It's not always about acting. But if she is sending that kind of email out

every day or every other day or weekly even, it would be annoying. Once you start getting too much of that, then I start deleting it without even looking at it. I don't even care what it is. Some people have a tendency to blast things on Facebook. I don't know if that's a mistake or not. There's no rule to this game. Everyone takes a different path. Find your path, and have fun along the way. That's what matters most.

Parisa Johnston

Parisa Johnston is represented by Houghton Talent.

Where you are from originally?
I am originally from Iran. I lived there until I was about 11 and my family moved after the revolution. I've had my home in many countries. I've lived in England, the UAE, the US, Thailand, Australia, New Zealand... And you'll find that quite common with people from Iran around my age because so many traveled around the world trying to find a new home.

When did you get into acting, or when did you want to become an actress?
I've always performed ever since I could remember. I was always singing and dancing and putting on shows whether it was in front of my family members or schools. So there was no real moment that I can think of where I decided 'This is what I wanted to do'. I just know I always loved it. It's just always been there. I was in England when it occurred to me that it was an option that it was something I could actually pursue. I was about

11-years-old and my school there offered drama classes so I took them and did some shows and competitions - little skits and little sections of plays.

Did you come to Atlanta while you were still in school or did you move here after? Your accent is almost negligible!
I came to Atlanta after I had graduated high school. I was taught the Queen's English when I first started learning English. When I was very young, my dad felt it was extremely important, so way before we even left Iran, I was taught to speak English. And I've spoken English pretty much all my life. The accent you hear is a mixture of British English and American, and goodness knows what else.

Your IMBD profile does not cleary state your ethnicity. Is that an advantage - to be ethnically ambiguous?
Yes. That's one of the advantages and that's really one of the things I think helped me with even getting an agent.

Iran seems to have a pretty vibrant film industry. Did you or does anybody in your family have any connections to the industry back in Iran?
We weren't in the industry directly, but Iranian culture is very much into the arts. My family was no exception. There's never a gathering when someone isn't singing, dancing, making a speech, or telling a story. There's always an aspect of performance or entertainment to our lives. Funny enough, I have an aunt who's married to a man who was the nephew of one of the most famous actors at the time in Iran, but that's about it. There's no other connection.

Do you speak Farsi?
Yes, I speak Farsi and a little bit of Arabic, French, Thai.

your look and ability to speak multiple languages, that's a great combo.

It has been an advantage but it is by accident. It wasn't something I actually pursued. It's just what happened in life.

Once you decided you wanted to pursue acting full-time, did you start taking classes in Atlanta?

When I finally said I'm going to do this, I took a class with the Alliance Theatre in Atlanta. From there, I've done some workshops with Ted Brunetti, Chez Studios, Sam Christensen, which led me to other venues and my current ongoing coach Vince Pisani from Houghton.

How did you end up at Houghton Talent?

I did a bit with the community theater up north in Dahlonega. With that and a couple of indie films on my resume, plus the workshops and classes at Alliance, I started submitting to every agency. I'd do it every two or three months. It didn't take very long that I got a new talent invite to audition from Houghton. They offered me representation at the beginning of 2010. They've been very kind. I did audition, I didn't just walk in, but being ethnically ambiguous also helped.

Were you working at a day job all at this time? How have you been supporting yourself since?

Yes, this was expected of me, right? This was "the right thing to do". I went to college, got a degree in computer programming and became a lifelong corporate employee. I have a regular day job and that's how I support my family. I work for a corporation. What's interesting is when I decided to pursue this dream of mine, my day job had reached a stage where I could work from home. I have quite a bit of vacation from my years of working and my years of service and flex hours. So all of those things allow me to keep my job, be fully committed to my job but also be fully committed to my passion, which is my acting career. And it affects so many things. It even affects how you approach an audition. Because, and I've learned this over time, if that audition means you're going to pay the electric bill, there's a whole different approach to it than if it's 'I just want to deliver my best and hopefully get the role'. Then I can focus on doing my best and providing my best performance.

What do you do in terms of marketing and networking?
It's one of those areas I probably need to improve on, but my networking is primarily, maybe even all, social media. I'm on Facebook quite a bit. I don't really have a website; I don't know that I'm quite there yet as an actor. I try to be on Twitter. I do post if I have upcoming roles that are gonna be showing on TV or film. Even though I feel like I should do more, it's surprisingly effective. I've had people in the industry reach out and say 'Hey I heard about you' or 'I saw your post' or 'I saw somebody talk about this and I'm doing this project. Would you be interested?' So in a way, yes, I'm surprised that it does work and I'm sure I could be a lot more effective if I was doing it more and in a structured way. There's definitely a balance though. You have to be very cautious.

What do you do in terms of staying aware of what productions are coming into town? Any specific newsletters or websites that you read?
I get the Back Stage Daily online newsletter so I see the goings on and the articles they have. I also have a couple of groups that I'm a member of on Facebook. My acting friends and contacts and Georgia Film and TV group. They post a lot of the latest articles and the latest news about the industry, especially as they relate to GA. As far as productions in town, it's basically what I read online. But truly what I audition for, I rely heavily on Houghton.

309

Are you going to stay in Atlanta to continue to pursue acting?
Yes, I intend to stay in Atlanta. I actually see Atlanta's future to
be very bright. Under one condition - if our lawmakers don't
make the same mistakes that some of the other states are
making - ending the tax incentives. Bottom line is it's a business.
For as long as we keep the incentives, the productions will
come. The GA market is growing by leaps and bounds. I
compare it to a gold mine. There's an existing, established,
much older gold mine in LA and one in New York. And everyone
in the world has heard about these gold mines and everyone
goes there wanting a piece of the gold. We just hit a new gold
mine in Georgia. Why would we want to be where people have
been digging for a long time? We have new ground to cover
here, where resources are limited and they need actors.

What do we Atlanta actors need to do to step up our game?
We've gone from barely getting auditions for one liners to
getting auditions for, guest star, recurring roles, some even
leads and series regulars. Not as often, but we definitely get
them, especially during pilot season. A couple years ago that
was unheard of. We need to stay consistent and do our due
diligence. Make sure we're doing the work and doing it properly.
Continue training and studying. We still have to pay our dues
and prove ourselves but as we do, as we prove we can be
trusted with the bigger roles, they will come. It's happening,
there's no question about it. Also, I have yet to be on set of any
production where I didn't learn something from just watching
the other actors, especially the LA actors. We talk about them
coming in and getting the bigger roles, but they really know
what they're doing and have the experience. We can watch and
learn from them.

Has your ethnicity ever been a limiting factor in any way?

When I started, the ethnic roles were limited to Hispanic, African American, and Asian. Ethnic meant those things and they didn't know what to do with Middle Easterners or Indians. Then for a while, it seemed for Middle Easterners, the only roles available were the terrorists. Every show had hostages and terrorists blowing something up and those were the roles Middle Easterners got. But in the past two years, there has been a significant change. For example, if you watch TV, there's a lot more variety of ethnicity in the shows, especially powerful ethnic women, which I love, of course. Even that is changing. I don't really see it as a limiting factor.

Do you have representation outside of Atlanta?
No, I don't. I have to evaluate that and see where and at what point would it be a good idea to start expanding. It goes back to being a professional. I want to make sure that if someone calls and says 'I need you to be in an in-person audition in the morning at 8 o'clock', that I have the means to do that without jeopardizing my day job.

How do you handle rejection in this career?
There are several things about it. One is, as difficult as it is, I learned very early to detach from the decision of whether I got the role or not. I do my best at the audition and then let it go. The other thing is that I know this is my thing. That this is where I'm meant to be, this is what I'm meant to be doing. So each rejection or lack of booking is just a step closer to the next opportunity. But the most important thing is to make sure that it's not the center of your universe. So balance in life is extremely important. Acting cannot be everything that you live and breathe and think about and do 24/7 of every moment of every day. You've gotta have something else. It might be family, exercise, or a hobby, something that sustains you so that your

entire existence is not your passion because otherwise it is very difficult to stay positive.

If you were to start your career over, would you do anything differently at all?

I have a motto, I don't believe in regrets but I believe in 'lessons learned'. If I could do it over again, I would have still gone down the path of getting myself self-sufficient, finding a secure job that pays my bills, but I probably would have started pursuing my passion a lot earlier and in parallel. But even then there's a reason why things happened the way they did. You make the best of it because you find it was for the best after all. I am convinced I started this exactly when I was meant to in order to truly make my dream a reality.

Ravi Naidu

Ravi Naidu is bicoastal actor with extensive film and TV credits. He currently resides in Los Angeles and also runs an audition taping service: http://www.lcaudition.com. More information about him can be found at his IMDB page, http://imdb.me/ravinaidu, and at his personal website, http://brownactor.com.

You've had a corporate career at a Fortune 500 company. How did you go from there to becoming an actor?

I was attending a show at Sketchworks. I was married at the time, and my wife decided that she wanted to become an actor. She had signed with Houghton. When we went to Sketchworks, some of the Houghton people were there, we started talking, and that planted the whole seed in my brain. The more I thought about it, I felt I should take some acting classes. I started at YourAct Studio and I really liked it. That, combined with the fact that I wasn't really that into my corporate job, got me thinking about doing it more. Nothing against my corporate job. It paid great and I worked with some great people, but I just didn't find the work that interesting.

I kept taking classes and I really enjoyed it. I was lucky enough to get signed on by Houghton, which is a great agency. They started having me come in for auditions and things just kept going from there.

Did you approach any other agencies?

I didn't approach anybody else, except for Houghton. And I like everybody at Houghton. They're super nice. I would go to auditions but I had no idea what I was doing. I still remember some of those auditions and I didn't realize it at that time, but now I realize how horrific they were. They were just God-awful. I hope the tapes have been destroyed. Terrible, terrible stuff. But I was enjoying it! When I first started, I didn't fall in love with acting. I fell in love with the idea that I could actually make a living as an actor. I fell in love with the fruits of being a successful actor even though I wasn't a successful actor. I fell in love with something I didn't have. And it's only since I moved out here that I've fallen in love with the work, and everything that goes into it. I'm not concerned about the fruits of what you get when you become a "successful" actor, because I feel like I'm successful already, because I'm getting to do this. I'm able to survive. I'm getting to do my own stuff, and I'm getting auditions.

But back to Atlanta. I was still working full-time, and that was really where more of my focus was because that's where all the money was coming from. And then, in 2010, I went to a 90-day silent meditation program over the summer. I had a lot of time to reflect, and I decided I didn't want to spend the rest of my working years doing a job that I was only doing for this thing called retirement. I wanted to choose the job that I will enjoy doing until the day I die, because I never want to retire. It just didn't make sense to me to keep the job, that the only reason I was doing it was to get to this point where I could quit doing it and then do other things with my time that I would really enjoy.

I decided to go for it 100%. When I got out of the meditation program, I met with Houghton and I told them I was seriously committed. I started taking three classes a week. I studied with Michael Cole, Vince Pisani, Dave Pillegi, and took improv with Brian Chapman and Matt Cornwell. I'm lucky in that I found the best in Atlanta. Houghton was great about recognizing that I was working really hard, and they were getting me out more consistently. Month over month, year over year, they would get me out more. And I thought, I've got to figure out a way to make this thing real, because I don't want it to be a hobby anymore. To appease my parents when I first got started, so that they wouldn't freak out everyday, I would tell them it's just a hobby. But I knew it wasn't.

What about at your job? Did they know you were doing this? Was your schedule already flexible in a way, or was it not as demanding already so you could do this?
It was very demanding, but it was flexible enough where I could do it because I was lucky in that I could work at home quite a bit. And then I only had to travel a limited amount for work. So a lot of the time, I was able to work from anywhere as long as I

had a good cell connection for conference calls, a good Internet connection to be able to log in. Both of the jobs that I had when I was an actor were great and flexible. Only a few people knew that I was doing it as a hobby. They would maybe see a show that I was in, like when *Homeland* came out in 2011.

And then 2012 and 2013, I booked some more things, and people would see me a little bit more. But everybody was very good about it because I got my job done. I had to work whenever I could work. I worked on set sometimes. I took my laptop and would request a PA to give me the wi-fi access. In between takes, I would be working on my computer or talking to a client...it was very stressful!

So it is possible to find a job that, if you can get flexible work hours and telecommute options, can work?
I feel very lucky that I was able to do that. If you can do that, or start an Internet-based business, or do anything that you can do that you can take with you wherever you go, and work during off hours.

Now in LA, you're not doing this. You don't have a corporate job of any kind?
No, I run an audition taping service for actors, called Lights. Camera. Audition! This was something I started in Atlanta and I truly enjoy it!

Do you do anything else outside acting? For emotional support, or just to get away from it, to recharge?

I'm sleeping, eating, breathing it at the moment. Because if I'm not prepping for an audition or prepping for a class, I read a lot. Growing up, I never had a really strong tendency to read, but now I enjoy reading more so I do read quite a bit. Granted a lot of the things that I read are industry related, so I think that one thing that I want to do is just to get into reading some fiction stuff that I'm interested in. And then, the other things that I do to relax is, strangely, exercise. Somehow that relaxes me a little bit because I'm not in front of the computer. When I'm exercising, I'm listening to podcasts that have to do with the industry. I'm really consuming mass quantities of knowledge, all the time right now. And it doesn't feel overwhelming because it's all very interesting to me. The other thing that I do that relaxes me a lot is watching TV and movies. Growing up, I watched tons of TV. Definitely made me a weak reader, but made me a lover of television.

If I'm stressed out or feeling overwhelmed, I plunk down on the couch, and turn on *House of Cards, Workaholics, Big Bang Theory*, a number of the shows. And now shows that are coming back are deep and good and varied. It helps me unplug from everything, just kind of lose myself in the show, whether it's dramatic or comedic. I desperately want to start taking music lessons as an outlet, and flying lessons. I ride my bike and go for walks. I go for hikes, but in all honesty, I'm all consumed by the industry right now.

What did you do for marketing when you were in Atlanta?
I was very weak in social media in Atlanta. I just did postcards. Atlanta, in hindsight, was much easier. It's a smaller market of

casting directors and industry folks. By smaller, I don't mean less significant...Atlanta and the Southeast is a rapidly maturing market. If I were at the level of pro-activeness that I am now in Atlanta, I would have known a ton of more producers, a bunch more directors. I would have done a lot more indie stuff. But that's just "would-a should-a could-a". I was working a full-time job, I was taking classes. I was doing things that I think I knew I could do. I just did postcards and the occasional casting director workshops. Shay (Shay Griffin, a casting director in Atlanta) is really great about that. She would always offer a lot of things for actors, to bring in casting directors like Alpha Tyler. Michael Cole is the same thing. He would bring in industry people as well.

And then sometimes casting directors from New Orleans would come to Atlanta and do workshops like that. Anytime I'd book something, I would make a concerted effort, and still do, to really make sure I foster and grow the relationship that I have, that I created now with that casting director. I feel like I've developed some good relationships with the casting directors in Atlanta. Of course, they all know that I'm not there anymore, so my opportunities and chances in Atlanta are quite limited compared to what they used to be.

What would you tell somebody who's a starting actor in Atlanta in terms of marketing or getting training?
Number 1, it's really important to know what their strengths and weaknesses are from an on-camera perspective. Meaning, if they're traditionally a theatre actor, then they should focus on on-camera training, and get with those top actors in Atlanta

who are also teaching. Michael Cole, Vince Pisani, Matthew Cornwell, Dave Pileggi and such. The people that are actively working and booking work, people who are building really strong resumes who're probably going to become the Atlanta A-listers. They probably are already the Atlanta A-listers, Michael Beasley, for example. Learn from those people, big time.

As far as marketing goes, a website is a very good idea. Having a domain with your own name, the simpler you keep it, the better. I did www.brownactor.com cause it happened to be available and it made me chuckle. I've stuck with it so far. But otherwise it was just going to be RaviNaiduProductions.com or something. Definitely start making a social media presence and learn what it means to be a professional in this industry. Because of my background in working in corporate America and having an Industrial Engineering degree, I didn't have to learn how to be a professional. I walk in the room and I'm already clearly a professional. I like operating that way. If somebody thinks that I'm not a good actor, I'll improve on that. That's something that over time, I'll improve on. But I've had way too much time to be a good professional, to ever get knocked down for being unprofessional.

The other thing I would say to anybody new is to be really honest with yourself. People told me, but I ignored them when they said this. They told me to be really honest with myself about why I'm doing this. So many people have said and continue to say if there is anything else that you would rather do, that you would also enjoy doing besides acting, do that. Because this is a really, really hard business. And I say it a little

319

bit differently. I don't want anybody to ever feel discouraged for going for something that they want.

But I think it's really good advice in that if your love is not of the work but it is for the fruits of the success that you perceive to exist once you become a successful actor, then I think you're going to have a very difficult time enjoying life. I think you're going to have a very difficult road ahead of you because there's absolutely no guarantee that you, no matter how hard you work and how good of an actor you are, will enjoy those fruits, that you will ever get those fruits. There is no guarantee.

Corporate America, 9 out of 10 times, you work really hard and you're really smart and you really bust your ass, you're going to climb the ladder. In the corporate world, people are going to pull you up that ladder if you helped make their jobs a hell of a lot easier. That's not the way in show business. It's been a journey for me to get to a point where I had to be honest with myself even though I said I'm in this because I love the work. I want to be an actor. It wasn't true, I was lying to myself and everybody. I was in love with what it meant to be a successful actor. I was in love with the fruits of that success.

Now, because I've been training with the people I've been training with, and I've been seeing the actors that I've been seeing, and getting exposed to so much, in such a compressed time, I've had a big shift. I genuinely like the work now. So I'm not merely as married or attached to the success side of acting as I am to the acting itself. Every individual scene, what am I doing, how do I feel when I get to the scene, how do I feel in that scene, do I feel authentic, am I being real? Am I putting on a show? Can I tell I'm being fake? Is this really good work? Am I doing good work?

If you are not honest with yourself, you are going to go through a period of time where you are confused as to why you hate your life. You're not enjoying your work. All of those things, you'll go through all of those things, unless you happen to be the 1 in 10 million that breaks into it and becomes a brash success. It happens but that's so rare.

And the other thing I would say is, if somebody told me – I don't think I have to really enjoy the work when starting in this career. I think it's perfectly fine for me to be getting into this because I want to be a multimillionaire actor with homes all over the world and private jets and things. I would say well, you know what? The first time that you actually do a scene that moves you, you may change your mind because that's a very significant moment in an actor's life. When you're in a scene and you, at the end of the scene, you have actually been moved by your own work, you know you've done great work. Not that you booked a gig. Not that you got on a show. But you did great work. It felt incredible. There's nothing like that feeling. That's why people fall in love with the work. It's too good. When you get the good stuff, it's too good. You can't not fall in love with it, but the business is so hard that you can fall out of love with it.

Is it possible to be in this consumed and driven in Atlanta? Or is it just because of being in LA where the opportunities and exposure are so much more, that you can be at that intensity

there? Can actors be at that level of intensity in Atlanta too?
They can do it anywhere. Absolutely. Atlanta has enormous opportunities for people to really just throw themselves into it. For me, it was difficult because I was overwhelmed and stressed out all the time. Getting into the business as a new actor was very difficult so it was like two full-time jobs. Also, I wasn't in love with acting yet. So I didn't love my day job or acting at the time. I kept doing the day job because the money was sweet and provided a great lifestyle. One of the reasons why I got into acting was, yes, I enjoyed the classes, but they were just introductory acting classes. It was doing something different from what I have been doing for several years out of college. It was nice to activate other areas of my brain that I hadn't really used a whole lot that way. It was a total novelty to be into it. But then, when I thought I want this to be my career, it wasn't because I was in love with the work (the acting). It was more because I could make a lot more money doing this. I wouldn't have to work in corporate America anymore. It was falling in love with the idea that I could not work in corporate America and have an even better lifestyle. So that's why it was really hard for me when I was there. Coming out here to LA, you're jumping into the deep end. And I quit my job so I had no choice but to really either check in or check out. I couldn't just keep doggy paddling my way into the pool, I had to get in and swim in the deep waters!

How can somebody jump into the deep end here in Atlanta?
Go see shows. Definitely take classes. Watch a ton of content. Read. Subscribe to things like The Wrap or Hollywood Reporter. Start reading the trades. Start reading up on the industry. Start

consuming like it's your job. Like you have a final exam on it at the end of every week. Consume, consume, learn as much as you can. Write your own stuff. Produce your own stuff. In Atlanta, you've got golden opportunities to do that because you've got so many people who would work for free there, because everybody is coming up. Everybody is trying to build a resume. It's tougher out here because getting crew for free is very tough. It's possible but I think it's easier in Atlanta, but Atlanta's becoming tougher too because crew people are constantly working in Atlanta too now. There's so much, there's legitimately no better place to be for film than Georgia, than the Southeast, for films. As crew. From a career standpoint. Those guys are constantly working.

What do you see as the future of Atlanta, having now seen it from the perspective of somebody being in LA, talking to people in LA? Are we living in an echo chamber here or it really is something that's perceived, even in LA, as a viable place to pursue acting? And second part, would you consider moving back to Atlanta?

Yes and yes. And no, Atlanta or Georgia is not, in my opinion, just an echo chamber. It's a legitimate secondary market now, and in 10 years' time, Atlanta will be a legitimate juggernaut in the industry. They'll be a globally known juggernaut in the industry. Atlanta and Georgia have been far more aggressive than the other states as far as putting in the infrastructure necessary to make that happen. Georgia, with the help of people like Shay and Ric Reitz and Wilbur Fitzgerald, and a lot of other very strong people, have lobbied heavily to make that happen. They've established the foundation that's getting stronger and stronger every month in Atlanta. As more cast and crew come out to Georgia, they fall in love with the place because it's beautiful. We get rain. Very minimal snow. The air quality isn't that bad. We also have a great airport. Hell, MARTA actually goes to the airport. So I think that there are some producers and folks who legitimately like Atlanta as maybe a possible home. That will cause a huge shift. For me, I would move back to Atlanta in a heartbeat if I booked the work that would mandate it. I wouldn't think twice about it because my mom is there. I miss Atlanta a lot. I was born and raised there. I lived there my whole life. It's work driven though. But am I considering moving back because things are so hard here? No definitely not. I'm going to make it and be brought back to Atlanta because I book the type of role that requires me to be there or the other option is it just doesn't work out here and I have to move back strictly for financial reasons. But I don't think that's going to happen.

I came to LA very quickly once I made the decision but a lot of the things that I have put in place before I came out here made that quick move possible. It was a calculated risk. I told myself at the beginning of 2013, if I booked a certain amount of work, I would have to seriously consider moving out here if I wanted to be a full-time working actor doing nothing but this business. It was only once I made that decision that the writing and the producing side came in and I realized I can do more than just be in front of the camera. My career goal now is to make all of my money either in front of or behind the camera. Some of the actors got in by producing. Eventually I'll also start directing. The other thing I'm interested in is editing. I want to because I think that a director who has an eye for editing makes for a better director. A director that is an actor and who also has an eye for editing. I don't know that I'll ever be a DP. I definitely will dabble more with editing.

If you were to ever come back to Atlanta because you were finding the amount and quality of work in Atlanta, do you think having been in LA would also bring a certain brand cache with it?

It used to more than it has now. The stereotype of LA actors coming back east is that you couldn't make it in LA so you come back here, which is not a good badge to wear at all. Now the one that I want, is the one that should be happening, is when I come back, for example, in April, for five days, to have writer-producer sessions for *Brown Town*. I'm booking in with my agent in Atlanta and hope that they'll get me some auditions. My hope is that the work that I have had out here will be very evident in the audition. I'll make that impression with whatever casting directors I get in front of there. It's just not he's been in LA for over a year and automatically should be accepted. No. It should be because I've been putting in a lot of work with my time. They can see how much stronger I am as an actor.

So I don't know, I feel like when I was living in Atlanta first, the impression that I had was oh no there's all these LA actors coming back to Georgia, coming back to get work. But then to be quite frank with you, when I would work with them and see them in classes and tape their auditions, I would say that 70% of them were not strong, were certainly not stronger than me.

In LA?
The ones in LA that came back to Atlanta. The ones that move
back because there's so much work here. And then when you
dig a little deeper you realize well the reason that they're back's
because they couldn't get an agent out here, or they couldn't
book any work out here. And financially they were getting
frightened and concerned and they felt like they had to come
back because they thought that their chance of booking were
better in Atlanta. There were a couple of actors from LA that
moved back to Atlanta where I got to tape them, because I ran a
taping service in Atlanta too. And in their case, I was like wow,
you are a very, very good actor. You are clearly a professional
working actor. Oh, oh you're from LA oh gosh, okay. And then
you look him up and you see their IMDB page and you realize oh
these people have a legitimate resume.

Yeah so there's that. In general I would say for Atlanta folks you
know, yes it's harder to be in the market a little bit, yes it's
making competition a little bit harder but you know what, if you
live in Atlanta and you've been in front of all the casting
directors there, I think you still have an advantage, a huge leg up
over the LA actors moving back because the casting directors
know you and like you and that is gold.

That is important, yeah.
Yeah, if you have Shay Griffin, Kris Redding, Chase Paris, Jackie
Birch (all casting directors) and Big Picture Casting, all fans of
your work, and they're bringing you in, then you are getting a
subtle preference over folks that they don't know regardless of

whether they're coming from London, New York or LA, or wherever.

From your perspective as a minority actor, is there enough work in Atlanta you think, that minority actors can jump into this 100% or is this something that still requires moving to New York or LA?
You mean to be a full time actor and not have another job to support yourself?

Right. Is it possible for minority actors to do that in Atlanta?
Yes, I think in many ways it's easier for a minority actor in the emerging market, especially in Atlanta to do that. I think so.

Meaning I think that as a minority actor in Atlanta, you have a distinctive advantage over non-minorities, if you're working hard and you're good. If you stink then you're going to make a strong impression that way. And if you stink a couple of times it's going to be tough for casting directors to trust you.

But if they see that you're curious and you're working, and you're improving, I think that you have an easier time getting opportunities in Atlanta. I definitely believe that. Now, the other part is I think that there are so many production companies now in Atlanta, there are so many studios going up. It seems like there would be ample work opportunities if somebody wanted to just be in the industry and doing nothing else.

So if you got into the production side of things, perhaps, that's a guess on my part, I would say that you're going to be able to support yourself for a pretty decent amount of time. Now the other nice thing is that they are casting larger roles in Atlanta, it's improving.

You have shows like Being Mary Jane and others that are casting some big series regular roles from Atlanta. It's getting better but I would say that it's going to take some time. I don't know how long but it's going to take some time for the mentality of production to shift to treating Atlanta actors the same way that they treat LA actors meaning, you know, a lot of people in Atlanta have heard of stories of various actors who've booked very prominent roles in TV shows, in Atlanta, and had to make some pretty severe concessions in order to get that job. From a pay standpoint, from a credit standpoint, and things like that. I think it's changing but that's still there. And that's because producers can get away with it. It's strictly a business decision, not anything against the quality of actors.

That's interesting. I would have thought, you would have said LA by far has still way more audition opportunities for minority roles than Atlanta.
Well, maybe that's true. I think I'm starting to tap into that now but it hasn't been a year yet that I've been with my theatrical agency, and it's only been this year that I felt like the number of auditions started opening up to me. So last year, you know, I didn't get my agents in place. I didn't get my team in place until this time last year. It's been a year, and so it took quite a while for me to start getting auditions. And I was shocked by that because I got so used to how easy it was to have auditions in Atlanta.

Now I think if we have the same conversation next year, I will probably tell you that, I better be telling you that yes there's way, way more audition opportunities here. Yeah. I think the other thing that you have out here that you don't have in Atlanta is that I feel like there are more opportunities to get involved in other projects that other people are doing. Although they might not be paying and probably aren't paying. They are opportunities to meet people who are in the industry and to work with people who are actively doing stuff. So there is most definitely way more of that going on out here than it is in Atlanta. For one Becky and Barry in Atlanta (which I love, by the way!), there are a hundred of those out here. I see breakdowns for web series on a daily basis.

It is overwhelming. From my own experience, my opportunities were much more abundant in Atlanta than it was in my first year here. Now by the end of this year that should be different.

Right. You said too that you felt like you'd pressed the reset button when you moved there?
Yes, which I didn't know. That's something that I would tell anybody when they're coming out here. If you don't already have agents lined up before you get here, be prepared for a lag. If you don't already know casting directors out here before you get out here, be prepared for lag because they have to see submissions from you, they have to see your face come across several times before they take a call from the agent and actually bring you in.

How do you handle rejection? Have you ever felt after you embarked on this - I don't know what the hell I'm doing?

Last year that happened a lot. Maybe from reading all of the stuff I've been reading, and from people I've been talking to, something's happened within myself to the point where I don't ever look at it as being rejected anymore. The reason is because I only look at it as whether I feel like I did the best job that I can do or not, if we're talking specifically about auditions, even in classes. And now there are a lot of times when I don't do the best job that I think I can do. Maybe it's because I didn't prepare as much as I should have or because I got really nervous. When I used to think of it as rejection, it was because I felt a certain sense of entitlement that I should be getting this job. I don't have that anymore because I don't care as much about getting an individual job, at least 80% of the time. 20% of the time you just get an audition for a show that you feel like you really want to be on, or a role that you want. The other 80% of the time it's an opportunity to make a good impression with very important business contacts and so when I don't book those jobs, I don't feel like I've been rejected from that job. I only look at it as did I do the best job that I could? If not, what do I need to improve, what adjustments do I need to make because I know I'm going to get another chance.

Sometimes you get pinned for a show and then dropped. It happens to every actor at some point. For me, it was a great role on an ABC Family show last year. And out here when they pin you, it's basically an avail check. They're saying they like you. It's between you and another person. Or two other people. You've gone to producers but they need you to block out something. I was on avail. There are two things that happened that felt like rejection to me. I was on avail for the show and the day before I was supposed to go for the table read, they called to say they went with the other guy. And that happened for me with *Being Mary Jane* in Atlanta as well.

Those things felt like rejection because I know I did a great job, I booked the job. And then they said we'd rather go with somebody else. So that hurts. Those are painful but then again, it's still good now because I did do well enough. I made a great impression with my casting director because they know that I was one of two choices out of the 750 that submitted. Last year I shot the *Mindy Project,* my first TV sitcom, a great show. And I was really happy about that. It was a great role and I was in a couple of scenes but all my dialogue got cut out at the end of the day. I had a really tough time with that for a couple of days because I became very, very concerned that the reason why my scenes were cut out was because they thought I was a shitty actor. Or maybe I did something wrong on set.

So my struggle was - what's the lesson for me to take out of this? I need a lesson from this bad situation, so that I can make sure it becomes a good situation next time. And the lesson is I don't think I did a bad job. All the scenes seemed to go very well on set. Everything seemed fine especially when I put them in comparison to the other work that I booked and the stuff that did end up making it in. When I went back and watched the show, I read the script - for a 21 minute show, they had written 31 minutes of scenes. So they already had 10 minutes there they were cutting out. In addition, they improv a lot on that show. So there was stuff that was added in that wasn't in the script so they cut out probably a good 13 minutes of what was scripted. I was the very last person on that call sheet, the very last actor on that call sheet. Simple math tells you that they're going to work from the bottom up. And they're probably going to cut the bottom guys first.

But it took me a couple of days and people talking me off the ledge to figure out that it's not that I have to give up acting because I'm a horrible actor just because my scene got cut from *The Mindy Project*. But it was tough because I'd put it out there on Facebook. I put it out there on social media that I was going to be on *The Mindy Project*. Everybody was watching. And every actor, when they watched it, knew exactly what happened because they knew I wouldn't be putting something out there if I were just going to be a background actor.

Now, if anything, I think what this experience made me do is it made me be even more serious about becoming a really good actor. I would like to be that actor who does something that just works so well that they have to figure out a way to fit it in the episode. Or at least, hopefully, get to the point where I never have a doubt that when my scenes end up at the editing floor, it's not because I did a bad job. That, in part, led me to get more focused on training and just always wanting to get better. Not just book more work, but become a better actor.

Ray Benitez

Ray Benitez's credits include The Watch (2012), Quarantine 2: Terminal (2011) and The Lost Valentine (2011). More credits can be found at his IMDB page: http://www.imdb.com/name/nm3918254/?ref_=fn_al_nm_1

Where are you originally from and how did you get into acting?

I'm a Cuban American. Acting was something that I always liked since I was a teenager but I never pursued it until my adult life. My background is in banking and it's great, but I always had a passion to be an actor. I once took my son, who is also an actor, to meet some casting directors. A couple of them came up to me and said, "Don't you want to do some acting?" So I decided to try it and realized I really liked it. I started taking classes. And soon agents started approaching me because there was a lack of Latinos in my age group and general lack of Latinos in the acting community in Georgia. It's been an interesting roller coaster ride because there are not that many roles for my ethnicity in Georgia. Most of the roles that are coming over here are mostly for white or black actors. Others such as Asians, Latinos, Indians,

Ethiopians, don't have that many choices. But everything is changing.

I am a SAG member. I am the board director for SAG in Atlanta and one of the representatives for the Latino community in the Southeast. Regarding opportunities in Atlanta, it's a great place for anybody who doesn't have a solid resume. They can start getting little roles and start building a resume because we have a lot of opportunities right here. But we have to be realistic. The big roles are getting cast out of Los Angeles because Los Angeles does not want to take the risk with us for the big roles yet. They're not sure what Atlanta has in their acting community, whether we have professionals who can handle that. But we actually do have fantastic people here, some with 300+ credits. Building up Atlanta's base of talent and perception is something we're all working together to do. I am one of the people in Georgia Production Partnership (GPP). We advocate for the tax incentive to stay here and for the local talent to get opportunities.

To back up a little bit, when you had your career in finance, were you already in Atlanta?
Yes, I came to Atlanta in 1991 just when the Olympics were announced to be happening here in 1996. I came to work as a banker. However, right now, I'm an independent real estate broker.

You've seen the city grow, in terms of the city itself and the acting opportunities?
Yes. When I first came to Atlanta in 1991, it wasn't such an international city. But now it's a global city. We have everything right here. And on a regular basis, I see requests from people– actors, directors, producers – in Los Angeles that are moving to Atlanta because they see the opportunity here. They love the

weather, the locations, and the tax incentives. It's perfect. But we need to continue to work together and prove to everybody that the talent is here.

What can we do for that?
Honestly, we need better classes, we need very good training. We need writers here who can create stories set in Atlanta or Georgia. We are all here, real Americans of all colors, races and cultures. We need writers that can create stories around the richness of our society here.

How do you handle rejection?
It's not easy. What I tell my children and what I learned myself is anytime you get a job, be thankful. If you don't get it, it wasn't meant to be...and if they call you back, that means they really like you and that means they'll call you again and again. Just do your best each time. You leave your heart in that room because you're showing them that you're ready. In the audition, I'm going to give them an experience that's very personal, comes from inside me. But I'm not going to take the outcome of that audition personally. And sometimes it's stuff you just have zero control over.

For example, I got three call backs for a scene with a huge star in a blockbuster Hollywood production but didn't get the part. I was way too tall! The male lead was somebody that's short and does not like to deal with people a lot taller than him. But the fact that they called me back three times means they like my work. You have to be patient. Be ready. Always be nice and always tell people thank you. Millions of people would like to be in your shoes...so if you are able to get into the room (with the director and producers), that means you already beat hundreds of people who were competing for the job.

No plans to move to LA?
At the present time, no. I don't think we have to do that anymore. LA is coming over here.

What made you decide to become SAG?
I worked in Los Angeles, and to work there you have to be SAG. The SAG-E (Eligible) doesn't mean anything. You either are in the union and therefore professional, or you are not. Of course, in Atlanta, most of the work is non-union but the big LA studios don't like non-union. They prefer union. It's been a challenge for me with regard to commercials because most commercials here are non-union. But we in SAG are trying to work with that and see how we can help non-union productions work with us to hire SAG actors.

Do you have representation outside Atlanta?
I have representation in Louisiana, Florida, Texas and also for specific stuff in LA.

What do you do in terms of marketing?
Start with classes and stay in classes. Always. I'm also on the board of the Atlanta Film Festival. Get involved with film festivals here and with the acting community. It's a small community really. When you get involved, you get known and stay in the mind of people who could hire you. Agents also like to see that you are involved with the community, being proactive.

What do you wish someone had told you when you started your career?
Follow your dreams. Don't wait. Don't believe anything is impossible. You can do what you set out to achieve because the clock never stops. There's gonna be ups and downs but never stop. It is hard, there are so many no's along the way before

that one yes. But when the yes comes, it makes it all worthwhile.

Scott Poythress

Scott will soon be seen in theaters again opposite Tom Cruise in Doug Liman's Mena, alongside Octavia Spencer in Robert Schwenke's Allegiant: Part II, and opposite Ben Affleck in Gavin O'Connor's The Accountant. He is represented by People Store in Atlanta. More credits and info at http://www.imdb.me/scottpoythress.

When did you know you wanted to become an actor? Was your family supportive?
I knew I wanted to be an actor while operating the follow spot from the light booth at Lassiter High School's production of *South Pacific*. My family has been and continues to be incredibly supportive.

How did you go about starting your acting career?

I studied theater in high school and started performing there and at church as often as possible.

What was your first paid gig?
My on-camera career began when I played the "Bad Dancer" in a training video for Chick-fil-A called Wayne & Mel: Super Guys. It was my first professional acting job.

How did you get your first agent?
A blind submission to a woman named Joan Taibbi with TMA Talent. She may or may not even be around anymore. This was 1992 in Atlanta. A very, very different time. She saw me as a "character type" (which I am) and then told me I would never play anything other than the "best friend." And I've never forgotten that.

What do you mean that you've never forgotten that?
I simply meant that this business is shockingly superficial, and the earlier you can remove your pride and feelings and see this as a business, the better off you'll be. So while she was right, to a degree, that also continues to drive me to push the limits of what people are willing to see me as.

What was your training like? How do you keep your instrument sharp between projects (if you have the time)?
I have studied theater since high school, graduated with a BA in performance from the University of Georgia in 1998, and worked the craft ever since in any capacity I could, which helped me grow as an actor. Sometimes I would work for free or little pay for friends making low budget commercials. Sometimes I would study a certain director's work and watch their entire ouvre. Sometimes I would focus on plays and read as many as I could get my hands on. Your instrument will never be sharp enough. Never. Anyone who tells you otherwise is lying to you.

What do you wish someone had told you at the beginning of your career? What advice would you give to an actor starting out?

I wish that someone had made me understand that no one owes you anything. This business is unquantifiable. Meaning, there is no amount of training, study or credits, which warrants you getting what you deserve. What you deserve is irrelevant. There is timing. There is training. And there is luck. If you can't handle that, you should choose another career path.

How did you support yourself when you started out? What were your survival jobs?

I edited trailers. I worked for a man named Stuart Harnell who ran Cinema Concepts. I cut and spliced 35mm film. The "Let's all go to the MOOvies..." trailers designed for specific theater chains? I cut those together. Loved it. I've also delivered hot wings. I've been a line cook. I've even sold speakers out of an unmarked, windowless van in Malibu (for one day only).

Do you do anything else to supplement your income today?

My wife and I have edited demo reels for actors since 2009 with a company we began called Back To One Creative. We also co-founded an acting studio called Drama Inc. in 2013.

What made you choose Atlanta?

I grew up here. But while living in Los Angeles and seeing the film/TV growth in 2008-09, we knew coming home was the right decision.

How do you prepare for an audition? For a role?

Read the script. Read the sides. Read the script. Read the sides. Repeat. Repeat. Repeat.

How do you handle rejection? Do you ever feel like giving up?
It gets easier and easier. The more rejection you face, the thicker your skin gets. Honestly, I feel like quitting every day. I kick myself for not choosing a different career but then shake that off and press on after realizing there is nothing else that would make me happy.

What is your favorite thing about being an actor?
All the free time.

What is your least favorite thing about being an actor?
All the free time.

Are you SAG?
I have been a SAG member since the day of the merger in LA. It was the right time for me to join. I had been SAG-eligible for 11 years.

What are some ways you stay on the industry radar? How do you make your mailings stand out? How do you keep your ear to the ground regarding happenings in the industry?
Social media can be a blessing and a curse. It's a necessary evil for generating our own heat and being our own manager, so to speak. Staying positive is critical. Not always the easiest thing to do when we're constantly reminded how often others might be working. But posting when you have a play opening, a TV episode airing, or sharing about an awesome class you're currently taking; all very good things. I only do mailings when I am certain I made the cut in a project that is about to air. I read the trades daily. I scour IMDbPro. It's a very powerful tool if you know how to use it effectively.

What do you see the future of acting being in Atlanta? What would you like to see happen in Atlanta to grow the film

business/opportunities for actors? Do you see series regular roles coming here?

The future of acting in Atlanta is growing (and has already grown) exponentially in the last six years since we moved back from Los Angeles. The problem is a lack of commitment coupled with a sense of entitlement with people "getting into this whole acting thing." There is no guaranteed payoff commensurate with the classes you've taken, the sets you've been on, or the number of credits on your resume. Your training never stops. Never. If you're not doing it because you love it, and cannot see yourself doing anything else with your life, I suggest you find another line of work because you're in for heartache. The series regular roles are inevitable. Productions saving huge money + ever-improving homegrown talent = only a matter of time.

Do you have representation outside Atlanta?

I am currently repped by the Daniel Hoff Agency commercially in Los Angeles, Brevard Talent in Florida, and The People Store here in Atlanta. And most recently I also signed with a new manager, Patrick Millsaps, based out of Los Angeles.

Tasia Grant

Tasia Grant has done at least a dozen commercials, and her film credits include roles in Tyler Perry's "Meet the Browns" and "Single Moms Club", "Breaking Up Is Hard To Do", as well as powerful roles in a number of independent films. Her TV credits include the Lifetime network series, "Army Wives", NBC's "Revolution", MTV's hit show "Finding Carter" and Tyler Perry's "The Haves and The Have Nots". You can keep up with Tasia's work via her IMDB page (www.imdb.me/tasiagrant), via Facebook and Instagram (@tasiagrantactress) or on Twitter (@tasiagrant).

Where are you from?
Washington, D.C.

When did you know you wanted to become an actor?
I started acting as a child in a theatre company and continued through college, but 10 years ago, I realized it was my passion

and wanted to make a career of it. After being on set for hours and not noticing the time pass, and leaving the set or the stage feeling so fulfilled, I knew that's where my passion was.

How did you go about starting your acting career? Was your family supportive?

I got back into acting classes, returned to theatre, and shortly afterwards, and sought representation from an agency. I have a really strong support system! My family is very understanding and encouraging, and many of my friends are very supportive. Even as hard as it was to hear that I was leaving corporate to be a full-time actress, they understood why I had to do it.

What was your training like? Do you have a formal degree in theater?

As a child, in the theatre company, Children's Urban-Arts Ensemble (CUE), we were professionally trained in acting, dance and voice. I do not have a degree in theater, but I received training in college as a member of the Hampton Players Theatre Company. As an adult, I have trained with several highly respected studios and coaches here in Atlanta, as well as coaches from New York out of Susan Batson's studio.

What made you choose Atlanta?

When I moved here, Atlanta was booming in the job market and THE place to live, especially for African Americans.

How did you get your first agent?

I submitted my headshot to about five agencies. I got called in by one initially, auditioned and got representation. I felt like that agency was doing pretty well with commercial and print work but not much television and film. At the time, when I was thinking about seeking additional or other representation, I was contacted by my current agent, auditioned, and 10 years later, we're still together!

How did you support yourself when you started out? What were your survival jobs? Do you do anything else to supplement your income today?

Starting off, my survival job was my full-time corporate job, but I realized it was also my crutch. Once I made acting my full-time job, I worked part-time as a Bank Teller, held seminars and workshops, taught classes, temp work and now have added multi-level marketing to the side hustle.

What do you do for marketing and networking?

I am my own PR person/publicist. I use social media as my primary marketing tool but I also network consistently.

How do you stay aware of industry news? Read any specific websites/newsletters?

There are so many but Backstage, Daily Actor, Actors Access, Georgia Film Commission, to name a few, are my primary sources of information.

What do you see the future of acting being in Atlanta? Do you see series regular roles coming here?

We are already on our way... in the midst of it really! With the major studios being built here and the numerous episodes and feature films shooting here, the doors have been opened for us to get more substantial roles. I personally have begun to audition for more guest star, recurring and even some series regular roles, right here in Atlanta!

What can actors in Atlanta do to step up their game, to be worthy of the bigger roles and to stand out from the increasing competition?

BE PREPARED!!! That preparation will give you the confidence to walk into the room and do what you know to do. Stay trained up, do your research on the project, the role, the director, etc. Then do your work with the script...put in the time and attention. And be professional about every aspect, from getting the audition notice to booking the job to shooting the job. This is your career... treat it as such. Believe that you are as worthy as any other actor, whether from LA, New York, or wherever...that is why you were given the opportunity. Own it!

What would you like to see happen in Atlanta to grow the film business/opportunities for actors?

I want Atlanta actors to continue to book more across the board and then follow through with great work. This is basically our proof in the pudding to those outside of Atlanta that the talent is here. They don't have to go outside for talent when they are shooting here and we are worth bringing to other locations to fulfill the needs of the roles. I also love that Atlanta filmmakers are creating their own content to showcase the talent here behind the scenes and in front of the camera, in hopes that major opportunities will grow out of it and provide more work for everyone.

What about roles of your ethnicity? Is it a limiting factor?

It is definitely an ongoing obstacle, but I must admit that as I see more people of color in leading roles on my TV screen and in theatres, I am increasingly optimistic about the opportunities that are in store for us in the very near future.

Are you SAG?

I am not. I am SAG-eligible, however, as a full-time actress, many of the opportunities, like non-union commercials and spokesperson work, have been most plentiful and have been my primary source of income. I have done SAG commercials, film and television, but until I am working continuously on a SAG project or the opportunities for recurring work increase here, It would be a hard hit financially for me to join. I have definitely considered how it may impact the perception of me as an actor if I joined.

Do you have representation outside Atlanta?

I have had representation in Nashville, New Orleans and New York as well, but experienced some conflict of interest, so for now, I am only represented by my agency in Atlanta. My Atlanta agent always had preference over the other agencies. I definitely plan to talk to agents in LA to look into representation out there.

Do you plan to move to LA/NY in the future?

I don't plan to relocate there but would live there during a season if cast as a series regular out of LA.

How do you handle rejection? Do you ever feel like giving up?

I honestly don't ever feel like giving up, but I most definitely go through periods of feeling impatient, frustrated and discouraged. Of course, I am disappointed when I don't book or even when I am not called to audition for projects/roles I am really interested in. It is all usually followed up by recognizing how blessed I am to have come as far as I have and to have the opportunities that so many are working toward right now. And it truly just makes me work harder and stay ready so when they come, I can really savor the moments and enjoy being able to live my dream, my passion.

If you had to re-do something in your career again, would you do anything differently?
This is such a difficult question for me because I really believe that things happen in the order and timing that it is supposed to, and that even the "bad" experiences are learning experiences. Deep down I know that my way couldn't possibly supersede God's way, so I guess, that's a "no". I will just continue to grow and do my best to make decisions with the best intentions, and trust God for the outcome.

Tony Guerrero

Tony is an internationally recognized Actor, Producer, Emcee and Voice-Over Talent.

He is a Spanish-language spokesperson for Ole Mexican Foods, Chick Fil-A, Lowe's, American Airlines, Wal-Mart and many more. He can be seen in Hollywood blockbusters like X-MEN FIRST CLASS, sitcoms like REED BETWEEN THE LINES and commercials. He has starring roles in the upcoming UNDOCUMENTED EXECUTIVE and PULSE OF THE INDIGO. Tony is also a sought after Latin-American emcee, appearing on TNT-LA, Univision and TV Azteca. He is represented by People Store in Atlanta.

Where are you from and how did you come to Atlanta? How did you start acting?

I'm originally from Mexico. I did some theater in school and I really liked it. It was something I really wanted to do, I decided to just give it a try and continued doing it. I worked in a few theater plays in Mexico when I was a kid, and eventually started pursuing my career here in Atlanta. I moved here 18 years ago. Back then, it wasn't even close to the thing that this city has become now - the new production mecca for Hollywood. But when I started living here, I noticed that some people worked in production so I decided to give it a try here in Atlanta at a 48-hour film festival. After that, I started applying for everything that had to do with acting – voice-overs, corporate events... everything that was related to film. I kept practicing, I wasn't taking classes, I was just doing my thing.

Did you ever think about moving to LA or New York?
I thought about moving to LA one time but I decided to stay here because I really like Atlanta and I saw this thing coming. I knew that it was going to be very big so I decided to stay and give it a try. I'm going to stay here because this is where I like to be – Atlanta. I love it. I can't move anywhere else. I tried, but I can't.

Has your ethnicity been a challenge to you in Atlanta?
Yes but it's not going to stop me. We always get typecast based on our nationality but I am good. I am happy with work, with what we can get. Even if it's a day player, it's good.

You do a lot of events as a host. Is that a big part of your work?
Yes. I'm big in my community. Being an actor is great, but I like to be involved in my community as much as I can. I would like to use my acting techniques to get us closer together, make folks in my community laugh and have a good time. I really like and enjoy being an emcee for my people.

Have you ever been cast as some other ethnicity, where they don't realize that you're Hispanic?

No, that's never happened to me. I've wanted to be cast as an Italian or Mediterranean but no, that's never happened. I think my face is really identifiable as a Hispanic.

And what about your accent?

My accent? It's funny because I'll try to get rid of it just to blend in, and people tell me no. Some other people tell me 'keep it', other people tell me 'don't lose it', and other people tell me to work on it. I think I'm going to keep my accent just because it is who I am. It makes me very unique.

What else do you do in terms of supplementing your income?

I just do acting, that's my main thing, and then I do voice-over work and emceeing. I also do corporate events and I have an acting school - Six Second Acting Workshop. It's a tiny little school teaching on-camera acting. We have about 20 students so far and it is located in Norcross. It's not specifically for Hispanics but it happens that way because Hispanic people here know me.

Regarding your voice-over work, is there enough voice-over work for you with your Hispanic accent?

Most of the things that I do are in Spanish. So there's a lot of work for Hispanics. There's a lot of voice-over in Spanish.

Do you look for work, for example, in New Orleans or Texas?

No, I don't look for jobs anywhere else because I'm pretty much busy here. I know a lot of people here don't have this as their main income but I'm very lucky.

How did you become so well known in the Hispanic community?
One of my main clients is Plaza Fiesta, I work directly with them. I work directly with the Mexican consulate in Atlanta as well. I work also with the television news channel, help them plan events because they pretty much always need an emcee or a moderator, and I can do that.

What do you do for marketing and networking?
I don't go to too many networking events. I want to go to more I just don't have the time, I stay very busy... but I try to go to get connected.

Do you believe Atlanta will continue to grow and we will get bigger roles in Atlanta?
Yes, eventually, it is going to happen. I see Atlanta growing to the point where people start moving here and there's going to be more competition but not right now. The bigger roles are going to come later on. For me, at least, it's going to come after the immigration reform happens. It's a hot topic among Hispanics right now. The American market is not quite considering big roles in movies for us quite yet.

What can we, in Atlanta, do to improve our game as actors? And what can we do as a city to make sure that we continue to get big projects?

As actors, what we can do is be more united, more educated and more proactive within the community and with each other. If we can get together and create more meetings and opportunities with producers, we will be able to attract more directors, productions and qualified people. They will start looking at us more seriously. I think we need to organize ourselves. As a city, we should be building more production facilities and state of the art communities for producing and editing movies. That would be excellent, to bring all these people here so they stop saying Atlanta is great but they don't have the infrastructure to film those big movies. We need new infrastructure and state of the art capabilities for studios.

How do you handle rejection? How do you stay positive and motivated?

The way I see it and the way I tell everybody is, when I walk into an audition I imagine that I'm walking into a party to which I have been invited. What do you do in a party? You try to have fun even though you don't know a lot of people. Sometimes you meet people and you just see them once or twice. And I imagine that these people who are in the room are my friends. And I like to think that in this party I am a part of the fun. Once I finish, I just forget about it because I believe that they're looking for somebody specifically and it's not about me as an actor, sometimes it's about physical appearance. I understand it's their job and I'm very thankful that they are looking at and considering me. Instead of dealing with 'Oh my God! The rejection!', I'm very thankful and see this as an opportunity to meet them. I'm so happy every time I go to an audition, I'm just happy to leave the room with a good flavor in my mouth, that I was invited to this nice party! If I go in there tense and thinking 'Oh my gosh, are they going to choose me' or 'they're not going to choose me', I'd be very nervous and stressed.

What do you wish someone would have told you at the beginning of your career?

I wish at the beginning of my career that I could have people to be more supportive. One of the things that you think in this career is that people don't believe that you can be an actor. People don't believe that you can pursue your dreams and when they don't believe in you, the road becomes more difficult because you have to face a lot of problems alone. If someone were to tell me, you can do this, just go ahead and pursue your dreams that would make my life easier. So now this is what I do for my students. I tell them that it's possible.

What do you think you might do differently if you could start your career all over again?

I wish I could have a better marketing strategy. I probably would have hired a manager or somebody that would do marketing for me, expose me to the right places, because one of the most difficult things for an actor is to be promoted. Sometimes we just sit down and wait for things to happen but we should be very aggressive in the marketing. If I knew that in the past, I would probably be in better shape right now. I don't sit around and wait for my agent to call me. I'm a proactive actor. What I do is every time a client or my agency wants to send me a check; I don't wait for the check to come in my mail. I always go get the check personally because I want to say thanks to the agent, I want them to remember me. I want to establish a relationship with the people who give me work so they can call me back again. Some of them insist sending it to me but I prefer to pick it up. But 80% of the clients, I go and visit them, and I shake their hand. I thank them for the job I got and they remember me. I recommend it to all the actors out there. Establish a relationship with all your clients.

You actively call potential customers or clients and you try to get work that way?
Yes, absolutely. Every other month, I update my demos or add something small and what I do is I send them an email with a little note saying you know what, I'm around, this is the new thing. I try to keep myself ahead of the game. So yes, I look for different ways to call their attention.

Towanna Stone

Ms. Stone has well over two decades professional experience as a Commercial and Industrial Film Host, Live Show Host, Actor, Model, Singer, and was crowned Miss TN USA '97 and 2nd Runner Up to Miss USA. Her administrative work includes spearheading print divisions at People Store and Houghton Talent in Atlanta, GA, founding Etched In Stone Productions in TN, casting independent productions throughout the southeast, and mentoring and teaching actors and models about establishing themselves in the commercial and modeling industry.
www.towannastone.com info@towannastone.com

Where are you from and when did you decide to become an actor and a host?

I grew up in Morristown, TN, and lived there throughout my formative years. I basically knew I wanted to act, sing and model when I was 8-years-old. My mother gave me a journal and that was one of the first things I wrote about. I'd say I've always wanted to be in this industry. I just wasn't sure if I was talented enough to do it because I was extremely shy. I would be in plays, but I would stay in the background. I would sing in the choir but it wasn't until I was 12-years-old that I started singing leads at weddings and at the Country Club. I made around $50 for a performance, and I thought how cool is it to get paid to do something I have so much fun doing.

I started doing on-camera work in Knoxville when I was 15. The first job the agency booked me on was hosting a Ford Motor Credit industrial film. I'd never seen a teleprompter before and had no idea what I was doing. I just watched what everyone was doing on set and never let on that I'd never done it before. Needless to say, I was hooked...the work was so much fun. I liked to play by standing in front of my mirror doing monologues and reading Reader's Digest like I was Oprah, so that really paid off because we had nowhere to go for classes at that time. I left Morristown, when I was 17, to go to college, and graduated from Middle Tennessee State University with a degree in Mass Communications. I studied Broadcasting and Theatre there. The theatre program was pretty strict and although I was doing professional work in Nashville, it was a balancing act with the professors to be able to miss rehearsals while performing in main stage shows to go host industrials or do commercials. That work helped pay my way through school, so it was important I continue to do it.

You also won a beauty pageant?
Yes, Miss Tennessee USA 1997 and I placed 2nd Runner Up to Miss USA. The woman who won Miss USA went on to be crowned Miss Universe and the woman who was first Runner Up went on to be Miss Universe. It was a really strong group of girls competing. It was a fascinating experience, because I had no idea what to expect. Competing was really an eye opener for me because I had never really been involved in pageants other than two small local pageants I did when I was in middle school

and I wasn't very good at it. It wasn't until I got to college that I started doing a lot of modeling work, mostly runway and print and I became more confident. There was one client I worked for who owned an apparel boutique and she kept asking me to do the pageant. I worked for her for about four years until I finally decided to do it.

That was the very first time in my life I had won something that I completely prepared for myself. Nobody really knew I was going to do it. I borrowed clothes from my friends, created my bio and platform, and worked with an acting teacher named Tina Van Horn. The thing I liked about the pageant was the onstage interview as well as the interview with the judges. I liked making the audience laugh at state...I was relaxed and in the moment. I really liked learning about that whole process. I had a negative connotation about pageants before I actually did it, but it made me a stronger communicator and it was a lot of fun. It was a very competitive atmosphere, but it was one where you have to rise above and bring your A game no matter what the circumstances are or if you woke up on the wrong side of the bed that morning. Miss USA was non-stop performing and being in front of people for a little over two weeks. In rehearsal, they had me do the telecast run through three times all the way to top three before the show was filmed that night in front of 28 million people. It was a positive experience for me. I'm thankful I was able to do it.

What did you study in college? Was it related to any acting or performing in any way?
I studied theater. I was a part of the theater program. I did several shows there and I also studied broadcasting and hosted shows on campus.

So you actually have some formal training there?

Oh yes. I've always been a proponent of class and studying. I think you should never quit studying. I strive to learn something new every day because we're evolving and growing continually. It's important to do that because you don't want to become stagnant, especially with acting and performance. If you're not in a class and working on your craft, you can become very stagnant and it can lead you to become insecure about what you can bring in an audition. You need to be able to work off of people and have that validation, get out of your head so to speak and it really helps you tremendously when you audition.

Did you stay in the Southeast or did you go to any other markets before coming back to Atlanta?
I worked in New York for quite a while. I went to New York right after I did the Miss USA pageant. I had a really great opportunity to work with a couple of different agencies there. Marla Maples hosted the Miss USA pageant and she introduced me to her commercial agency, I did really well with them, they were a great fit. I brought all my friends to work with them. It was a fun time to be in New York. Gary Bertalovitz was my agent. He's over the women's division at Images now. They were primarily a commercial agency and I primarily did commercial work in New York. Towards the end of my time there, I started to work with Wilhelmina.

You were able to support yourself that way?
Yes, I did. I worked in New York. I lived in Manhattan. I had a roommate and it was expensive but we made it happen. I moved to New York with $600 cash and a couple bags. I lived in Astoria Queens for two months, then found a place and moved into a studio on 72nd and Central Park. I was across the street from the Dakota building and Central Park, and I was steadily working and being sent out on auditions, so I felt like I was in the right place at the right time. I moved over to 97th and Lex

my last year being there. Taye Diggs was our neighbor. That was while he was in rent. It was the 90s and we were making good money. Our day rates were $1,500 to $2,000. It was a different market altogether and it was a stark difference from when I was working on-camera in the 90s and when I started working as an agent. I saw the rates drop and a lot of it had to do with the advent of the Internet and people being able to book themselves. It just drove the rates down. When I was in New York, we were making great money and it was just a different world. When you're able to not only work as an actress, but also as a model, you know it's even better because it's good to diversify and have different streams of income. I was hosting Digital Cafe at that time and was coming into my own on-camera.

You were still getting acting training in New York as well?
Yes, I trained in New York. I studied with many different acting teachers and I studied voice. And then when I decided to come back to Tennessee, I started teaching and I taught theater performance privately and on the collegiate level and it was very rewarding to be able to do that work. I still keep in contact with some of the students I had. But I think it's important whenever you are exposed to really good training, to be able to come back and share the information with others. I wanted more opportunity and I saw that more things were happening in Atlanta, and that's when I moved.

You applied for a position at Houghton at the time?
No, the first agency I worked at was People Store. To get my foot in the door, I worked the front desk for about four months. I saw market potential doing print and I was given the go ahead to spearhead the Print Division there. Working in New York gave me the right foundation in terms of Print. I knew how to secure

clients and really go after the jobs and negotiate rates and contracts. I knew what they were looking for in models and I understood how to prepare models and talent for the job. So it was just a perfect fit for me. Sometimes agents have never done the work and don't know how to connect with talent. It isn't just an administrative job. You have to know how to coach and intuitively bring out the best in people, even when they don't see it themselves, and be willing to be patient with them while they grow. Developing talent while catering to clients' needs is an area I've always felt confident. After working there, I spearheaded the print division at Houghton and was able to continue working on-camera as well. They were always good about that. That's one of the reasons I preferred to work as a print-booking agent because I could still maintain the on-camera work. It was the perfect match.

Do you think being an agent or working in an agency helps actors in the sense of being connected to the industry and possibly having a flexible job?
Absolutely, because when you work with agents, you not only learn about the industry but they understand the business. They understand when you need to take time off to do a job and are willing to work with you and that is definitely a positive. It was important for me to work in an agency because it's good to stay in that environment. You know there's something great about being in an environment where you can learn what's happening in the industry.

Do you do anything else to supplement your income right now?
I've been consulting actors and models who are interested in getting into the industry. I tailor a package to suit the needs of

the talent depending on their level of experience and goals. We identify the areas of weaknesses in relation to their overall package and help them to become stronger. Also, I share information about how to circumvent pitfalls. This year I've cast an independent TV series called *Atlanta Law* and an independent short film called *If I Should Die Before I Wake* written by award winning author Eric Ayala.

You're fully focused on your career as an actress and voice-over talent?

I'm actually going into the studio tomorrow to do a new voice-over reel that I'm really excited about. I'm fully committed to this work and feel most fulfilled when I'm on set and working on a production.

What else do you do for marketing and networking?

Casting Networks is a really good resource for me, and 800Casting. It's important to be listed with as many of the different casting sites as possible because you can stay privy to what's going on. Scouring the Internet is a good idea, too. I'm always researching what's going on in Atlanta and what productions are coming to town. It's important to do your own research and not only rely on your agent to find the work for you. I also have friends who work in Production and it's good to be able to know what's coming to town before production starts.

It's good to have connected friends, right? This industry is built on relationships.

Relationships are cornerstones to careers. Cultivating really solid relationships with people that you trust is tantamount. It's good to have people you can bounce ideas off of when you're working on something. If you're writing, it's good to be able to pop that over to a friend of yours who works as a Director or Writer and get their opinion on it.

What do you think is one of the best ways for a new actor in Atlanta to build relationships that way?
There are several different ways to do it. The first thing is to get into a really good acting class. The way to do that is to audit as many different classes as possible, study with as many different teachers as possible, and then decide out of that batch of teachers who really resonates with you. Where do you think you're going to be most challenged? Where do you think you'll grow the most and then study that. You'll create relationships with people in the class and you'll keep your nose to the grind. In those environments, you're inevitably going to learn what's going on in the industry. You find out what techniques work for different people, what shows are being put up, what auditions are happening and who is booking. It's just a great way to stay connected.

I also met a ton of people working as an agent. Even now when I go to an audition, I'll see at least a handful of people I know. One of the things I love so much about this industry is that it's really communal. You can go to an audition and see someone, catch up and have a great conversation about the industry, what they've been up to.

Do you believe that we will be getting bigger roles out of Atlanta?
I do believe that. I do believe it's coming just because I've seen how the industry has changed in the 12 years I've been in Atlanta. It really wasn't until about five years ago that I started seeing a vast change in terms of the kinds of films that were coming into Atlanta. Big box office films, especially in the last two years with the tax credit, are drawing big name celebrities.

It's inevitable that we'll be offered bigger roles and meatier parts. We need to continue to grow in the area of top-notch training here. It's absolutely critical. That's one of the areas I'm starting to see a change. Hopefully, there will be incentives and more top-notch teachers will come to Atlanta. That's at the core of what's needed. I can tell the difference when I'm in an improv class. I see the difference in the roles I'm cast for and the frequency that I'm booked when I'm in a long form improv class. The same holds true for film classes. It's a tangible connection that I make between earning dollars and studying. The thing about Atlanta is I came across so many actors and models that want to book but they're not willing to put in the work to make it happen. There are specific things you have to study to become great at this craft. Every other profession, people have an understanding that you have to go to school to learn to do it. The people who study and prepare themselves really stand out.

Are you SAG?
No. Working all those years in a 'Right to work' state, I never made the decision to join SAG. Most industrials and commercial acting jobs I've booked were non-union and those are the bulk of my work. But I will happily join when I book a national SAG commercial.

Do you have representation outside of Atlanta for yourself?
I work with an agent out of Nashville and Knoxville and I'm meeting with different agencies in the Southeast. I have a goal set to have representation with other agencies in the Southeast and I'm trying to decide if I want to go back to New York.

That can get expensive very quickly.
Yes it can. Flying back and forth only makes sense when the client is paying travel or you have someone in that area you can visit when you go in for an audition or call back.

How do you stay positive and motivated?

I've worked for 27 years now in the industry and I've taken time off from auditioning twice. I became discouraged because of the rejection and what I learned to help circumvent that is to stay grounded and to exercise. Today I ran two miles, lifted my weights and swam. Tomorrow I'll do yoga. For me, staying connected physically helps me stay mentally grounded. If I'm mentally grounded and spiritually centered, then I'm better able to go into situations and not be attached to the outcome. The Casting Director or the client is going to make whatever decision they're going to make, and there are too many variables that come into play to take it personally. All I have to do is show up, do the work and know that I left everything in that room that I could possibly bring to the table. After that, my job is done. If it works out that I book the job then marvelous, but if it doesn't I can walk away knowing I gave it all that I've got. For me, that's been the best approach.

So you're basically saying, I have my pillars of support, my physical, emotional, spiritual support and I don't put all my happiness and satisfaction in the outcome of the work that I do as a performer?

Yeah, it has nothing to do with the outcome. That's a hard statement for me to make but I've finally accepted that. What it has to do with is preparing before the audition and being as ready and prepared for that moment as you possibly can be, knowing that you have created a character out of words on a page. It really is important to be able to let go. That's one of the things about acting. I believe you have to be able to let go of the end result just in terms of auditioning. Yes, we want it. I'm not saying we don't want it but just in terms of how you deal with it when you walk out of the room and you leave the audition, you have to be able to let go because when I don't let go is when I get in my car and I'm going over and over and over everything that I did in the audition. How could I have done it differently? Why didn't I say it like this? Why didn't I do it like that... and it's just not a good place to be. I found out for myself, it's a stronger choice to be able to let it go. It's a challenge to really believe it and live it. It's taken years for me to get to that point.

What do you wish someone had told you at the beginning of your career?
I wish someone had told me acting was one of the noblest professions a person could pursue. I wish someone would have told me you're being used as a vessel, as a conduit, to communicate something that has the possibility to change someone's mind, to change someone's life. I wish I would have known what a special thing this is because I battled with it for years. I was thinking I should have followed in my dad's footsteps and worked in the financial world or done something more stable. I was thinking that acting wasn't an important career. Now I understand how powerful communicating is and I'm still very drawn to it. God made me this way and there's nothing I can do about it, so now I have more peace about pursuing it. But I really wish I would have known that in the beginning. It is so interesting because I've seen where I've grown and changed just by choosing this industry. I was so shy. I got anxiety going to certain functions because I knew I'd have to talk to people. I really found my voice from doing all of this. Speech classes helped. Private coaching helped tremendously. That's what it's all about - growing past your insecurities, facing your fears and being willing to go to the places that really scare you. That's when we grow the most.

Vince Canlas

Vince Canlas is an actor with 26 years of experience in movies, television, commercials, corporate films, live events, print and voice-overs. He is originally from Manila, Philippines, but grew up in the Southeast. Vince can currently be seen in the films A.C.O.D., The Reluctant Fundamentalist with Keifer Sutherland, Kidnapping Mr. Heineken with Sir Anthony Hopkins and HBO's East Bound & Down.

When did you know you wanted to be an actor and how did you go about getting started?

I was in high school in North Carolina and I was involved in doing the lighting for plays. I saw that the actors weren't that good. I thought I can act, but it was a small town and they weren't ready to see an Asian in tights doing Shakespeare. I thought I'd just wait and move to a bigger city. I also didn't actually do anything in high school, because I was painfully shy. After college I moved down here and decided to take some classes to see if it's even something that I do decently. I went for two years to the Alliance Theatre, taking all the various courses. I didn't do the full program, but about two years worth on and off. I really liked it and realized this might be a viable living for me. Two other actor friends and I moved to LA back in the mid 80s to see if we could make it work. A couple of events happened that kept us from getting there in a timely manner. One person's car broke down so the other guy and I went ahead to LA. We rented a place in Korea town, but then the other friend got homesick and left LA shortly after his dad came in town for a meeting. So, there I was, by myself, and no job. I interrupted my two years at Alliance with that move. In retrospect, we probably headed out there prematurely. Because things weren't working out, I moved back here. My girlfriend was still here, so I thought maybe this is not a good time to be in LA after all.

Did you study any acting in college?
No. The closest I got to performance was as a male cheerleader. It wasn't until Alliance that I started being serious about it. It was at the Alliance that I met Rebecca Schrager of People Store and she signed me up. It was around 1986. I have been with them ever since. Back then you could multi-list, so I was with at least eight agencies, but I've never left the Store.

Well, they are one of the top agencies, so that's great.
Yeah. Although, because of that, everyone wants to be on their roster. I've heard people say they feel like they get lost there, especially if you are new talent and there are many of your type in a category.

I imagine that's not a problem for you though?
No, there are not many Asians in my category, and even among Asians, I'm in that category of "ambiguous." I'm lucky that I get

sent for a lot of things, not just Asian roles as a wildcard. That's preferable since you get to audition for a lot of things. You know it's all about numbers. Even if you're not right for that particular role, but you did good work, they'll remember you for something else. It just happens.

When you were in LA, did you feel that it was hard to break through just because of the competition or did you just feel like it was too expensive to live there? What was the challenge?
The first time I went out in the mid 80s, the timing was wrong and I was still very green. It was just about survival mode. We went out there with all our possessions in our vehicles, no job, and not a place to live. That was just a wasted trip, and yet also a learning opportunity. But then, jump forward. I tried again in '91 but I was about to get married, so as far as having a family out there...I had to take on that decision. I did get married and we had a child, so going back to LA was closed. It was not even in the cards. It was only after my divorce in the early 2000s, did I keep a place out there. I was trying to do bicoastal. I kept the place out there for a year, but every time I tried to go out there, I'd book something here. I had to keep changing my plans and life. I felt that was like an omen that it wasn't meant for me to be out there.

Back then, the Atlanta market wasn't as big a market as it is today. Did you do mostly commercials then?
From the 80's when I first started, it was mostly print work. In the early 90s, corporate stuff, print and commercials. There was also a little more TV and film. And then the economy went south

in 2007 and the corporate stuff went away. A lot of things went away. It really was very slow times. And then the tax incentives finally started to take hold. Then it became, mostly TV and film auditions. I hardly got any corporate bookings anymore, but I started to do audio books. I was also trying to do about one theatre production a year, because it's fun and it's a good work out.

Right, keeps your craft sharp.
Yeah, in lieu of classes, indeed. This year, I started to take improv classes. I was taking two a week. Improv is something you always have to have handy in your tool kit. Even with scripted work, improv is really a value-adding skill.

You mentioned briefly that you got your agent, People Store, without any audition or submission process.
Right, Rebecca (Schraeger) didn't have a lot of Asians in her file. However, because I didn't audition to get in, she was mostly just sending me out for print. I didn't realize that because I didn't audition and we didn't have a discussion, she wasn't aware that I was capable of on-camera acting. That was my mistake for not following up to be submitted for acting auditions, not just print work. It took me a couple of years before I actually started to get industrial auditions. Times have changed so much now, though. Newbies have a hard time getting a top tier agent here...there's a lot more competition. It's frustrating for them, all this work coming to town and they don't have a chance to submit for it or go after it. But then, even if you have an agent, it's a struggle to be submitted. And even if you are being submitted, it's a struggle to book.

How do you stay on your game and make sure you don't let it get you down?

First and foremost, it's not all encompassing. I have a great part-time job that I've had for 24 years in corporate video production and photography. It's a job that I enjoy, but it's a double-edged sword, because I have a great job so I'm not as hungry in the acting. I'm getting lazy. Because it's a great job, I have satisfaction in it. I don't feel the desperation to book acting work. But sometimes it keeps me from focusing as much as I should when I do have an acting opportunity. I feel scattered and distracted when I should be learning lines, because I have a project due, so sometimes I feel like that hurts my audition when I don't give it 100%. Or, I feel too tired after work or feel rushed to do my own taping while at the office, yada-yada. I've never felt the audition process to be a chore though. It's part of the actor's job. The actual booking is gravy.

If you're not having fun anymore with prepping, memorizing and auditioning, then that's going to be reflected in your attitude or performance. After all these years, I still find the process challenging, fun, and entertaining. Clients can feel the attitude, especially if it's a face-to-face audition. You come in there jaded, desperate or frustrated, that will come off in your performance. I remember going into auditions with Mike Pnewski (another Atlanta actor also interviewed in this book) many, many years ago. He was already in the mindset and owned the room, not just when he was auditioning. He owned the room when he was just standing there, waiting to go in by his attitude, his mindset. He had game face, and body. You're already auditioning even when you're in the waiting room.

I detected it myself, so when he and I went in there to read together, it's like I wasn't even there, because he was so big in that room. I'm not saying physically or his acting style, but his presence was so big, I was insignificant. He owned that scene. That was a hard lesson for me.

When you say, "owned the scene," do you mean he was just able to be the character throughout?

It's not like he was acting like the character he was reading for, but he had this presence and his charisma without even saying anything. He had so much confidence and self-awareness when he first walked in there, the way he carried himself. Yeah he's a big man, but it's not so much his size, but his presence was large and palpable. He's a seasoned veteran, so he had that level of confidence. He's been to LA. He worked at the largest market. That audition was in the 90s.

What else do you do?

It's a fine balance. I am able to enjoy life and attempt to maintain a relatively stress-free lifestyle. Being naturally laid-back doesn't hurt. You have to be able to let things roll off. I've seen ex-girlfriends who are actors where the business just ruins them, because you're under the spotlight, so there's the self-doubt and criticism, maintaining certain looks. For a woman, that's hard. It's hard for anybody, if you can't let it go. People come and go (in the biz). It's because they think, oh wow, I'd like to do that. It looks easy. Well, that's the hard part, making it look so easy that anyone thinks that they can do it - until they realize how many steps are involved; the marketing and constant networking to stay relevant...there's a lot of different steps actors deal with to be able to book a role and get to say one line.

A lot of people not in the acting industry don't realize how much work and preparation goes into trying to get the job and how big a deal getting that one-liner is.
Yeah, especially nowadays. There are many hoops to jump through. Even that one small role is precious and difficult to obtain, because of competition and they're spending money on you once you book.

Tell me more about your job and how it gives you flexibility.
Back in the late 80s, and early into acting, I thought - what's the best way to stay in the face of casting decision-makers when I'm not acting? I started working as a PA and eventually worked every department I could. I even worked at PC&E studios back when they had a studio on Clifton Road sweeping the stage, checking in equipment and lights. I was lucky enough to know people in that business to allow me to get work on Michael Jackson's Bad tour. He was doing a documentary and they had a week of concerts here in town at the old Omni. I worked as a lighting grip. It was these little opportunities that came my way and I took advantage of it and learned as much as I could. It never got me acting work, since I was not hired for that purpose. They didn't really want to hear about your other aspirations. It's very cliquish, this production work. And it was difficult to break into the cliques and get regular work. I had a

friend in production that said to try corporate audio-visual to fill in the gaps. Putting up screens, setting up projectors. So I got some on-the-job training and the more I learned, the more I was able to market myself in different areas. For four years, I freelanced in audiovisual work and finally landed at my current job where I maintain part-time status for schedule flexibility. They are okay with it. In 24 years, I've only had to turn down four major acting jobs. Can you believe that? It's just that flexible. The sweetest gig ever! That reason also made it difficult to move to LA.

You have golden handcuffs.
That's exactly what someone else said, I have golden handcuffs and I've got a great work environment at the office where I do video production and photography. I don't pursue production work outside of that job because I try to focus on acting when I'm not there. But it's still fun and its good living.

You mentioned the production work that you did, and trying to be on set, and being in front of the decision makers. It really doesn't help you as an actor because they don't want to hear about that?
That's correct. They don't want to be bothered with you trying to sell yourself while you're there to do a job. And in retrospect, that's true. It just cheapens you. Don't burden them with having to think about other things. Instead, you should be thinking about what you were hired to do. I wouldn't recommend that strategy to anybody now.

What do you do for marketing?

Tooting my own horn has always been a difficult thing for me. Even in the day job where I have to do the performance evaluation is tough. You've got to toot your horn on Facebook, to show this is what I'm doing. When acting in the late 80s, early 90s, there was an actor who was renting a room from me. He had soap opera good looks, but he could not act his way out of a paper bag. He was wooden. He took some classes, but he was so great at networking, schmoozing. He could work the room like nobody's business. He had self-confidence, self-awareness, and he would book work just on that. He would keep getting called. And he would turn work down! We were amazed that he could turn work down. It's money in your pocket. "Well, I've got this other stuff that I've got to do," he'd say. He was trying to start a limo business. The point is, he wasn't desperate and his lackadaisical manner equaled confidence. He looked good on-camera. Horrible actor, but a great interactor and he knew the right things to say. The agents kept calling him even when he said he was out of the business. It amazed me how much he still got called. I wanted a piece of that skill. I watched him, but it came so effortless that it was just something in him that allowed him to exude that self-marketing skill. Some things can't be taught.

It is essentially a people's business we're in.
Yeah, and so he was always marketing himself without knowing it. And that's what I sometimes have to remember. That even in the non-acting situation, you are 'on', you are marketing. Because a friend of an acquaintance might know someone. And before you know it, you've created a little buzz. It may not happen often, but it has happened where you're remembered.

Do you see the market continuing to grow here?

I see the market continuing to grow, because we see the investment the big production companies are putting down with their big studios - probably more than I'm currently aware. That's just the big ones. We have many smaller offshoot companies, too. With that growth, we're getting LA actors and actresses submitting and working as locals. Since you can electronically submit, the reach is greater. So yes, the market will grow but will our acting opportunities increase? Probably not to the degree the laymen think it should. I live downtown and they shoot a lot of movies here. It's kind of depressing when you're driving by three different productions in your hood and you haven't been called to audition for any of them. It's a reality check. There's more work and more auditions, but you won't necessarily book more.

The people that continuously stay immersed in it daily, they're the ones that I see continually book like Michael Cole, Ric Reitz, Claire Bronson and Wilbur Fitzgerald. I don't know who has a corporate job and books regularly.

What else can you do to get yourself completely immersed that way?

You find that balance where if you're not at your day job, you're working on your craft, you're working on your marketing, you're getting out there networking, you're doing indie films and plays. And that's what I'm trying to do, but I just enjoy life. Sometimes I just want to ride my bike. I don't have to always be reading the book on how to get the part without falling apart. I do try to take the opportunity to interact with my agents, because its about being human and just saying, hey we're not here to always talk about acting, but just to say hello. It helps to have a hook, something they remember me by. For instance, every time any of the agents email me for an audition, my answer is always the same for an affirmative response, "I'm your Huckleberry" from the movie *Tombstone*. They know me as their Huckleberry, meaning I'm they're go-to-guy. You try to brand yourself someway, somehow. And that's what people who are in a crowded category need to do. I have a unique look. I don't need to do it so much, but I do it anyway. Even more so for someone who is a white, middle-aged guy, he needs to have a hook. You've got to do what you can to be remembered.

Looking back, anything you think you could've done differently? Or what advice would you give somebody starting out in Atlanta?

Your basics are most important. When I don't update my headshots, what does that tell my agent? I don't care enough about my career to do the bare minimum. So I need to rectify that. This laziness looks like I don't want it enough to change my headshot; maybe I don't deserve to get a booking. That's more of a regret than a mistake. Get your basic fundamental marketing tools out there and up to date. Continually do something that keeps you sharp. Get in class, get together with your fellow actors and work on scenes...because, as many auditions that come your way, you don't want to get cold. You always want to do good work and you can't do that if you're coming in cold. If you don't have your bare essentials in place, then you have no right to complain.

Vince Pisani

Vince Pisani is an actor, teacher and coach. His credits include Halt and Catch Fire, Reckless, Complications, The Vampire Diaries, Banshee and more. More info can be found at his IMDB page: http://www.imdb.com/name/nm2079627/?ref_=fn_al_nm_1. He is represented by Houghton Talent in Atlanta.

Where are you from originally and when did you know you wanted to be an actor?

When I was 7-years-old, my dad was trying to figure out what to do with me that summer and he found out a local play that was going to be cast that needed kids. He brought me to this community theater called Gainesville Community Playing in Gainesville, Florida, where I was born and raised. I hadn't really done any plays before. When I got to the audition, they put all the kids in a semi-circle on the stage. And in order to get the kids to relax and have fun, they made us all get up and say the Pledge of Allegiance. I didn't know what was really going on. But the director picked me and said, "Stand in the center of the semi-circle." And he took a helmet that was from one of the soldiers that was going to be in the show. It was called *Ruddigore*, which was Gilbert Sullivan, of all things. He put this helmet on me - it was three sizes too big for my head because I was the smallest kid in the group by far. It plopped down on my head and everybody laughed. I distinctly remember thinking at that point, "If they're gonna laugh, they're gonna laugh because I make them laugh, not because they're laughing at me."

That was an important moment for me. I started realizing I can have control of being able to make people laugh. So I started doing theater and grew up a theater rat. I did my first professional show *Evita,* at the age of 11, at the Hippodrome State Theater of Florida. That gave me my first taste of what real actors do, and the fact that they were living out of suitcases. It was pretty amazing at a young age to have been exposed to that.

Coming out of that, I had the opportunity to audition for the Mickey Mouse Club down in Florida but I ended up being too scared to take it. We didn't want to move to Orlando, but the people who were in the show with me from the theater pushed me to do it because they'd worked with Disney a lot already, and they knew that I would do well. We never fulfilled that, but from that point onward, I kept doing only occasional stuff.

I also got a little bit freaked out at how professional actors lived, because I saw that they were constantly traveling, and not around their families all the time, it made me nervous. So I went away from it during my high school years. Went to college at Oglethorpe University here in Atlanta and got my degree, of all things, in Economics, which is not in any way, shape or form related to acting.

I was planning to be a business major. The funny part is, it ended up being a very good thing for me because I understand business and how to run and navigate a business, which has ended up helping me as an actor. When a lot of actors get started in the professional realm, they fail to see it as a business. They see the art of it, but they don't see that there is a big business side of it, which is going to be your living. Effectively, you are the CEO of your own business and so that's why my degree has paid off.

Back in 2000, right before I graduated, I was an extra for a friend of mine in a short film. When I did that, the bug bit me again. I knew this is what I'm supposed to do and I knew I had passion for it. I was sitting in the final Capstone business class for my degree and they were talking about decisions in business models. The final decision was to cut human capital. In other words, you had to fire a bunch of people. And I realized I couldn't do it. I wasn't cut out to be that guy that could just eliminate tons of people.

Being an extra in my friend's short film led to something inside me that was saying, this is what you're meant to be and this is what you're meant to do. So I stayed put in Atlanta and immediately auditioned for an action short film, which was terrible, but I got in. Then I auditioned for the play *Twelve Angry Men,* at a theater here in Atlanta. I booked the first four auditions right out of the gate coming out of school, and the rest is history. I started building it from there and I never left Atlanta. It's funny how things worked out because it all fit right into place for me.

So you had no idea that Atlanta was going to pick up and become this big?

380

No idea. For those of us that have been here in Atlanta as long as it is, if you had told me in 2000 that Hollywood would be on our doorstep, that we would be having multi-million dollar studios and shooting Marvel comics movies here, that I'd have a career in film and TV here, I would have laughed at you. It was a dream and it was what you're hoping for, but it was never anything that I would have thought would have been near the horizon. You'd see maybe one or two film auditions in an entire year back then but now we get that in a week. It's a different world now.

What did you do then training-wise?
I think training is important. I was trained in the Meisner Technique through the Actors Express here in Atlanta. I was trained at the Professional Actor's Studio for five years. Then I trained in Meisner up in New York as well. And then in Atlanta with Shannon Eubanks, for on-camera stuff, who fundamentally changed my life in a lot of ways. And a lot of the school of hard knocks.

The benefit for those of us that have been at it for a long time is that we made a lot of mistakes. Because there were fewer opportunities for great training here, you had to learn on the job a little. Nowadays, a lot of people don't have that luxury because of the amount of people that are in it. But back then we learned a lot by doing it, which I don't recommend for people now. Because the mistakes I made were bad.

If I'm honest, the best training I think I could have ever gotten was in theater. I did show, after show, after show. Some back-to-back, sometimes I was in one show while rehearsing for another. I'd go from one play to another, and doing lead roles, I learned a lot about interacting with an audience, how to affect an audience and how to handle the volumes of dialogue quickly, what works or what doesn't work, listening, the power of your imagination, all because you were simply playing make-believe in front of people and you learned some very valuable lessons that if they didn't buy you, if you couldn't affect them, you couldn't do your job. So you learn how to adjust to and quickly get to where it can affect people. Understanding storytelling is something essential to all good actors because that's what our job is, to be a storyteller, and not to be a movie star. Sometimes it'd be a small part in a play, sometimes it would be the lead. But I had a job to do.

So make sure you understood how to take something from the script, to the stage, to the audience, in a way that was powerful and affecting them. And that was a valuable lesson because you go through that school of hard knocks of being on stage telling those stories but you're not making any money, you're doing that for free. You do it because you're passionate about affecting an audience for storytelling, and not about fame and fortune. The best actors are the people who are in a place of service. Of service to the audience, of service to your fellow actor, and service to your director and producer.

This probably ties in to why, maybe, we're seeing a resurgence or emergence of British and Australian actors who cut their teeth doing so much theater?
Yeah and it makes sense! Because I think that the problem for the American actor is that they don't train a lot. But when they do train, they're training just to make sure that they can get a part. And we do live within a society of reality television where people can become famous pretty quickly for having, let's be honest, very little talent.

So it all depends upon what your goal is. I think something that British and Australian actors have understood better than we have recently is that your commitment is not to the success, the money you make or the jobs you get, but really, it's about telling the story and being the best storyteller you can be. And having a passion for that.

Those of us who are successful in this market, and have been for a while, we are all passionate storytellers. We all write or direct or study the art of storytelling. And have done theater. Because that's our avenue, that's our place to be able to learn and affect an audience and grow as an artist. And that way when you get to film and TV, instead of doing it to move forward for fame and fortune, you're doing it in service to the audience and the story. You stop needing it for yourself as much.

It boils down to sales. If you buy from a salesman, and he comes in, and he's going, I definitely need you to get this car, I need you to buy this car, it's a great car. Here are all the wonderful things about this car. I'll do anything you need me to do, just take my car. You don't buy from that person because they're desperate and they want something from you. They're selling to you. You feel sold to. Whereas you know if an actor comes in and is not trying to sell anything but is trying to solve the casting problems and is there to help tell their story, that's what they're looking for. Someone who can solve their problems for them.

So that's what they need in casting - somebody who comes in and solves the problem they have?

You got it. They rarely go to the best actor. They go to the appropriate actor. There's a difference. Is this person the appropriate one to tell our story? There are a lot of factors that go into appropriateness. Age and ethnicity, look, talent, essence, feel, timing, politics, there's a lot of things that go into making someone the appropriate person to tell the story.

To the actor that comes in self-serving, they're missing the point as to what their job is. So if that means I come in and I say one line, deliver a pizza, I say my line, I deliver a pizza. That's what I do - I do the job. That's all it takes to move that story along, to serve that story. I've done that job. I'm not gonna come in and be that drunk pizza delivery guy or draw more attention to me because I want to advance my career. You advance your career in serving the story and being trustworthy, somebody they can count on to do the job and do it well.

Working for my talent agency (Houghton) has been incredible training too because by watching hundreds of auditions a week, I got the most valuable training. I saw what worked and what didn't work. Why working actors work and why people who weren't working didn't work. I also got a great lesson in understanding the difference between characteristics and character. For example, certain people have characteristics such that even if they are moderately talented they could be appropriate to cast and use to tell the story because of their characteristics.

So what you said about British and Australian actors is definitely right. You have to learn both sides to this. You need to get better at your craft and you should always be training. The day I feel like I've achieved it is the day I should quit because that's not true. I don't care who you are, you always can get better.

That is the mentality that the top people in the market take - is to always look and go, who's doing this better than me, and how can I learn from them. Different people do different things better than I do. So if this person here is a better improviser and they teach classes in improv, I'm going to learn from them. And I still do that. I'm getting ready to do long form improv coming up here soon just because I wanted to learn it. And it keeps me sharp. I do my teaching too because to be able to teach someone the skills that I got under my belt helps me make sure that I know my own technique.

As far as success, financially, fame and fortune-wise, I guarantee nothing that way. But I can at least be prepared for when those opportunities do come up, to do my job and do it well.

That's all you can do really, isn't it?

That's all you can do, because the other stuff is outside your control. So we do live in a time right now where I think with the advent of YouTube, the little cameras, you can learn the craft of storytelling, not just the acting side, but also the writing. You can produce your own stuff. And more and more, it is an avenue for storytelling, a legitimate opportunity for people to expand and grow. Actors are foolish if they don't participate in those things, if for no other reason but to keep sharp and quit relying on an agent or market to provide the opportunity. Make your own opportunity.

Is it valuable for actors to learn to write and use the technology available to publish, distribute, etc.?

Absolutely. You create vehicles for yourself, you create footage for yourself. You show people what you can do. Far better than sitting on your butt waiting for someone to hand it to you.

How did you get your agent?

It was not easy for me to get an agent. In the early 2000s, the market here was primarily commercials and industrials, very little film and television. And my look and feel being more Italian-American, people didn't know how to cast me.

I must've been in somewhere between 10 and 12 showcases in the Actor's Studio. The agents all knew me by name when they'd come and see these showcases of me. But I wasn't getting an agent, and could not understand why. I kept thinking it was a comment on my talent at first. Then I began understanding it was a comment on my type. They didn't know what to do with me. They didn't want to represent me. They didn't believe that the acting by itself could sway people in the commercial and industrial route.

I tried everything, I submitted by mail to the different agencies, wasn't getting callbacks. They all know me by name. But looking back on it, God was giving me a gift, in a sense, that I kept getting into theater just to get better and better, and keep working on my craft and training. Mentally, I was thinking, man I have got to get better if they're going to find me an agency since I had no knowledge of the business and didn't understand that I wasn't the right type.

I'm thankful for it now because it was making me a better actor despite my type. But finally I did a monologue I'll never forget - I dyed my hair blonde for this play I was in. I was reading for Virginia Wolf in the advanced class studio. I was reluctant to do this showcase but did it anyway. And lo and behold, I get signed on by my first agent! I'm sitting there with blonde hair, feeling totally weird that I finally get signed. This what it takes - me having to be blonde for me to get this!

Most people think this is the end – you've got an agent, you're ready now. Well, I went through a year where I went on three auditions in that first year. I didn't know any better to know that that wasn't very good numbers. So I went through the year and I wasn't getting anything. And I go and do another showcase and another agency sees me in that showcase and calls me the next day for a commercial audition at Stillwell, for a national commercial for the College Loans Corporation.

The description was for a Michael J. Fox-esque character. I do my first commercial audition ever, and I book it. And I'm thinking, of course, this is how it's supposed to be.

I just get this gig in Charleston, I go and shoot it. I didn't have a good contract at the time. I made $1,100, which I thought was a bundle. I didn't realize that it was basically a complete buyout of my image, for that spot, for three years. That commercial aired everywhere. It was in Hawaii, Alaska, Texas, Florida, New York, Los Angeles. My current agent estimated that I probably could have made somewhere around $30,000-$50,000 on it. But instead I made $1,100 because I had a bad contract. I didn't understand the business yet.

I also thought, I just booked these commercials so now these people were going to send me out all the time. But those agents proceeded for six to seven months to not send me out at all. And I couldn't understand what was going on. Then a director saw me at a theater gig where he was directing commercials in town. He worked primarily with People Store Agency, and so he tried to call me in for a commercial to the People Store. People Store called me up and now I was repped by People Store. Agents number three. I worked with them for a little while but they weren't getting me out very much and I didn't understand why.

Then I proceeded to get on my own project down in Florida, a lead role in a film on PBS. They needed another really good actor to do the film. So I got Michael Cole on the film with me. It started a very good friendship and he's still one of my good friends.

Michael introduced me to his agency, Houghton. But this is back when casting and agencies had just started to use email communications in a big way. They had the wrong email address for me. So I go another 5-6 months and no sign of anything from Houghton either but I'm used to it. Now I'm thinking this is how it goes. Houghton calls up and says you never answer any of our emails. We found out they had my email address wrong all along. So here is a great lesson for new actors – I needed to speak up but I didn't. Be proactive without being annoying.

Next, a free spec commercial comes up. The director chose me for it, I didn't even audition. They just give me the part. I go and do this free job for the agency. There are a lot of actors that are so hesitant to do that type of thing, especially nowadays. And when I did that, the director wrote a letter to my agent, saying how good I was. He was so thankful, and that started to build my relationship with Houghton to where they could trust me. They sent me out on Commercial Computers. I book that commercial. It did very well, so much so that they called me directly to do industrials. But knowing the business now, I called back and asked them to go through my agent. The next thing you know, career is building because of trust and my relationship with my agency has never stepped back since.

I had to prove to them that I could be successful, despite the fact that I didn't know what to do at the time. I'm persistent and consistent in working, accepting a lot of things for free, just to work on my craft and to be good at it. And building a business partnership with the agent where I'm making them look good despite the fact that I'm not making a fortune on any of these projects. But its really built respect from my agent and the casting companies, because they can rely on me.

And from there on, I was very professional, on time, theater taught me that. How to be constantly prepared and build a good reputation. It's not just being good at your craft, it's about being good at what you do. Be easy to work with, professional, on the ball, on time and not a diva. When you're that guy, you'll work.

How did you start supporting yourself especially before you started booking bigger jobs?

I was a personal trainer for 12 years at the YMCA. I found flexibility that way. I worked very hard at that job as well. It's no longer about just waiting tables. There's nothing wrong with that, but you can maintain a living through multiple ways. For me, it was personal training, side jobs, I dish washed, I did floor training, I worked in the maintenance department of the YMCA.

Did you get your physical trainer certification after you decided to pursue acting? Or was it something that you were already doing?

It was both. In other words, I worked at YMCA all the time, I put myself through college, I had scholarships, and I was a collegiate athlete. College athletics taught me hard work and made me focus. You only had so much time to practice for track, and only a certain number of hours to work to make money to pay bills. The rest of the time I had to stay focused on my studies.

So it wasn't that big of a shift when the studies turned into studying acting. To pay my bills, I still worked at the YMCA. Instead of focusing on collegiate athletics, my focus was on building an acting career. Not becoming a trainer. I did the physical training so that I could be a professional actor. There's a certain thing to be said for finding financial stability but not getting too comfortable. It was about never losing sight of the fact that my goal was to become a professional actor.

So because everything you do is within the industry, that gives you a certain amount of added bonus in terms of marketing and networking and knowing what's happening?

Yeah, I constantly have been able to have my thumb on the pulse of the industry and I've been able to see the industry from in front of the camera and from behind it. From the agency and casting perspectives. There's a big information gap between the way the real game is played and the way most actors think it's played. As an actor, you're taught theory, about the craft, how to be the best actor you can possibly be and make strong choices.

But what they don't teach you sometimes is the living, breathing machine that you're stepping into. The real position as an actor is that you're loaning people your artistry to serve a business. And sometimes the business uses art and sometimes my job has nothing to do with art, but everything to do with serving my role. And about networking and relationships and people you can trust and at the end of the day, money.

There's a lot of money involved with this. It's a very expensive art. You're gonna use people that you trust and can rely on. It makes sense that casting directors are gonna trust actors that they've been with a long time, that they know can do it. They work well together and they've been successful together. As a new actor, you have to be of service to someone and do it well. Network, but not from a needy standpoint, from a problem solving standpoint. Instead of making it about you, find ways to serve others and when you do that, you'll serve yourself.

There's a great book, Dale Carnegie's *How to Make Friends and Influence People*. It's a wonderful book and those principles hold very true in the acting world.

Not everybody can have jobs within the industry. What do you recommend they do in terms of marketing and networking?
Anytime there's an industry event, where you're getting a chance to be in front of industry professionals, take advantage of those things. Get involved in the Georgia Production Partnership (GPP), the local organizations where producers and crew and filmmakers are. Go to the local independent film scene by working in teams and getting involved in those production companies. That way you meet people who are working on better levels than you are.

If you are always hanging around with people who are working on your level or lower and you're not around people who challenge you to be better, you're in the wrong arena. You want to be around people and find events and productions that work with people better than you.

Good classes help you meet people who already are working with the better agents in town. Be strategic about your marketing. Bonnie Gillespie has a great book for actors, about targeting, being smart about using IMDB Pro and keeping up to date with what projects are coming into the market, Showfax and Actor's Access, using all your tools that you have available to you to be able to keep your finger on the pulse of the market, and knowing which shows will need your type and your characteristics.

Also learn about your product – yourself. Sam Christensen has a class on that. He has been a tremendous influence in my life because it made me better understand what I bring to the table that is different than anybody else. And that ties in to stopping looking to other people to give me something and instead focus on what I can bring to the table.

If you're brand spanking new, do a little bit of extra work to be able to understand what's going on and get involved, possibly to do some stand in work. Learn set etiquette and terminology so it's not a foreign place for you. You don't want to do what ended up happening to me. You don't want to end up being the first time on set, forgetting all of your words in front of a camera.

Also for networking, casting workshops are becoming viable options because you can get in front of agents. When I was in New York, it was essential because the industry was moving so fast, that was a way for them to see me. But be smart about the workshops you choose. Choose the one with the person who is casting a show that you could be on.

What it really boils down to is knowing what makes you unique and different. What do you bring to the person as an actor? And if you don't know those, then you can network all you want but you really don't know what you're bringing to the people.

You can't go in with the mentality that they're going to give you something. You have to go in with the attitude that I'm going in to learn, to meet this person and start to build a relationship. Not to seek out something from them. There's a difference. You approach it the way a good salesman does, that I want to meet this person and start to build this relationship with a person, not come in and try to sell them.

What do you for the future of acting in Atlanta? Do you see us continuing to grow and book bigger and bigger roles here?
It's already happening. The number of opportunities for better parts is growing. Like every other market, not everybody is going to get opportunities for those roles though.

What it amounts to is, for actors in this market, being able to do the work consistently and building a solid product that people can trust and rely on. There are those of us that have been successful at blazing trails to get people to trust us more. It's going to take some of those people saying no to smaller parts given out to make room, and start to bridge the gap between bigger parts and the actors that we can provide. Be willing to never stop growing. It's gonna take some time but five years ago, we weren't seeing any guest stars and now we're starting to.

Where are we gonna be in five more years? As long as the market continues to grow and people continue to get better, I guarantee casting will start being nationwide.

It boils down to not waiting for those roles to get here to get good. It's about the training and constant investment in becoming a better storyteller, as well as possible investment time outside this market.

It's also about us accepting that us getting to read for big parts is not such a big deal. It's just what we do. If you get to read for a big part, you can't get overexcited about it. You hear it all the time on Facebook. It puts so much weight on one audition. But what you begin to realize is that when you work with people on a higher level, this is the norm, nothing earth shattering.

Casting and producers and directors can sense when you have that right mindset, the difference?
They absolutely can. I almost can guarantee every time someone says that statement – pray this comes through, this is going to change my career –that they are not going to get this part. Their desperation will come through on the camera. Who are they doing the audition for - are they serving the producer

or the director or are they serving themselves? Our job as an actor is to behave truthfully, given imaginary circumstances. If that act of circumstance is I want this to make my career, not this character and this moment in this story - that's the problem. Am I worried about where I'm going or am I really truly in this person's moment right now?

You briefly moved to New York to get training and check out the market. You have no plans to move out to any of the bigger markets permanently?
If there were something to pull me there, I'd go. Going out there on a whim at this point in my life doesn't make any sense. Not when people are coming here.

How do you handle rejection and how do you stay in a positive mindset to pursue this?
Any actor who doesn't say to you that at least once or twice a year I'm sitting here thinking, what the hell am I doing, they'd be lying to you. Every actor has those points once or twice a year when they're going, am I just going crazy?

The more you endure the highs and lows of the business, the more you understand the business and what you bring to it. It's easy to weather those storms. I'm very thankful for my spiritual support because that ultimately determines whether I stay in this or not. But the other thing is that the job can't be the reason to do it. I do it because I don't have any other choice. This is what I love, this is what I do, and I knew I was born to tell stories. If I measure it by my booking, I'm in trouble. If I measure it by getting feedback from the people who do this at a more successful level than me and know that I'm moving towards the level that they work at, then that's how I can measure how I am doing.

I focus on improving my product to the best of my ability from others that are doing it better than me and are more successful than me. If I can do that, and I seek out avenues constantly to do that, then I have faith that the rest of the stuff will take care of itself. There are times when you're marketable and there are times that you are not marketable. That doesn't mean that I quit or that I'm an awful actor.

The other thing is sustainability. Right now, I'm on a five-month drought for me in film and television. That's a long time for me. But I'm doing a short film here in a month or two. I did a 72-page play, two-man show, professional level, getting on stage exercising my craft and getting better as an actor. Hardly made any money. But the show made me better as an actor and also sustained me artistically so that I can go back and do these day players and have it not be about me expressing myself. You have to find sustainability - financially, emotionally, spiritually, socially, artistically, so that the work can just be that. Do the work. Do the auditions. Do it to the best of my ability and not have it be a definition of who I am as a person.

Also actors get so focused on just themselves and their acting. I say, no, don't postpone things like having a family or being around family or friends and doing things like playing an instrument, painting, or volunteering.

As for rejection, it stops being rejection when you're sustained in so many different ways and you're able to say - sometimes they need your assistance and sometimes they don't. That doesn't mean that the solution I presented them wasn't a good one.

There are a lot of wonderful things about being an actor. But if it's all about making money, there are tons of other ways to make money. If it's about fame, you get into a speedo and parachute off the I-285 overpass; you're going to be famous. The problem is people are looking for the approval of other people to adore them and that's what's giving them meaning. That's unfortunate, because people are fickle. Fame is fickle.

I always tell people if I can make money and provide for my family through what I love to do, then just because I'm not a star doesn't mean I'm not an actor.

Of course, you set your goals high and you set your tone but maybe we should stop worrying about becoming famous and start worrying about making a living. Do what you love to do and try to be better. Understand there are times when you tell stories in 28 seconds on a commercial, there are times when you tell stories when you're teaching someone about kitchen safety in an industrial, and there are times when you are a lead in an independent film or the lead in a play, and there are times when you are a day player in a television show and you come in for one scene and you're done for the day. All of them are storytellers.

We get actors sometimes at the agency that say that they don't want to do any commercials or industrials but that can feed you and pay your bills. Instead they'd rather sit there and struggle financially about things when they could have done one industrial and paid their rent for the month? It happens all the time.

I still do Union extra work. Is there anything else that I can do today that's going to make me $350? If not, then why not do this? But again it's because I don't see the $350 as my artistic worth today. I see it as this is my job and I use my art to be in my jobs. But ultimately it's just my job.

If you had to do your career all over again, what, if anything, would you do differently?

I would have tried to get into a major performing arts academy or school. I'd invest in more training early on.

Do you believe that a formal degree helps?

I don't know if a formal degree helps. I would have gotten to a major studio or teacher earlier on. I would have gotten as quickly into William Esper's School for Meisner's technique up in New York, maybe done that early. And improv training. For me, personally, my college education helped me in other ways. It helped me in the business side. If I absolutely knew that I was going to be an actor, and that was going to be my passion and my thing, I'm not saying that I wouldn't have pursued my degree, but I would have got into a major performing arts studio like William Esper or worked with a master teacher as quickly as possible.

The other thing I'd say is I would try to find a good balance between all parts of my life. I wouldn't postpone other things in my life. I would get more experiences and make sure that I was doing the things that a good person does, because I know that was going to bring material that makes me a better actor. I think that there's a correlation - being a better person trained well becomes a better actor. And the reason why I say that is because of one word - empathy. The ability to empathize with words on a page, and another person's circumstances, that may not be the same circumstances that you have had. So in order to do that, it takes strong imaginations, and that takes a lot of life's experiences early on. For someone that doesn't have a lot of life experience, you don't have much to go off of. Because think about it, most of the time, our imagination begins with our own reality as the foundation.

There was nobody who could guide you or mentor you?
I had none of that. I was just going at it myself, and that's how I've done my career. People who have come before you, who have blazed trails before you, you find them, and be gracious towards them, and they can help guide you. I'm only where I'm at this point because of the people who've helped me. You know, Shannon Eubanks and Michael Cole, and Mystie Buice, my agent at Houghton, Sam Christiansen for my branding. I think Will Smith said that behind every actor is a good teacher. And that's what it boils down to. So I think that as a lesson, we have also the responsibility to help teach and mentor people who are coming behind us. And if we do that, then the market will go to a much higher level.

Wilbur Fitzgerald

Wilbur has appeared in over 100 feature films and television shows. His recent credits include Anchorman 2, Hunger Games: Catching Fire, The Founder, and television shows like Dallas, Prison Break, and Friday Night Lights. More information can be found at his website: http://www.wilburfitzgerald.com

Where are you from?
Atlanta, born and raised.

How did you get into acting?
I went to law school and was practicing law here. But I was restless doing the law practice and not really having landed in an area of practice that got me all psyched up. I had a good time though cause I did a lot of different things which have come back to help me later as an actor and also as an activist for our industry because I ended up working for one group that represented cities in the state of Georgia. So I ended up doing some early lobbying work at the state capital, writing legislation, and so I kind of got back into that when I worked on the tax incentive program in Georgia back in 2007-2008.

But I started acting out of curiosity. I took a course over at Emory University, one of their night courses for non-students. At that time called "Evenings at Emory." And they had a couple of actors in Atlanta who taught the course, just an introductory course. I didn't know anything was going on in Atlanta. It was all very much under the radar, especially production - Film production, Commercial production. So I took this course and then an agent came and spoke and I thought, "Well, this is interesting, I think that I'll take this a bit further." I ended up studying with one of the local teachers at that time. Wonderful woman, Sandra Dorsey, who was from Atlanta but spent several years on Broadway. She had studied under a teacher in LA, one of the fine teachers out there. And so, she brought her experience and her skills back to Atlanta. So I studied there.

Does this still exist?
Good question. Don't know. But, she was a good example of someone who should be teaching. Trained under a wonderful, established teacher in LA. Experienced in New York. And also was a working actor as well. But her primary business became teaching, not acting. So she was very good for Atlanta at that time.

And you studied on-camera audition technique with her?
Not really audition technique, more just acting, method acting. There may have been some on-camera work at some point but it was mostly just the basic craft of the work and scene study typically, which I happen to think is probably the best way to go for a young actor. So I did that, and because of my age and look at the time, I was approached by an agent, and started going out for TV commercials, and having the voice that I have, ended up doing voice-over work. It opened up that whole world in Atlanta for me of doing TV commercials, radio commercials,

corporate training films, and then eventually I started doing some TV and feature film work.

How did you get your agent?
It was different back then. You didn't necessarily sign anything exclusive with any one agent. There were three or four agents. The agents knew all the good acting teachers in town. They would come occasionally to an acting class and speak and so sometimes an agent would say, "Hey, Wilbur, nice to meet you, why don't you come by and see me and we'll talk about representation?"

So you know the agent would typically find the actor, which is always the best way to sign with the agents when they somehow find you. And I've gotten my best representation that way. I have a voice-over agent in New York that I've had for 20 years. Wonderful agent. And still maintain a connection with an agent in Austin, Texas that found me somewhere. I sort of grew from there, I spent a number of years in New York doing primarily voice-over work, and some work in TV commercials, a little bit of work in television.

During classes and while booking work, you were still working as a lawyer?
Working some as a lawyer at my own practice.

So you could set your own hours?
I could set my own hours. And also during that time in my career, there was constantly work of various kinds available to actors. It's changed a little bit now. But for me, I was doing a lot of industrial work, corporate video stuff. What's called now the "Co-ed Contract" in group SAG-AFTRA. I was either doing an industrial, or I was doing a TV commercial or a radio

commercial, occasionally a film would come to town, or a TV movie. Had a lot of those back in the 80s and 90s.

I was always doing something. Working a pretty good bit. Occasionally there was some travel to places like Charlotte, NC or some place in Alabama. The work was mostly in Atlanta, but a lot of it was regional. I did some work down in Florida. And for about 12 years, I put most of the emphasis on voice-over work, which is when I went to New York to do national commercials, promos, and movie trailers.

You moved to New York?
Yeah I bought a place in New York on Central Park West. But I didn't move full time. I would go up and spend about three months at a time and do primarily voice-over work which was very rewarding and successful for me. And living the life of an actor and going on anywhere from 3 to 5 to 9 auditions a day. A day! It was great. At some point, I decided that I really wasn't doing what I originally set out to do as an actor, which was to do film and television. And it wasn't working for me in New York. I came back to Atlanta to jump back into that, and that has worked out.

Did you ever go to LA?
I did some work out there but New York was a better fit for me, it just had the right energy for me. And coming back to Atlanta worked out because there was still a lot of work in the region, film and TV work, and then jumping ahead several years, a lot of the work shifted to Canada because of the dollar exchange rate and tax incentives. And then the tax incentive thing started to happen in various states.

Georgia got involved in about 2004. And then Louisiana upped the game and as soon as they did, it was going to be really changing the production in Georgia because we were no longer competitive. So that's when I got involved with casting director Shay Griffin and Ric Reitz and Ed Spivia, the former film commissioner, and we approached the then governor Sonny Perdue back in 2007 and said we have an idea to make our incentive more competitive. He listened to our presentation, and he liked it and he put us to work on a business plan. We were successful in convincing him that this was the way to go and then we lobbied for this and got it passed in 2008 and the rest is history. Thank goodness. It's been huge.

That's fantastic. A huge impact.
So it's been good because we were doing this, in all honesty, not only for our own livelihood but because we loved the industry that's going on in Georgia for so long. The last thing we wanted to see was the industry virtually going away, in a very short time. We had too many friends in the business that we wanted to make sure still live and work in Georgia. And as soon as that bill was passed and signed into law in 2008, business immediately started coming back, people started coming back, crew people and we've grown beyond even our wildest expectations to where we are today with the economic impact, the infrastructure growth, the studios, and I think we'll have this sustained growth for a good number of years.

Which is great for the actor in some ways because there was a time when there were any number of different roles which might be available for an actor in Georgia. One of my first good roles on a TV show was a recurring role on a show called "In the Heat of the Night" with Caroll O'Connor, and I ended up working on that show off and on for about five years. That's become more difficult to pick up that kind of role because a lot of what we have here now are the smaller, day player roles. It's a little bit more challenging for the new actor to grow beyond that simply because of the way that the casting landscape has changed.

So what do you see as the future of acting being in Atlanta? Because, like you say, the opportunities sometimes are not made available to starting actors and then I've been on productions where they've flown in talent from LA to work here.

A lot. And many times you might look at that talent that's been brought in and think, we have that person right here. This is what casting director Shay Griffin did for years when she was trying to sell the state many years ago. She would go to LA and she would talk to a producer and she would say the magic words, "We can save you money." They'd be like, "What do you mean?" "Well let me see your cast breakdown. Oh, I've got that person in Atlanta, I've got that person in Atlanta, I've got that...in other words you don't have to fly that person in." "Oh you do?" "Yeah we've got that person."

And so, Hollywood started to trust people like Shay on those casting decisions because it comes down to money, trust and relationships, and so she was able to show them in many cases that they didn't have to fly the entire cast in from LA to shoot in Georgia. We have those people here. For some reason, that's not the case anymore because though they are saving around 30 percent on their production costs, because so much of the production has left LA, the creative is still in LA and New York and my personal opinion is that they're trying to hold on to as much as they can. Knowing the production is going to be done in Georgia, they're still trying to hold on to all the creative decisions and protect their turf.

It doesn't come down to, well, yeah we can get that actor in Georgia. It's not about that necessarily. This is a very competitive business. So like I was talking to you about, I'm trying to up the game with my audition self-tape videos and headshots and things. The most basic way an actor can up his or her game is by being well trained and it's important to seek out the very best and this is why, if I were sitting here talking to an actor who's excited about getting into the business and all that, my advice still would be to start in LA or New York, and find some of the best teachers and spend a period of time where it's not going to be about your getting out and auditioning, it's going to be about your craft. It would be going to LA, or New York, or London and training so that, because you hear that over and over, the actors that people like to work with are the best trained actors.

And we see that with these British actors booking all these roles in Hollywood.
Yes, I'm sorry, but they're just terrific. It's a trend, but it's a trend with logic behind it.

But we do have good training in LA and New York.
We do. We absolutely do. And I studied with a woman in New York, who's just terrific, it's very intense scene study. And, you know on a show, you have to not just audition, but when you're on a show, you have to make split second decisions to go in a certain direction emotionally or you have to be able to go in and be prepared to go with the flow with some of the changes of who you're working with. This is why improv training is also, to me, very basic stuff that you need to look at in becoming an actor.

I was on a show last year with Samuel L. Jackson and John Cusack and the first day I went into work, we called a little meeting off to the side and Sam Jackson said, "I don't like these lines, I've written my own thing here." Cusack said, "Yeah, I've made some changes here" and talking to me he said, "You feel comfortable taking these lines and we'll switch these around?" And I said, "Sure". We were just sitting there, in a way just cutting and pasting. And the director was looking at us like, "What are you guys doing?" But you know this is what happens when you have really good and experienced actors like Cusack and Jackson, they want to get in there and change the material and make it their own.

You've got to be able to do that dance or it's just not going to work out. I learned that early on, you might have those lines down, but when you get to the set, especially on a TV show, they might call you aside and say, we've changed all of this, we're going to be shooting in about 30 minutes so you might want to go back and work on this new material. You've got to be able to do it. It's just the way it is so a lot of it obviously comes with experience, but it comes with good training too. Sort of being quick on your feet.

So one good tip then is that if an actor wishes to pursue acting even in Atlanta, get the top notch training that, I guess, unfourtunately doesn't exist in Atlanta today?
I don't think it does, still doesn't exist, certaintly not at the level that's available in New York, LA or London. It seems that in Atlanta people are excited about getting in the business and they can take an eight-week course and they're camera ready. Ready to go out and rule the world and work on a show and it's not to say that you can't sort of get ready for something, to be at a certain level in eight weeks, but not the level that you really need to be, not at the level compared to the LA actor that's been training for years.

An LA actor that gets a call for an audition goes and spends an hour or two with their acting coach. They're accoustomed to that heavy, intense competition. And I've seen some of the auditions and audition tapes that come out of LA, they're really good. That's not to say that every LA actor is great, but a lot of them understand the demands of the business better than we do in Atlanta, on average.

So we have all of these studios coming up here, a lot of production. People see all this coming up and go, "Oh you should be getting all these roles." No, it's still about getting the best training wherever it is and then coming here.
That's right. And, I think there is an awakening to this that we have to be prepared that just because the production is here, does not translate into "Oh I've got all these great job oppourtunities awaiting me." And we have these agents that represent far too many people that are not good yet, and that's a concern. They wonder why they're not working or they're not getting the opportunities.

It's fine for a person to say "You know, I think I want to try this acting thing." You never know. And they try this acting thing. My advice is as soon as you realize that, wow, this is what I want to do, then you should be on that journey to become the best at what you're doing and what you're planning to do, and that may really require that you go off and pursue this in a place like New York or LA.

You might even want to stay there and pursue the work at some point, but it becomes about the training. And for somebody at my state of the game, it becomes about the experience. I'm able to walk in the room with a certain level of confidence because when I'm going to go into the room to meet a director or producer, I'm going to be prepared for anything that they throw at me. To me, that's the fun of it. There was a time in my life where I wasn't excited about auditions, that day is gone. I love auditions. I love to go in and immediately try to be part of the team. Like here I am, let's have fun, let's create something.

Auditioning is the job, really.
Yeah it is. In some ways, I snap my fingers and I become whatever it is that I'm playing. Totally committed. And that's the fun of it.

So you believe that the industry is going to continue to be here in terms of production?
I do. But all that always depends on what the political landscape is. But as it exists currently, with a very supportive government, a very supportive governor, very supportive legislature, it looks like we have a good long-term future here with production. Obviously there's a lot of investment, which is not incentivized like the studios. It would be a surprise if somebody popped up on the legislative scene and decided to pull the rug out and change the tax incentive, but you know what? It could happen.

This is one of those things where you never can become too comfortable. You have to be diligent. Look what's happening in the state of Louisiana. They're having serious problems with budget shortfalls and will probably continue to for the next few years. But, their legislature is proposing a cap on their tax incentive. Like 180 million dollars. It's passed in their House. It's going over in their Senate. I have no reason to believe that that won't pass in the Senate. That will cut their production perhaps in half. Certainly for 2016. A lot of the studios plan their feature films 12 to 18 months out. They've planned their TV shows. They've planned to go in and have a show and maybe have it there for five years. So, this will certainly change the planning for the studios as it relates to working in Louisiana.

And that will probably have a positive impact on Georgia. So I won't say it's a fragile sort of thing. But when you have groups like Georgia Production Partnership, which are very involved politically, and are very diligent with their planning and pay attention to relationships with the governor, with somebody who might be the future governor, the speaker, and who might be the future speaker.

It's about never becoming complacent. And my sense is some of this complacency came into play with North Carolina and had something to do with the loss of their incentive. I know that North Carolina has a steep history, and I love to work there. I always enjoy working in Wilmington and other places in the state of North Carolina. It's a great place to work. And you know I think you can start to feel like you're entitled. Your business is here, you've had a history and we're entitled to keep having that history.

But the business industry does not respect history or entitlement. It respects the bottom line. Always. You will have some states that are favorites to shoot in that will pick up production work no matter what. Like Texas. People just enjoy working in Texas. I've done many shows out there. So you have some shows that are driven by not as much the money as perhaps, in some cases, the landscapes and locations. But before, it used to be all locations driven. That's no longer the case.

What about the perception of actors in Atlanta? Is there still a perception gap in terms of talent level and quality? If you were to get top-notch training, really get good in New York and LA and come back here, would one have a chance at getting the bigger roles?

I think there is a perception that the highest industry standards are still in LA. Or in New York. I think that a lot of that is perpetuated by those people who want to continue to make sure that the LA talent is up for the good roles - that's where you do your hiring. My experience over the years has been that the directors and producers have been surprised sometimes at how good the talent is here. But you have to realize that we're a very mature market. We've been doing this work since at least the early 70s here. We've had film and TV here for a while. So we've built up a nice little talent pool of experienced actors.

And there are some recurring roles booked out of here too. Absolutely. A lot. I've been fortunate to pick up recurring roles on a number of shows that either shot here or in Texas. The industry feels more comfortable if they're hiring the day players here and if they're hiring the series regulars in LA or New York, especially with some of the younger actors. For somebody like myself, because I've been around for a long time and I've got a lot of experience, I feel like I can go in and compete with pretty much anybody because I've been doing this for so long. It's been my career. But so many of the LA actors, young actors, they go there, they make a commitment to train, it's what they're going to do. They might have to work other jobs to do that. This is what I tell other actors. If you really want the real world of commitment, go to New York or LA. There's a perception here that if you go to the right weekend seminar with the right LA casting director, that's going to put you where you need to be, but that's not going to happen. And the same thing is true with voice acting. We have some good voice coaches here. But I think it's like so many things in life. Here's an odd but valid comparison. If you've got some sort of illness, you go out and seek out the best doctor. You don't go just to the emergency room at Emory Hospital and hope for the best. You might start there. But you go and find the best man or woman who knows what you've got and who has done thousands of hours of diagnostic work on it. And that's where you go. Go to the specialist. And I think that for acting you go to a specialist. Because it's not just something you want on your resume, it's something you want to have inside of you.

What do you do in terms of marketing and networking?

Not enough. If I were a younger actor, I would think more about the marketing that's done through social media. When I was working on this film in North Carolina, I met a social media person for Nicolas Sparks. And I asked her, how important is social media for this movie and for Nicolas Sparks and for this whole promotional aspect and casting and all that. And she said, "Oh it's very important, it plays a big role in our casting, especially for these young leads. We know that if they have hundreds of thousands of followers, we look at that as a built-in audience." So the actors own development and network comes into play, especially for the younger leads. For somebody like me, it doesn't make any difference. It's not the group that I'm in. So I think the best marketing involves being able to show off good work and have good demos. That's what you want it to come down to. I don't think you want your marketing to get ahead of your talent and your ability. It's like rigging a number on IMDB. If you can rig a number through some sort of algorithm on IMDB and rank at number 562 and you've done two short films, what have you really accomplished? Nothing.

The star rating on IMDB, you mean?

Yes, the star rating. But I think you bring up an interesting question because to me, the best marketing is developing relationships. And part of developing relationships, in my opinion, is doing the kind of work where you become known as a person that is, perhaps, not only getting the job done, but you're fun on the set, you're low maintenance, you're dependable.

Somebody once said to me, casting is sort of like problem solving. In other words, if Wilbur walks into the room, and I'm in a nice, dark pinstripe suit, they look at my resume and go, "Oh, you're reading for this lawyer, and you're also a lawyer." So, fine. And the conversation is, let's go with this guy. He knows what he's doing. That's his background. He read very well. And so you've solved that problem. On to the next person.

This is how fickle the process is sometimes, but it's just the way that it is. I had a guy who was head of ABC casting one time. I walked into the room to shoot for a TV pilot that was shooting here in Atlanta. And the guy looked up, pointed to me and said, "You are exactly what I had in mind for this character, I hope you're good." And I said, "Well, we'll find out." I ended up getting the role. But it was a very interesting lesson that could cut both ways, especially in television. I happened to walk in and I was what he had in mind for the look. That became more important than what I was going to do in the performance. Fortunately, it worked out and everything fell into place. But if I had walked in and been not even close to what he had in mind, my performance would not have mattered at all. I did not fit the look. There was nothing that I could do about it. No amount of preparation would have made any difference, especially in television. It's so driven by type. You are stuck, for better or for worse. Now feature film, probably a lot more wiggle room. Certainly a lot more wiggle room if you're doing stage. Because of the kind of things they can adjust.

It's funny because actors worry so much about "Did I say this one word right or not." When in fact, 90 percent is out of their control.

Out of their control. So what you do is you try to figure out what you are in control of, and you make sure that that part of it is at 100 percent. Whatever that is. It's interesting. But I want to get back to this thing about relationships. What you'll see is when you develop good relationships with not only colleagues, other actors, but when you work on a show, when you work on something or another, whatever it is. People are going to remember that you were a solid team player. And you want, even with your friends, you want to be around people you enjoy being around.

And because there certainly are a lot of people we don't want to be around whom we run across. I think that our business is no different than that. I remember one time I worked on a TV pilot or something and it was a funny role that I did. It was great. Then somewhere, a year or two later, I got hired out of the blue to be in this national TV commercial, and for the life of me I couldn't figure out why until I got on to the set, and it happened to be the same director who I worked with two years prior. So, good relationships come back. And the other, "not-so-good" relationships will also come back, but not in a good way. So...

What're your thoughts on the other things that the actors try to do in terms of sending postcards, sending gifts, or trying to get into casting director workshops, trying to get in front of them...are those useful?
I think they're all very tempting, because we're always looking for something to connect. I really can't speak to the effectiveness and of course the way that social media has changed the landscape of promotion, I want to once again go back to the relationship aspect of the promotion. I want to ask the question, if the actor has an agent or is looking for an agent, what kind of relationship already exists between that agent and

the casting directors because that's still where the challenge is for the newer actor.

A casting director typically already knows any one of the 5 to 10 people who can go in and get the job done. A casting director does not want to take chances. The casting director never wants to be embarrassed. So why should a casting director see a new actor they've never heard of when he or she knows they've already gotten 10 actors that can fill that role. Now, if you're a new actor, your agent will submit you but beyond that, how does an agent get to that casting director and say, "You really need to see this new client." As the agent, you've got the challenges of somehow getting the actor into the room or in front of the casting director. This is where it's important for you to have a good relationship with your agent so that you can have this conversation because that's who you're selling yourself to first – your agent, and then the agent is selling you to the casting director. And this is where managers really come into play in markets like LA and New York where a manager can build a relationship with a casting director and say, "Boy, you really need to see Wilbur for this role, Wilbur's a terrific actor, he's also a lawyer in real life, he's done so and so and so and so, he's just got cast on this." That's what a manager does.

Unfortunately, the agents in Atlanta, because of the volume of people that they represent, that's not as likely to happen anymore, where they can really go to bat for you and pick up the phone. And truth of the matter is that a lot of the casting directors don't want to have a conversation with an agent because they're combing the entire Southeast for a role. They can look at the thumbnails of 300 videos in front of them and think that just by doing that they can select the right actor. And maybe they can.

Are managers becoming available in Atlanta?

I hear that they are but I tend to doubt that that's going to become the norm here because first of all, managers don't necessarily fit the traditional landscape here where that manager can get a casting director on the phone and try to sell somebody. It's common in LA and New York. It's not common here. I don't know if the casting directors will go along with that. I heard that they won't.

So what else can an actor do in Atlanta to stay connected?

I think that the best information ends up being the information you hear from other actors about what's going on. I'll give you an example - I read for the director and casting director on this movie confirmation a few days ago. When I first got the call to put it on video, I looked at the breakdown. There were a number of roles on there in my email from my agent. So I called a buddy of mine in LA and said, "You know, the star of this movie is so and so and you just worked with her recently. I bet you there's a role for you in here. Have you heard about it?" So he called his agent, calls a couple of other people, checked it out, and ended up getting a reading for one of the leads in the show. I tipped him off at something he had not heard of.

Early in my career, I was tipped off by some friends about shows that I ended up reading for and getting cast in and I had some very good friends that knew that I had certain training, certain talent, etc. and they called the agent and said, "Maybe you should submit Wilbur, yeah he's pretty funny, does a lot of improv, I've seen him do a lot of improv." That kind of conversation actually led to a role for me on a film that shot for two months. So network with your other actors because that will put you in that loop of perhaps doing that weekend film, that short film, that will give you some experience, that thing may not lead to anything, but you're working with your colleagues. To me, that's the best networking you can do.

And classes.
That's right. Yeah. But you know it's about any kind of good exposure that you can have. And not the fake publicity that you're always doing for yourself, or some people are always doing for themselves on Facebook and you can sort of figure out pretty quickly that that's just B.S.

What do you wish someone had told you at the beginning of your career? Or if you had to re-do your career all over, what would you do differently?
I think once I realized that I wanted this as my career, I would have treated it the same way I would have treated law school. I would have gone to school.

Get a formal degree?
Perhaps. But certainly found a great teacher. A curriculum where I'm in for a year or two. I think that sort of being pushed, to where a good teacher can push you, to very uncomfortable places, so that you not only learn how to go to those places, but you develop confidence that you feel like "I can pretty much do anything. I've been challenged and stretched." It's a workout.

And also it gets you thinking. One of the most important things about this work is script analysis, breaking this script down and knowing who your character is, and also knowing who you are, knowing what your casting is. So that if somebody says, "Wilbur, let's do this scene again, and this time I just want you to be yourself." What does that mean - be yourself? That person knows what they're asking you to do. Do you know what that means - to be yourself? It can be difficult.

So if I were to start again, that's what I would do. What, you can't afford to go to New York? Well, figure it out! Make sure that those first few years are not about getting an acting job, but they're about getting the training that will sustain you for the rest of your career. For a lot of people, that's working in the theater.

I had a buddy of mine that was working on one of the Atlanta shows. And they were block shooting. Which meant they were shooting all the scenes in one particular direction that they had lit. And he had to do 12 continuous pages without stopping. Yeah. And four different scenes. And he's had theater training, very good actor. So, he took several days to prepare, knowing that there was going to be some version of that stretch. And I don't think that he even anticipated that they were going to go 12 straight pages without cutting, bam, bam, bam, bam. He killed it. But he was prepared.

So it's about preparing. Over preparing. And running the lines with your girlfriend, your boyfriend or your spouse, whatever it is, just over and over and over because you're going to be doing it over and over and over and over on a set. You might end up working like I did one time. David Fincher, he'll do maybe 25-40 takes. And part of his reasoning is that at some point you are going to break down, and maybe in those last takes, something is going to come out that you've never even rehearsed.

So it's interesting. I didn't always enjoy the audition process, but I actually love it now because in the preparation, you discover things. You discover something in that fifth or that tenth time around that didn't occur to you. I wish I had time, don't always have the luxury of time to do a video audition, do a self-tape, sleep on it, look at it the next morning and then go, oh, that wasn't so hot. I can do better than that. I came up with something overnight. And I can re-shoot it.

In many ways, the self-taping phenomenon has given us an advantage in that you could, if you had the time do that, go back and change it.
That's right. Take advantage of it. And some are on such short notice. For example, the other day, I was asked to put on tape and only had three hours to turn around but my day just didn't allow me. Disappointing, but it just didn't allow it. Most of the times we have 24 hours. And you can do a lot in 24 hours. So, yeah, take advantage of that.

The other thing is think about the quality of whatever it is you're turning out. Maybe you can get by with an iPhone and a bed sheet that's not quite fully ironed as your backdrop and the sound is going to be echo-ey. Is that how you want to present yourself? I don't. I want to present myself as somebody who makes this as real as possible, as technically beautiful as possible. I want the sound to be absolutely perfect. Of course, it still goes back to the performance, but I want to leave the impression that I'm a person who goes after quality, I want to put the best presentation out there.

And when you talk about setting up the cinematic look, little things make a difference, the little touches.
It's like, wow, this is interesting. Little touch. Something a little interesting. And sometimes I'll do this with a script. The words are not sacred to me. I will improv things, if I can come up with something that makes it a little bit more interesting, I will do that. The words can be sacred later on if they have to be. But I want this to be interesting, or else I'll find some way to have a more interesting lead-in. I think it's challenging to do an audition where there's just one line, or something like that.

You talked about being a lawyer, and being able to have your own practice and have the flexibility. Have you practiced law throughout your acting career?

I don't really practice anymore. And I don't have to. So I've even put more of my focus now into the work that I'm doing as an actor. And so I'm afforded more time to do that. I think that's helped me because I'm not really professionally doing anything else. Except for the volunteer work that I do and will continue to do in the industry. But my focus is on my film and TV career.

Yolanda Asher

Yolanda Asher *has performed onstage from New York to Ohio as well as in film and TV. She sang in the opera workshop* A Blessing on the Moon *at Emory. She performs in the annual Atlanta Community Food Bank fundraiser* Lend Me an Ear. *Yolanda serves as Secretary of the Atlanta local SAG-AFTRA board and is Co-Chair of the SAG-AFTRA Atlanta Indie Outreach Committee. She also volunteers on the Agent Relations, HealthNet and other committees. She's a past member of the Atlanta Area Equity Liaison Committee. She is represented by the Jana VanDyke Agency.*
resumes.actorsaccess.com/yolandaasher

Tell me where you're from and how you got started.
I was born in New York and raised in New Jersey. I graduated from NYU's Tisch School of the Arts with a Bachelor of Fine Arts in Acting. Part of my NYU training was with the Stella Adler Studio. I was thrilled to get into NYU because it wasn't easy and they're one of the top acting training colleges in the country. I was also grateful for the scholarships. It was an amazing

education that opened me up to so many things I didn't know about, like experimental theatre.

For as long as I can remember I always wanted to be an actor, singer and dancer. My mother and father sang in a choir, and my mother told me that she sang when she was pregnant with me. So I had my first on-stage experience while in utero, and then when I was four, in Polish school productions.

My father said that his mother always wanted to be an actress, but she had a family to care for in Poland and was denied being able to follow her dream. So I guess it's in my genes. My parents were supportive in that they liked seeing me perform, but my father always told me to "Get a real job." Yet, when I settled on something else that nurtured my soul, he still didn't consider it a "real" job because I was self-employed as a Shiatsu (Japanese Acupressure) therapist. He wanted me to have a steady job. My mother was happy that I was fulfilling my dream. I'm a healing artist and a performing artist, and both careers intertwine.

So that's one way you supplement your income as well.
Yes. What's wonderful about Shiatsu is I can make my own hours. So if I have an audition or a shoot coming up, my Shiatsu clients are very understanding about that. I previously worked in the corporate world as an administrative assistant and also did temp jobs. It's important to be able to have the freedom to take time off for auditions and shoots.

Tell me more about your training and experience after NYU and Stella Adler Studio.
I continued my training with workshops and classes. You can't say, "I have a BFA. I know it all." An actor's job is always to grow and learn more. You have to keep the acting muscle flexible and keep perfecting your craft. Don't let it get rusty. Acting for film

and TV is much different than for the theater. My initial training was in theater. I studied Shakespeare and the classics. After I graduated, most of the parts I got were in stage musicals because I sang and danced. I was glad to be able to use my classical training when I played Maria in *West Side Story* in Summer Stock, Michigan. I also performed as a singer and dancer at Radio City Music Hall's *Magnificent Christmas Spectacular*. When I was cast at Radio City I thought, "Oh wow! I've got it made." But once the show was over, I had to look for the next gig, and that's the hardest part about being an actor. There's no job security.

How did you end up in Atlanta?
I moved to Atlanta because I felt like I needed to be in a new environment. The Atlanta film industry was growing and it was close enough to New York so I wouldn't be too far away from my family, yet still be able to be on my own. I thought about moving to L.A., but it would have been too much of a change for me. I didn't have any connections there and I knew some people here. So I came here. I used to say it was the trees that pulled me here. I needed a kinder environment than what New York was. I was in a sublet in Hell's Kitchen, but that expired and I had to find another place to live. I had a great job as an independent contractor in the corporate world and made good money. I was interviewing with New York talent agents and one agent felt like a good fit. We really liked each other. But then then I found a place to live in metro-Atlanta and moved.

My New York film jobs were mostly background work. They liked that I had a car and often used me with my car. It paid well because I was SAG. I also got some work on AFTRA shows. In NY, you must belong to the unions, so each union card I earned felt like a great achievement. But Atlanta is in a right to work for less state. I am still glad that I'm in the unions here, and that SAG and AFTRA have merged.

I don't think people should join right away. They first need to get some training and acting credits. Join when you're ready. If most of your work is coming from union projects then join and pay your dues. Step up to the plate as a professional and get your pension and health credits. Don't believe anyone that says you don't need to join in Georgia. It may not be a requirement, but you might lose out on opportunities if you're not SAG-AFTRA. A friend told me she wasn't considered for some roles because she wasn't union. Another friend told me he got more bookings after he joined.

Has being a SAG-AFTRA member been a challenge in Atlanta?
Yes and no. At one point, when things were slow, I wondered what it would have been like if I weren't union, but then realized it would have been no better. Lots of hard work for very little money. I've heard horror stories from non-union actors who have worked jobs where they ended up not getting paid, or had to wait months before getting paid. They also complained about other issues. They always prefer to work on union projects and benefit from the negotiated conditions. So in that respect, I'm grateful SAG-AFTRA is there to protect me.

Oh! And the term SAG-Eligible? Many actors who have no intention of joining will use that moniker as if it means something. All it means is that you're non-union. It doesn't impress anyone.

Do you believe that we will book bigger roles out of Atlanta?
Definitely. Our local Talent Agents are working on that. Because of Georgia's growth in film and TV production, the opportunities can only get better. We have a very strong financial incentive for producers to bring their projects here and I think that will keep

expanding. Studios have built facilities in Georgia and more are planned. We have good support for that within our local government. Georgia lawmakers are seeing the value of the film industry and wherever a film or TV show is shooting, local businesses are experiencing the financial support it brings. I find it interesting that actors from New York and Los Angeles are moving to Atlanta because of the work being shot here. That raises the quality and quantity of our talent pool.

What do you think is the most important thing that an Atlanta actor can do to raise their game?
It's important for Atlanta actors to be professional. I'm talking about those who are originally based out of here and haven't seen the way things are done in New York and L.A. Read everything. Respond to everything. Follow the instructions. Don't be flaky. And take classes. Everybody says this and it's so true. Really perfect your craft. Acting is a muscle that needs to be exercised. Don't treat it like a hobby.

I have heard many talent agents are cutting their rosters so they can focus on the serious actors. If you take your job seriously, then they will take you seriously. Take a pro-active role in your career.

When I see a breakdown online that fits me, I submit myself for consideration. And my agent is glad about that. Some agencies don't want you to do that; you need to know your agent's stance on self-submissions. If you have an agent, make sure you're following their instructions on how they want you to be. I can't stress enough to follow instructions. Read all the fine print twice, three times, and make sure you have it correct. And when they ask you to label a file a specific way, label it the way they requested.

I have heard of casting directors deleting an audition video file just because it wasn't labeled the way they wanted it to be labeled. If an actor can't follow simple instructions on how to name a file, then what are they going to be like on set?

Go and train with the best teachers in town as well. Don't study with someone who's going to stroke your ego and say "You're wonderful" without giving you pointers on how to improve. Don't be afraid to fail either. Do things outside your comfort zone.

Having studied at the New York University Tisch School of the Arts and the Stella Adler Studio, do you believe that kind of formal training is useful or valuable to actors?
Definitely, yes. Structured, focused training is really important. I don't think I know of anyone who is a good actor who hasn't had any training at all. I don't know of any actor who is just a natural. You can tell when somebody has had coaching or training - it's more real.

Do we have good training here in Atlanta?
Well, I know we have several universities here with theatre programs. I'm not sure what kind of training they provide, since I haven't monitored any classes. But I have attended theatrical performances at Emory University and Oglethorpe University, and there was a lot of talent there. Emory also hires professional actors to perform alongside the student actors, which benefits the student.

There are also many different acting training studios in town. I'm always excited when L.A.-based coaches like Crystal Carson and Ted Brunetti come here with intensive Film and TV acting workshops. They're amazing and really work you hard.

You don't plan to move out of Atlanta any time?
No. For one, I don't have as much family up in New York as I used to. And with the film industry growing here now, this is the place for me to be. I would consider moving to New York or Los Angeles if I was offered a role on a TV series. That would be sweet. But to tell you the truth, I really like the Atlanta community! We're a nice supportive family.

If you had to re-do your career, would you do anything differently?
I probably would not have left New York when I did. I have wondered what my career would have been like if I had stayed there instead of moving to Atlanta. What other opportunities I could have had if I had signed with the NY agent who was courting me.

How do you deal with rejection? How do you stay positive?
Don't take anything personally. There are many other factors outside of your control. So do your audition and then forget about it. Like for *IVIDE*, (The Indian feature film shot in Atlanta that I helped cast) when I submitted my headshot and saw the character breakdown, I thought "My God, that's me! That's me!"

But I didn't hear back for months. So I let it go and thought, "Okay, moving on to the next audition!" And then I finally got a request to submit an audition tape. It was a nice surprise. So I taped my audition and sent it in. A week later, I was asked to come in to audition in person. I appreciated being told afterwards that the director really liked me, was interested in me, and wanted to meet with me. It gave me hope while I was waiting to hear if I was cast. You usually don't get that kind of feedback.

Yeah I know your pain.

Thanks. But auditioning, that's part of my job. It's a free performance that eventually ends up with a paid gig. I just go from one to the next, to the next, to the next, to the next, and stay positive. If I don't get cast in something, then I will be cast in something else. As long as I'm continuing to be called for auditions, then I know I'm doing something right. Casting Directors don't waste their time calling in people they don't think can do the role. It ends up being a numbers game. Eventually something will land.

It's really hard not to obsess about your auditions. But you have to let them go! Always plan something else to do afterwards to get your mind off it. If you think you made a mistake in any way, then make a mental note to learn from it so you don't repeat it next time. Keep learning and growing.

Any final thoughts for new actors starting out in Atlanta?
Register with the main casting websites serving Atlanta: Actors Access, Casting Networks, Now Casting and 800 Casting. Some charge a fee and others are free. All the agents require having an online profile at these sites because that's how Casting Directors list their breakdowns. So while working to get an agent, you'll be ahead of the game. You'll receive casting notice emails and be able to submit yourself for projects. Some projects don't go through talent agents and only post online. That's how I got my role in the film *IVIDE*.

Be wary of other sites that promise you the moon. When in doubt, ask around.

Keep studying. Do theatre. Do student films. Participate in the 48-Hour Film Project. Take improvisation classes. Do play readings. Read aloud to children. Do whatever it takes to exercise your acting muscle.

Also, don't be a prima donna or a diva. And that goes for men as well as women. Don't be overly demanding or hard to work with. Do your homework. Come prepared. Pay attention. Take direction. Relate with your partner. Hit your mark and say your lines. I know an actor who was cast in a film because someone on crew saw her name in the list of actors they were considering for a specific role and said, "Oh, I've worked with her before. She's really great." Boom! She got the job. It can be as simple as that.

Additional Resources on Acting in Atlanta

- http://www.actorsanonymousatl.com
- http://www.thedinnerprojectshow.com
- http://www.ozonline.tv/oz_sourcebooks1_gfvs.html
- http://www.georgiaproduction.org
- http://pdavidalexander.com/getting-into-the-acting-business-in-atlanta
- http://www.houghtontalent.com/links.htm
- http://amtagency.com/client-resources
- http://peoplestore.net/resources

About Rafiq

Website: http://rafiqbatcha.com
IMDB page: http://imdb.me/rafiqbatcha

Grab a hot cuppa milky n' sweet Indian chai and gather around for a story.

I kinda stumbled into acting in Atlanta. I was born in Mumbai, India, home of Bollywood. So the desire to act can't be helped ☺. I'd acted in plays, break-danced and sang (slightly off key) on-stage throughout school, college and grad school. I even performed the role of Shylock in "The Merchant of Venice" three separate times - in elementary, middle and high school. So you could say I am "trained in Shakespeare" ☺. I made short films and even took some classes but never seriously considered acting a real career.

Until one day in 2008, while dreading yet another trip to a client site when I was working as a management consultant, I realized I just couldn't continue this. I was too unhappy. I had to make a massive change in my life. So I decided to make a full length movie, the first Hindi language Bollywood style feature film set and shot in Atlanta, called "Mumbhai Connection", about the struggles of an Indian IT salesman forced to sell IT services to the Atlanta mafia. Getting the movie made and released was one of the most challenging things I've ever done. The mistakes I made alone are worthy of a separate book. But I finally got distribution and released it in theaters across India in 2014.

Almost in parallel, as I was going through an existential crisis, in 2008, the Georgia Entertainment Industry Investment Act got expanded vastly, and the number of film and TV productions in Atlanta began to grow. So when I got done with shooting Mumbhai Connection, and the long process of post-production and finding distribution was underway, I decided to try my hand at getting professional representation. I got signed on by Houghton Talent, and have pursued professionally acting in Atlanta since then.

Looking back, fate/chance/luck has had much of a role to play. Kismet got me to live in a city that's turned out to be such a hot acting market, where I'm in a niche (South Asian male).

I continue to take classes. Houghton sends me out on auditions. I self-submit as much as I can. And I sustain myself day-jobbing at a large technology company doing product marketing – basically telling stories using PowerPoint. I'm grateful to have a job that gives me the flexibility to pursue acting and keeps me from being desperate to book.

Dear future superstar,

I hope you enjoyed reading "Acting in Atlanta" and that you find it useful. I've tried to create a book that I would've loved to help me when I started out.

I'd like to ask you a favor – please share your thoughts on Amazon whether you loved it, hated it, felt it was "meh". It will be immensely helpful.

Thanks!
Rafiq

Made in the USA
Columbia, SC
04 February 2018